# DISABILITY AND SOCIETY

# DISABILITY AND SOCIETY

## IDEOLOGICAL AND HISTORICAL DIMENSIONS

Patrick McDonnell

BLACKHALL
*Publishing*

This book was typeset by Ark Imaging for

BLACKHALL PUBLISHING
33 Carysfort Avenue
Blackrock
Co. Dublin
Ireland

e-mail: info@blackhallpublishing.com
www.blackhallpublishing.com

ISBN: 978-1-84218-137-9

A catalogue record for this book is available from the British Library.

Printed in the UK by Athenaeum Press Ltd.

# Table of Contents

# Preface

This book has grown out of a number of research projects that I was involved in as well as various courses that I taught at University College Dublin and at Trinity College Dublin. Running through all of this work were two key questions: what is the nature of the relationship between perceived impairment and society and how has this relationship changed over time? In attempting to answer these questions, the book starts with the premise that disability is a socio-political rather than a psycho-medical matter. It locates disability within a broad political and historical framework and links changing responses to disability with other important social, political and cultural movements.

In recent years disability has become a significant, and sometimes controversial, issue in public discourse. This higher public profile is reflected in the increasing number of education and training courses and programmes that have become available, not only in disability studies per se but also in areas where disability interacts with disciplines such as education, law, medicine, psychology and the social sciences. This book is intended for undergraduate and postgraduate students in all of these fields. It will also be of use to trainers and participants in disability awareness and disability equality training programmes, to professionals and allied workers in disability related services, and to general readers with an interest in disability issues.

# Acknowledgements

I take this opportunity to express my appreciation for all the support and encouragement that I received during the production of this book. The award of a Newman Scholarship at University College Dublin during 2001–3 enabled me to complete a great deal of the preparatory work. My sincere thanks are due to the Disabled Persons Trust and the National Disability Authority for funding the scholarship and to the Equality Studies Centre, where I found a dynamic and supportive academic environment for the research. I am also deeply grateful to my research and teaching colleagues and the many students at the School of Social Justice and the School of Education and Lifelong Learning, University College Dublin, and at the School of Linguistic, Speech and Communication Sciences, Trinity College Dublin, with whom the themes of the book were explored and discussed.

Particular thanks are due to Professor Kathleen Lynch, Equality Studies Centre, University College Dublin, for providing the initial encouragement to undertake the work, for reading and making valuable comments on early drafts, and for her support in bringing the work to a successful conclusion; to Teresa Whitington, Librarian at the Central Catholic Library, for assistance in getting access to valuable source materials; and to Dr Mary Kelly, School of Sociology, University College Dublin, who provided me with a copy of her doctoral thesis. Special words of gratitude are also due to the many individuals who were so generous with their time and expertise and who made constructive suggestions at various stages of the work – John Baker, Carlos Bruen, John Bosco Conama, Pauline Conroy, Dawn Duffin, Edel Foley, Rita Kwiotek, Lorraine Leeson, Tina Lowe, Frances McDonnell, Joe McDonnell, Lucy Moran and Helena Saunders.

I am especially grateful to Elizabeth Brennan at Blackhall Publishing for her insightful advice and her unfailing courtesy and efficiency in overseeing the publication process.

# 1

# Introduction: Ideological and Historical Perspectives on Disability

In contemporary Ireland and indeed internationally, the relationship between disability and society is being transformed. Change is manifest in fields as varied as legislation, education, research, service provision and even in the meaning of disability itself. The promise of these initiatives is that they will end or, at the very least, minimise decades of discrimination and exclusion. However, the development of more equitable structures and practices in relation to disability requires a thorough understanding of how things came to be the way they are and, by extension, what exactly needs to be changed. The challenge for today, then, is to ensure that new and promising initiatives are not subverted by what we have inherited from the past. The central aim of this study is to identify and describe the major ideas, values and practices that have shaped disability relations in Western society in general and in Ireland in particular and, by doing so, to highlight those ideas, values and practices that are likely to influence planning and policy making in the future.

A brief analysis of the membership and report of a special education review committee, established in August 1991, provides a revealing introduction to the place of disability in modern Irish society. In the context of education, the Report of the Special Education Review Committee, published by the Department of Education in 1993, was a landmark document. It was the first comprehensive study in the history of the Irish state to deal specifically with special education and as such it constituted an important review of past practice and provision as well as being a signpost towards policy development and planning for the future.

The review committee initially consisted of fifteen members, representing key interests in the primary education sector (see below). This number was later increased by eight to make it representative of a wider range of interests in the system, including the post-primary sector and the guidance services of the Department of Education. Thus, the major interests represented on the committee were: the Department of Education, various managerial, educational and teaching associations, the national parents' councils, teacher education, and the Department of Health. By comparison, the single representative of the Disability Federation of Ireland cannot be regarded as an adequate level of 'service-user presence' on the committee. Membership of the Review Committee was as follows:

## Chairman

Mr Declan Brennan  Former Secretary, Department of Education

## Members

| | |
|---|---|
| Mr Liam Buckley | National Association of Boards of Management in Special Education |
| Ms Lola Heffernan* | Association of Community and Comprehensive Schools |
| Mr Michael Shevlin* | Association of Secondary Teachers of Ireland |
| Mr Kevin O'Meara | Catholic Primary School Managers Association |
| Mr Sydney Blain | Church of Ireland National School Chairperson's Association |
| Mr Liam O'hEigerata | Department of Education |
| Mr Liam Hughes | Department of Education |
| Mr Seán O'Dubháin* | Department of Education |
| Mr John O'Leary* | Department of Education |
| Mr Paul Barron | Department of Health |
| Mr Éamonn Ó Murchú | Disability Federation of Ireland |
| Mr John Carr | Irish National Teachers' Organisation |
| Mr Anthony Bates | Irish National Teachers' Organisation |
| Mr John McKay* | Irish Vocational Education Association |
| Sr Eileen Buckley (Daughters of Charity) | Minister's Nominee |
| Professor Áine Hyland | Minister's Nominee |

| | |
|---|---|
| Mr Paul Niall | National Parents' Council (Primary) |
| Mr Patrick McCarthy* | National Parents' Council (Post-primary) |
| Mr Páid McGee | St. Patrick's College of Education, Drumcondra, Dublin 9 |
| Sr Rita Fennell (Sisters of Mercy) | Secretariat of Secondary Schools |
| Mr Donough O'Brien* | Teachers' Union of Ireland |

**Secretary**

| | |
|---|---|
| Mícheál Ó Flannagáin | Department of Education |

*Members representing mainly post-primary interests who, as mentioned above, joined the committee some months after it was first formed.
*Source*: Report of the Special Education Review Committee (1993).

The Report of the Special Education Review Committee expressed in microcosm many characteristic responses to disability in Ireland. The most striking of these are: firstly, the extent to which disabled people are excluded from ordinary society and its functions; secondly, the dominance of perspectives which define disability in individual and clinical terms; and thirdly, the privileged and controlling roles assigned to professional experts, especially those in the fields of medicine, psychology, welfare and education (National Rehabilitation Board 1994; Dept. of Equality and Law Reform 1996). In addition, there is a widespread assumption that the history of institutional policy making and intervention in relation to disability is primarily a history of humanitarian progress: advances in welfare and social reform, undertaken for the benefit of disabled people (McDonnell 1992).

With reference to exclusion, membership of the committee by and large represented administration, management and teachers – all the interests responsible for organising and delivering special and mainstream educational services. Not included, however, were any people who had actually experienced special education as pupils. Neither did the committee appear to be aware of the significance of such exclusion, even though the membership was actually increased when it was felt that a more representative body was necessary. It is hard to think of any other circumstances on the eve of the twenty-first century in which an officially appointed body, engaged in the examination of a public service, would completely exclude direct representation from among the people who actually received the service. In short, members of the key population for whom and on whose behalf this report was prepared were seen as passive participants in the educational process; they were people to whom things were done, things best left to the administrative, clinical and pedagogical specialists.

The individualised and medically oriented definition of disability adopted in the report is particularly evident in the discussion on deafness and deaf students. The report re-states the classically disabling definitions and categorisations employed in an older report, The Education of Children who are Handicapped by Impaired Hearing (Dept. of Education 1972). In this model, two main criteria are used – the degree to which hearing is impaired and the degree to which children are unable to speak (Dept. of Education 1993). The report of the Review Committee then goes on to note:

> Research has shown that severe deafness can disrupt almost every aspect of normal socio-psychological development ... All pupils with more than a mild hearing loss will experience a significant degree of difficulty in the development of language and speech ... (106)

No sources are given to substantiate these claims about development and language in relation to deaf pupils. The committee appeared to take language as being synonymous with speech and the report made no reference to at least thirty years of research on sign languages and Deaf[1] communities, nor to the implications of this research for the development of educational programmes for deaf pupils. The report gave no indication that there is an alternative perspective on deafness – that, for members of Deaf communities, deafness is a matter of culture and language rather than a matter for medicine and clinical audiology (Kyle and Woll 1985; Padden and Humphries 1988; Gregory and Hartley 1991). It ignored evidence showing that the low levels of achievement among deaf pupils has more to do with the lack of linguistic access to an appropriate curriculum and pedagogy than to a hearing impairment (Dant and Gregory 1991; McDonnell 1992a).

The composition and work of the committee reveals the existence of deeply embedded assumptions and beliefs about special education and the individuals who are placed in special educational settings. It assumes, for example, an identity of interests between the pupils and the professionals who plan, administer and operate special educational provision. It concedes to professionals an exclusive right to define problems and formulate solutions. The knowledge, experience and opinions of current or past pupils of the special education sector were counted as being of little or no value compared with the knowledge, experience and opinions of teaching, managerial and administrative professionals.

A report on gender issues in education, which excluded women from the relevant committee, would be considered unacceptable and offensive. Why then were no former pupils of the special education sector included in the committee? Why did the report accept individualised and clinical models of disability in spite of existing and well-established critiques of these perspectives (Finklestein 1980; Hahn 1985; Borsay 1986; Abberley 1987; Oliver 1990)? Why were the major problems defined primarily as matters of assessment, provision and administration rather than as matters of structural inequalities and discrimination (O'Hanlon 1994)? Why was an identity of interests presumed between a population defined as having 'special needs' and a body of professionals who plan, administer and operate services intended to meet those needs? Why did professionals so unquestioningly assume the exclusive right to define the problems and formulate the solutions?

The assumptions and practices that informed the work of the Special Education Review Committee reflect the nature of the broader relationship between disability and society (Oliver 1990; Barnes and Mercer 2003). In its exploration of this relationship in Ireland, the Report of the Commission on the Status of People with Disabilities (Dept. of Equality and Law Reform 1996) gives cause for very serious concerns. In hundreds of submissions to the Commission and at listening meetings throughout the country '[t]he picture that emerged was one of a society which excludes people with disabilities from almost every aspect of economic, social, political and cultural life.... Many people with disabilities felt that they were being either kept at, or pushed to, the margins of society'(5).

Any attempt to understand and deal with these inequalities requires an exploration of what we can call the deep structures of the relationship between disability and society – the underlying and often taken-for-granted beliefs, ideas and values that shape that relationship (McDonnell 2000a; 2003). These have become so entrenched in social consciousness that they are adopted as 'fact' and commonsense (Oliver 1989). In the next section, I focus on the general connections between ideology and disability. The discussion includes an examination of the concept of ideology and how it is used in this study.

## DISABILITY AND IDEOLOGY

Because people have multiple social identities, inequality can be generated in many different domains. Baker *et al.* (2004) argue that the sphere of cultural relations, where ideas and values are created and legitimated, is one of the key contexts in which the inequalities and injustices experienced by disabled people are produced. In their development of a social theory of disability, disabled scholars have also identified particular ideologies within Western culture as major sources of discrimination and inequality (Oliver 1990; Morris 1991; 1993; 1996; Shakespeare 1994; Barnes 1996; Thomas 1999; Barnes *et al.* 2002).

Oliver (1990), drawing on the work of Gramsci (1971), identifies a set of core and peripheral ideologies which were linked to the rise of capitalism and which underpinned and shaped modern interpretations of and responses to disability. A core ideology of individualism provided a foundation for the social construction of able-bodied and able-minded individuals who were assumed to have the capacities to operate the new machines and cope with the disciplines of factory based work. Oliver contends that the emergence of concepts of able-bodiedness and able-mindedness in relation to the development of wage labour also made possible the idea of individual pathology which became the defining characteristic of disability. The particular focus on the body brought about the involvement of the medical profession and the appearance of peripheral ideologies of medicalisation, normalisation and rehabilitation. Oliver argues that the ideologies such as individualism, medicalisation and normalisation underpin the social creation of disability in modern society and, while he attaches considerable significance to the role of culture in this process, his argument strongly suggests that these ideologies are ultimately grounded in the economic and material realities of capitalism.

Following the work of Campling (1981), Fine and Asch (1988) and Lonsdale (1990), and employing a feminist critique of the early materialist accounts, Morris (1991; 1993; 1996) introduces a distinctly cultural perspective in her analysis of disability. She notes that women have been disabled not only by the material barriers of society, but also by the patriarchal values implicit in early disability theory and by the psycho-medical values of mainstream feminist writing. While the typical focus of early disability theory had been the public domain of paid work, education and the built environment, Morris highlights the personal and the private issues – sexual and marital relationships, housework, abuse and violence – that had been marginalised both in theorising and in political campaigning. In addition, she argues that the experience of disabled women has been overlooked by feminist theorists and researchers and that, where it is addressed, it is frequently informed by disabling psycho-medical definitions of disability. Thus, for Morris, values and attitudes produced in the cultural domain have a profound effect on the social creation of disability.

Shakespeare (1994) also stresses the autonomy of culture and the need to highlight its role as a primary source of the oppression of disabled people. He maintains that people are disabled not simply by material discrimination but also by prejudice and stigmatisation, that these are ingrained in cultural representation, language and socialisation, and that a social analysis of the individual experience of impairment is necessary in order to make sense of these processes. Referring to the disabling imagery found in literature, the cinema and television, Shakespeare suggests that people with perceived impairments are objectified as 'other' and that the consequent practices, which can range from avoidance, control and exclusion to extermination, have been found not only in the modern period but also in societies that pre-date the emergence of capitalism.

Barnes (1996), however, identifies two problems in prioritising the cultural sphere. Firstly, not all cultures necessarily interpret impairment in negative ways and, secondly, there is the danger of reducing 'explanations for cultural phenomena such as perceptions of physical, sensory and intellectual difference to the level of thought processes, thus detracting attention away from economic and social considerations' (49). Nevertheless, Barnes acknowledges the importance of cultural values and observes that the cultural oppression of people with perceived impairments can be traced back to the foundations of Western society. Greek, Roman, Christian and Enlightenment traditions have discriminated against disabled people in a variety of ways, from the practice of infanticide in Greece and Rome, through the witch hunts of the medieval period, to the systematic institutionalisation of the nineteenth century. Barnes believes that responses to perceived impairment cannot be explained in terms of any single factor, such as economic relations, general cultural values, or a particular belief system.

Another, more recent, line of analysis that also draws to a significant degree on culture, is one that focuses on the body (Corker and French 1999; Paterson and Hughes 1999; Hughes 1999; 2000; 2002). Thomas (2002) points out that postmodernist and poststructuralist accounts concerned with the body refer more to cultural representations of the body than to 'real' bodies. These mainstream accounts, however, rarely explore impairment or disability, even in more recent studies that urge an engagement with real bodies. In relation to disability, Hughes (2002) calls for a sociology of impairment to counter a prevailing discourse of bodily perfection which has its roots in Western culture. In the past, such beliefs found particular expression in eugenic ideology and practice and have recently been reinvigorated by two important developments – firstly, by the growth of 'new genetics' and the 'geneticization of explanations of human behaviour' and, secondly, by the production of new forms of discrimination in popular culture which focus on embodiment and appearance and which 'constitute the aesthetic invalidation of disabled people' (Hughes 2002: 73). These developments, Hughes argues, constitute major contemporary threats to inclusion and emancipation.

In a study that sets out to integrate feminist and materialist, personal and public perspectives, Thomas (1999, Chapter 4) proposes that, like patriarchy, disability is a social relational construct, and that both have been responsible for the oppression of men and women. The feminist and postmodernist emphasis on personal experience has been criticised for being too individualised since it runs the risk of bringing fragmentation into a movement that already faces powerful opposition (Finklestein 1996; Barnes 2000). Thomas, however, affirms the importance of subjective experience as a means of understanding the socio-structural world and argues that it is necessary to conduct disability analysis at both micro and macro levels.

Recent disability theory, then, has placed increasing emphasis on the importance of culture. It suggests that disabling outcomes, whether they are thought to stem from the unequal distribution of resources, the exercise of power, or the oppressive nature of personal experience, are invariably underpinned by, or associated with, particular systems of meanings, ideas and values – or ideologies – from the cultural domain. Moreover, as Baker *et al.* (2004) point out, ideologies may be influenced by economic and political forces but are not determined by them. Such relative autonomy means that ideological systems are not unitary; ideas may serve not only to reinforce but also to challenge dominant economic or political values.

Ideology is one of the most elusive and contested concepts in the social sciences and, while it has acquired both positive and negative meanings, it is most often used and understood as a pejorative term (McLellan 1995). Its negative connotations are evident in the main Marxist tradition where it has been regarded as a mechanism deployed by a ruling class to subordinate other social groups; its positive meaning is found in the Enlightenment tradition where it is defined as a science of society for the unmasking of irrationality and prejudice. In his analysis of ideology, Thompson (1990) distinguishes between neutral and critical conceptions. In a neutral conception there is no implication that ideology is misleading, illusory or aligned with a particular interest group. It may be present in revolutionary or conservative political programmes and is in principle available to any group with the capacity to acquire and use it. On the other hand, a critical conception of ideology carries negative, critical or pejorative connotations and implies that it may be biased, deceptive or partial.

Gramsci (1971) proposes an interpretation in which ideology may have two very different functions. Firstly, symbolic forms can interact with relations of power and, accordingly, patterns of meaning can be mobilised to reinforce individuals and groups who occupy positions of power. In this sense, ideology refers to '*the ways in which meaning serves to establish and sustain relations of domination*' (Thompson 1990: 56, italics in original). A key point here is that symbolic phenomena as such are not ideological; rather, they 'are ideological in so far as they serve, in particular circumstances, to maintain relations of domination' (Thompson 1990: 56). Thus, ideas and values can be employed by the powerful to sustain their position and promote their interests – to establish a hegemony, to use Gramsci's term. However, the symbolic field is also a particularly important site for resistance in contemporary societies (Baker *et al.* 2004). It is possible to foster ideas and values that challenge the domination of the powerful and promote an alternative account of how things might be – to advance a counter-hegemonic set of meanings and interpretations. Gramsci's understanding of ideology both as a hegemonic process and as an instrument of social transformation is adopted in this study since it is particularly relevant to an analysis of disability relations in society. On the one hand, as we shall see, relations of domination have been among the most characteristic features of disability in Western societies since early modern times, articulated through ideologies such as medicalisation, individualisation and normalisation. On the other hand, the emergence of disability rights movements and the development of a social model of disability reflects a counter-hegemonic challenge to these oppressive symbolic forms and material practices.

A focus on ideology is worthwhile and relevant for several reasons. Firstly, the whole field of ideas, meanings and values in relation to disability is a contested one. This conflict and uncertainty makes an exploration of ideology particularly important for understanding the relationship between disability and society. The current debates about the causes and meanings of disability demonstrate that the realm of ideas and values constitutes an important site of struggle for disabled people and their movements. The way in which disability is defined, for example, will influence the kinds of solutions to problems that are proposed and how resources are allocated.

Secondly, ideology constitutes a relatively invisible element in the relationship between disability and society (McDonnell 2000a; 2003). Relations between society and phenomena such as disability, gender or race can be regarded as operating at two levels (Drudy and Lynch 1993). There is a relatively visible or surface level of practice, structure and organisation. The differing educational arrangements that Irish society makes for boys and girls, or the particular legislation that it enacts for people with perceived impairments, are examples of visible structures and relations. But there is also another less visible or deep level, consisting of ideas, theories, values, beliefs and so on, that underlies and informs these surface arrangements. This is the level of ideology. The use of terms such as 'surface' or 'deep' does not imply that one level is more important than the other, or that one necessarily precedes or leads to the other: ideas and practices are intimately connected with, and influence, one another. The distinction is intended to orient our analysis towards those aspects of the relationship between disability and society that are not readily discerned or are more easily masked, that are often taken for granted and, thus, are less open to critical scrutiny.

Thirdly, we live in an information age in which our understanding of social phenomena, such as impairment and disability, is mediated through global communications networks. Power and control are exercised not only through political and economic systems but also through ideas and symbolic systems (Baker *et al.* 2004). It is essential to critically examine the ways in which social phenomena are named, defined and understood. Finally, current debates make it clear that disability inequality is generated through complex combinations of material structures, institutional practices and cultural relations. Because ideology operates at interfaces that involve culture, the economy, the body politic and indeed the personal, an ideological analysis can reveal important interactions and linkages between these different domains.

## A FRAMEWORK FOR ANALYSIS

In this study, the relationship between disability and society is explored in the context of two different but related and interacting sets of ideologies – organising ideologies and legitimating ideologies. The framework presented in Table 1.1 is intended more as a heuristic device to facilitate analysis and discussion rather than as an indicator of clear-cut and rigid demarcations between different ideologies. This framework makes it possible to identify and track the many different strands of ideas, values and practices that have shaped the relationship between disability and Western society and to examine the complex ways in which they have interacted with one another.

**Table 1.1: Ideologies**

| Legitimating Ideologies | Organising Ideologies |
| --- | --- |
| Individualisation | Exclusion |
| Humanitarianism | Medicalisation |
| Expertism | Institutionalisation |
| Social Cleansing | Eugenics |
| Economic Efficiency | Normalisation |
| Disability Rights | A Social Model of Disability |

It is possible, however, to make some important distinctions between organising and legitimating ideologies. In terms of how they function, ideologies such as exclusion, medicalisation and institutionalisation represent characteristic sets of ideas, concepts and practices around which responses to people with perceived impairments have been organised. They express dominant and influential beliefs about the nature of impairment and how it should be managed. On the other hand, legitimating ideologies are employed primarily to explain or justify the introduction, exercise and operation of their organising counterparts.

The two sets of ideologies also differ in terms of their historical development. Responses to disability were organised in characteristically different ways at different times. Beginning with exclusion during the early modern period,[2] through the institutionalisation of the nineteenth century, and down to contemporary social model theory, organising ideologies represent a sequence of concepts, structures and practices that became established in Ireland and in Western society generally. Each successive organising ideology did not wholly replace its antecedent; rather, it was presented as a conceptual, administrative or structural 'improvement'. Thus, new perspectives reconfigured rather than displaced earlier approaches. Successive ideologies of medicalisation and institutionalisation, for example, framed exclusion in very particular ways; in turn, medicalisation was framed in particular ways as a result of institutionalisation and eugenic theory. Legitimating ideologies, on the other hand, were typically concurrent rather than sequential. 'Expertism' (see Troyna and Vincent 1996) and economic efficiency, for example, were employed in an on-going way to justify and explain organising ideologies as they developed. Similarly, every organising ideology was accompanied by a humanitarian rhetoric, claiming that what was being done was in the individual's best interests. It is important to note that every legitimating ideology did not always and equally interact with every organising ideology, nor to the same degree in every instance when there were links involved. What is being suggested here is a general pattern of relationship and interaction.

Many, if not all, of the ideologies listed above have been identified and discussed to a greater or lesser extent in the existing literature (see, for example, Oliver 1990; Barton 1996; Shakespeare 1999; Thomas 1999; Barnes *et al.* 2002; Barnes and Mercer 2003). However, their distinctive characteristics, the manner in which they emerged and became established, the different ways and contexts in which they function, and the particular patterns of interaction among them – the primary concerns of this study – have not been explored to any great extent. In the literature, the organising ideologies of exclusion, medicalisation, institutionalisation and eugenics have been seen as maintaining relations of domination with regard to disabled people. Normalisation, in contrast, is regarded as a more ambiguous ideology. In its rehabilitative sense, normalisation is seen to oppress (Oliver 1990); on the other hand, the idea of normalisation has also been employed to challenge the more oppressive ideas and practices of institutionalisation and eugenics (Wolfensberger 1972; Kirkebaek 2002).

The emergence of a social model of disability marked a major paradigm shift in disability relations in Western society (Barnes 1998; 2003). Under earlier ideologies, the economic and social difficulties experienced by disabled people were put down to the deficiencies, incapacities and limitations of the individual. Social model theory challenged the idea of disability as an individual deficit or tragic condition and proposed instead that it is a product of an environment that excludes and oppresses by the particular ways in which it is organised or structured. Social model theory revolutionised thinking about disability and has been responsible for a great deal of anti-discrimination legislation as well as the introduction of structural reforms aimed at creating more inclusive societies (Barnes 1998).

With regard to legitimating ideologies, individualisation reflects two dimensions of how disability has traditionally been interpreted – as an individual condition that, in turn, is regarded as a form of pathology. Individualisation constitutes the centrepiece of what has been called the medical model of disability (Oliver 1990). The ideologies of humanitarianism and expertism are closely connected. Humanitarianism is frequently linked with measures that are proposed or implemented in what are claimed to be the best interests of individuals with perceived impairments, and ultimately, 'for their own good'; expertism implies that any such determination is best made by a professional. The ideology that I have termed social cleansing is particularly associated with ideas and measures that seek to remove elements from society that were perceived to be defective or deviant, by eliminating them, for example, or by forcing them to conform with dominant norms. Such responses can range from eighteenth and nineteenth century efforts to clear the streets of people with perceived impairments to more recent attempts to forcefully assimilate Deaf people into hearing society (Lane 1984; 1993). Throughout the period under investigation, the idea of economic efficiency has been a persistent factor in shaping public policy responses to disability. In this respect, new structures and practices were frequently promoted as being for the public good or in the interests of society. The rhetoric of economic efficiency was extensively used to promote eugenic policies, for example.

In contrast, a disability rights ideology differs from other legitimating ideologies in several respects. In terms of how it became established in current thinking about disability, it offers an insider perspective and developed, as it were, from the ground up. It proposes an alternative and countervailing set of ideas and values because, unlike other legitimating ideologies, it is ultimately grounded in concepts of equality and social justice. For disabled people today, the struggle for disability rights implies the need to transform existing social structures and relations (Oliver 1990). Thus, a clear understanding of both the ideological and historical nature of these structures and relations is an important part of this struggle for change.

## A HISTORICAL PERSPECTIVE

Several theorists have emphasised the importance of incorporating a historical as well as an ideological perspective in studies of disability. Oliver (1990: 62) maintains that the experiences of disabled people 'have to be located within a framework which takes account of both history and ideology'. The historical analysis proposed by Finklestein (1980), for example, demonstrates the importance of the mode of production in the creation of disability, especially in relation to the transition to a capitalist economy. His analysis enables us to understand how disabled people were pushed to the bottom of the labour market, how they came to be regarded as a social problem, and how they were increasingly segregated from mainstream public life and removed to institutions such as special schools, asylums and workhouses. Armstrong *et al.* (2000: 3) stress

> [t]he importance of a historical perspective in relation to understanding the nature of exclusionary policies and practices … First, it will act as a timely reminder that current practices are neither natural, inevitable or unchangeable. Secondly, how key concepts are defined and applied within particular professional discourses will provide an antidote to individualised and deficit models of disability.

Pointing to the neglect or even explicit rejection of bringing an historical awareness to bear on contemporary policy development, Radford (1991: 449) stresses that 'we bury the past at our peril.' Albrecht (2002: 33) also emphasises the need for disability studies to be informed by an 'historical sensibility' and Borsay (2002: 98) observes that an historical perspective 'is a missing piece of the jigsaw in disability studies'.

Disability theorists have emphasised the need for research to be emancipatory, that is, to incorporate a capacity to bring about change in the lives and experiences of disabled people (Oliver 1992; 2002; Barnes and Mercer 1997). In order to change the complex nature of contemporary disability relations, it is first necessary to understand how they have been shaped, constrained and oriented by the past. A historical perspective makes it possible to identify and track the pervasive and recurring presence of disabling ideologies and practices in society. Moreover, it will help to overcome the tendency to treat disability as if it were an isolated phenomenon, unrelated to broader historical forces. An analysis informed by history will demonstrate that the ideologies and practices that have shaped responses to disability do not stand alone but are part of more general political, social and cultural movements. Thus, it is fair to claim that an understanding informed by history is essential for the transformation of disability relations in contemporary society.

A striking feature of disability relations in the period under investigation is the degree to which they transcended national boundaries. Although there were national and regional differences in the timing of the appearance of particular ideologies or the intensity of their effects, the general pattern was remarkably consistent. One example that stands out is the establishment of schools for deaf children of the poor. The National Institution for Deaf-Mutes, which opened in Paris in 1794, was 'the first public school for the deaf in the history of the world' (Lane 1984: 6). Not long afterwards, the first Irish school was established in Dublin 1816 and the first American school in Hartford, Connecticut, in 1817 (McDonnell 1979; Winzer 1993). Thus, while developments in Ireland constitute a major focus of this book, these are always located within the broader international context.

In a more general sense, the Irish experience serves as an excellent exemplar for investigating and understanding the ideological infrastructure that shaped the relationship between disability and Western society. Much of the literature, for example, suggests that the institutionalisation of disabled people was closely associated with urbanisation and industrial capitalism (Topliss 1979; Finklestein 1980; Ryan and Thomas 1980; Stone 1985; Oliver 1990). As Jones and Tillotson put it, 'The drift to the town and the growing complexity of industrial machinery at the time meant the development of a class of industrial rejects for whom it was clear that special provision would have to be made' (1965: 5–6). The development of institutional provision for people with perceived impairments in Ireland, however, does not bear this out. The Irish experience was more directly linked to a process of governance than to urbanisation or industrial development. Thus, the use of modern forms of institutionalisation to regulate and control populations perceived to be problematic is not necessarily tied to any particular mode of production.

A historically crucial turning point in the relationship between disability and society is marked by the emergence of techniques of scientific classification in the late eighteenth and early nineteenth centuries (Foucault 2002). These techniques created the means that permitted disability to be identified and categorised as a specific social and political issue and, because of this, ideologies such as institutionalisation, eugenic theory and normalisation could be, and were, brought to bear on perceived impairment in very direct and visible ways. In contrast, in the period before the development of techniques of scientific classification, disability was far less visible as a distinct social and political phenomenon. The development of centralised state responses to poverty and of the tools and procedures associated with scientific medicine during this earlier period, prepared the ground for scientific classification and set up particular ideological and technical frameworks for interpreting and responding to perceived impairment. Consequently, in the early sections of this book (especially Chapters 2 and 3), considerable attention is devoted to exploring the ideas and practices that were central, firstly, to the regulation of poverty in the early modern period and, secondly, to the development of scientific medicine during the eighteenth century.

In this study, then, a historical perspective is expressed through the identification and analysis of a sequence of organising ideologies that emerged and became established in Western Europe, beginning in the early modern period. In developing this perspective, I refer particularly to the ideas and work of Michel Foucault (1971; 1976; 1977; 2002). Although he did not write specifically about disability, Foucault's work provides a powerful 'box of tools' (Allan 1999: 18) for analysing how society defines, identifies and responds to perceived impairment. His major themes – dividing practices, scientific classification, the relationship between power and knowledge, the role of the human sciences in regulating individuals and social groups, and the focus on the human body – are precisely those that resonate in the relationship between disability and society. His work is especially valuable in helping to detect shifts in how society has identified and responded to individual and social anomaly.

## THE STRUCTURE OF THE BOOK

The appearance of what Foucault calls 'dividing practices' in early seventeenth century Western Europe (Rabinow 1991: 8) provides a starting point for Chapter 2. A dividing practice identifies certain individuals and social groups as problematic and, in the interests of better government, segregates them from mainstream society. Essentially, a dividing practice constitutes a form of exclusion. In this early form, exclusion was not specifically directed at people with perceived impairments; rather it encompassed them as part of a very mixed population of the poor. Chapter 2, then, examines the ideological and institutional roots of exclusion. During this process, poverty was redefined and consequently private troubles, such as old age, impairment, sickness, homelessness, unemployment, and being orphaned or abandoned, became public issues that both municipal and central governments desired to regulate.

Chapter 3 examines the genesis of the medical model of disability, when from the eighteenth century onwards, the techniques of scientific medicine and health administration created the first formal tools for defining individual impairments and for classifying people accordingly. This process of medicalisation enabled finer distinctions to be made 'between the different categories of unfortunates to which charity confusedly addresses itself' (Foucault 2002: 93). Linked with the demands of mercantilist economics, the dividing practices of the human sciences enabled systematic distinctions to be made between health and disease. In this process, and because of its preoccupation with pathological anatomy, scientific medicine incorporated both illness and impairment within a framework of disease, and people with perceived impairments began to be categorised in terms of having particular kinds of disease. The increased use of medical criteria to create new classifications was accompanied by the emergence of a new body of professional experts – doctors – and by distinctive institutions, notably the modern hospital.

As medical and administrative systems developed during the nineteenth century, they acquired the capacity and power to underwrite more specialised forms of categorisation and segregation. Chapter 4 explores this theme with particular reference to Ireland, where institutionalisation affected a variety of social groups deemed to be in some sense deviant or deficient. Institutional expansion was characterised as an explicitly reforming and rehabilitative endeavour and was accompanied by a growing body of professionals who administered, managed and operated the institutions. Thus, responses to disability became professionalised. Institutionalisation also led to the emergence of resistance among disabled people to professional and institutional perspectives. Institutions created communities of people whose shared experiences made it possible to create alternative visions of how things might be and to challenge imposed regimes of discipline and rehabilitation.

After the optimism that accompanied the first stages of institutional expansion – regardless of whether we see this in terms of humanitarian reform or as a mechanism of social control – perceptions about the reforming or curative potential of institutions became increasingly pessimistic. Chapter 5 describes how such a shift in perspective gathered force and, towards the end of the nineteenth century, found its most powerful expression in the eugenics movement. This chapter explores the implications for disability of eugenic ideology and practice and how the shift towards a more pessimistic view of human possibility turned on the question of mental health. Other major themes in the chapter deal with eugenics as a discourse of expertism, the preoccupation with 'mental incapacity' as the primary source of a whole range of social pathologies, and the disabling measures proposed and implemented as a result of eugenic policies.

Chapter 6 is devoted to an analysis of what came to be known as normalisation. Initiated among professionals in fields such as education and mental health, normalisation represented one of the first major ideological challenges to the exclusion and institutionalisation that had dominated the field of disability in Western society for centuries. Normalisation was one element in the intense post-World War II questioning of oppressive ideologies such as patriarchy, colonialism and racism. This chapter describes how normalisation was articulated in different parts of the social system in Western society. For example, in special education, it was expressed through the integration movement and in mental health through de-institutionalisation and community care initiatives. The chapter also explores the limits of normalisation from a disability rights standpoint.

The final chapter discusses the emergence and critical development of social model theory, in which disability is defined as a form of inequality rather than a physical or psychological condition. The chapter explores disability in an egalitarian framework consisting of four core contexts and sets of relations (Lynch, Cantillon and Baker 2001; Baker *et al.* 2004): an economic context and relations of distribution and redistribution; a socio-cultural context and relations of respect and recognition; a political context and relations of power and representation; and an affective context and relations of dependence and interdependence.

## A Note on Language and Terminology

Sensitivity to terminology is evident in the unstable language that has appeared in debates about disability over the years (Oliver, cited in Brennan *et al.* 1991; Jenkins 1998). Zenderland, for example, notes that what was once called 'feeble-mindedness' later became 'mental retardation' and, later still, 'developmental disability' (1998: 6). In the field of disability, yesterday's definition may have become today's term of abuse (Digby 1996). Examples that spring to mind include 'idiot', 'imbecile', 'moron', 'spastic'. Much of the language used to refer to disability in the past is, today, seen to be judgemental and pejorative (Barnes 1992*a*). This is particularly evident in eugenic discourse (see Chapter 5). In this study, the terms 'disability' and 'disabled people' are used in a socio-political sense, that is, they denote a particular form of oppression or discrimination; the term 'impairment' is used to refer to a perceived difference in physical, sensory or intellectual functioning. Where other terms are used, they are intended to reflect the thinking and usage of particular historical periods.

Terminology is important in other contexts. I have already used the term 'Deaf' in this chapter. This term is used to refer to deafness in linguistic and cultural senses (Wrigley 1996) and where membership of a distinctive Deaf community is apparent. With regard to the relationship between deafness and disability, some theorists in Deaf studies (see, for example, Lane 2002 and Ladd 2003) reject the notion that Deaf people can be seen as disabled. This particular view, and the cultural and linguistic model of deafness that informs it, can certainly be sustained against some contemporary definitions of disability. However, it is much more difficult to maintain this distinction in the context of disability as a social, political and cultural creation (see the introduction to Chapter 7).

Morally loaded language is also evident in the ways in which oppressed and disadvantaged people have been described in the past – 'the idle poor', 'the defective', 'the unfit', and so on. To avoid overusing quotation marks, where these and similarly loaded terms occur in the text they are unmarked and reflect usage during particular historical periods; quotation marks are reserved for atypical instances. The relationship between language and disability is discussed further in Chapter 7, in the section 'The Socio-Cultural Context and Issues of Respect and Recognition'.

## NOTES

1. The term 'Deaf' is used here to reflect the distinctive cultural and linguistic implications of deafness (Wrigley 1996).
2. The early modern period in Europe is usually seen as beginning in the late sixteenth and early seventeenth centuries.

# 2

# The Ideological and Institutional Roots of Exclusion

In June 1623, Jane Sellars was discovered on the streets of Norwich and promptly dispatched to the town's Bridewell to be put to work 'till she be reteyned in service'... In April 1624, she was again found 'livinge idely' in the city. In Michaelmas 1625, Thomas Robinson of Yarmouth retained her for one year, but she broke her covenant and ran back to Norwich where the beadles discovered her 'vagrant' in April 1626. After the statutory whipping, the bench issued a pass and told her to return to Robinson but Sellars never left Norwich and was back in Bridewell a few days later. At her discharge in August she was allowed two days to leave the city. Typically Sellars ignored the order, and was discovered 'vagrant and out of service' in October 1626 and was once again committed to Bridewell 'till she be reteyned in service'. She was probably discharged without such employment, however, for she was found to be 'idle' in November 1626 and was confined in Bridewell 'till further order'.... In 1627, she ran away from two different masters, and in October found herself back inside the now familiar walls of Norwich Bridewell where she also celebrated Christmas 1628. In 1629, Sellars was whipped for 'ill rule' and 'michery' – her first recorded theft. Her first appearance at Quarter Sessions was in April 1630, when she was charged with stealing six pairs of stockings. By now she had an illegitimate child who was 'put' to a wife of St. Swithin's parish in the following month. Eight months later, Sellars was 'punished at the post' for 'lewdness and ill rule', and again prosecuted for 'ill rule' at the close of the same month. In April 1631, she was acquitted of petty larceny, and in August was returned to Bridewell ... for begging. A few days later, Sellars was branded for 'felony under x shillings'. She was discharged in October and promised the court that she would go 'forthwith to Yarmouth to gett ... a service'. An entry in the Sessions' minute book for December 1631 simply states, 'Jane Sellars to be executed'. This could refer to an outstanding action or it may be a reference to a verdict reached elsewhere. Sellars makes no further appearances in any Norwich records...

Paul Griffiths (1996), *Masterless Young People in Norwich,*
*1560–1645*, 146–7

## INTRODUCTION

Although it may not be immediately obvious, the dividing practices reflected in the experiences of Jane Sellars provides us with a starting point for an analysis of exclusion in relation to disability. Sellars belonged to the most characteristic problem population of Western Europe during the early modern period. Her circumstances were regarded as problematic because she was unemployed and homeless, when to be normal was to be in service in the charge of an older householder and to have a fixed domicile. Having been identified as problematic, the principle institutional response to Sellars' situation was segregation from mainstream society and confinement in the Bridewell, an institution especially created to segregate the problem poor from the rest of the community and to facilitate the implementation of measures designed to treat their presumed problem.

The relationship between poverty and disability is usually explored in economic terms. This chapter, however, is concerned with the historical and ideological links between them. In particular, I argue that the dividing practices that ultimately became such a dominant feature in the experience of disabled people in Western society have their origins in early modern political, social and cultural responses to poverty. The dominant institutional and ideological responses – exclusion, confinement and the notion of rehabilitation – to the poverty of people like Jane Sellars provided a template for the later treatment of disabled people. At this point in time, if disabled people were excluded from mainstream society, it was as a result of poverty rather than perceived impairment (Finkelstein 1980). Consequently, this discussion focuses on the ideological rhetoric and institutional innovations associated with poverty during the early modern period.

In developing the discussion, I firstly describe how poverty was redefined as a pressing social problem rather than being an acceptable, even commendable, moral state. With the implications for disability in mind, I then explore the ideological nature of exclusion and its associated practices – the exercise of professional power and knowledge, the construction of a problem such as poverty as an individual pathology, and the creation of new institutions involving segregation and the notion of rehabilitation. In the final sections, I discuss these developments with particular reference to Ireland and I conclude with a brief analysis of the legacy of this ideology of exclusion.

## POVERTY REDEFINED

From the late middle ages, distinctions were beginning to be made between the able-bodied and the deserving poor, and civil authorities had begun to restrict begging to the latter group on the basis that its destitution could be attributed to natural or accidental causes – age, the death of a spouse, sickness, impairment (Grell and Cunningham 1997). People with impairments, however, were not always considered to be among those deserving relief. In her analysis of the distribution of relief to the sick poor in early modern Norwich, Pelling (1998: 73) observes that 'dumbness, deafness, limb-loss and perhaps lunacy' were not among the conditions for which the authorities made provision. Attitudes to those considered deserving were also tempered by anxieties about the spectacle of public begging, by fears concerning the spread of disease, and by suspicions regarding the authenticity of particular cases (Beier 1985; Bogucka 1997; Jütte 1997). As far as the authorities were concerned, it was not always easy to determine who was deserving and who was not. The Surveyor General of Ireland Arthur Dobbs (1729), for example, believed that impairments were not always natural or accidental but were caused intentionally to excite charity, and in Thomas More's *Utopia* there were no 'strong and lusty beggars who feign some disease as an excuse for their idleness' (2002: 52).

There are compelling reasons for locating most disabled people within the broad and heterogeneous population of the poor in this period. Firstly, even in today's far more affluent Western society, disability is one of the most significant indicators of poverty (Harbison 2003; McManus 2003). Secondly, at a time of sharply rising levels of poverty, a very large proportion of the population as a whole lived at subsistence level (Lis and Soly 1979). Thirdly, if there were comfortable or affluent disabled people, their material status was indeed precarious. In the early modern period, the legal codes of countries throughout Europe imposed substantial restrictions on people with perceived impairments: 'they were deprived of the rights of inheritance, forbidden to testify in a court of justice, and not allowed to make a deed, contract, note or will' (Winzer 1993: 22). Thus, the ideologies and practices that impinged on the poor inevitably affected the vast majority of disabled people.

Before going on to explore the ideological and institutional character-istics of exclusion, it is important to establish why poverty, especially in the form of unemployment and homelessness, became a significant ground for exclusion. During the sixteenth century, in a process that became common all over Western Europe, a number of critical perspec-tives coalesced around the issue of poverty. Although attitudes to poverty and alms-giving in medieval society were never unanimous, there was a general consensus that the Christian community had a special obligation to the poor. It was accepted that to give alms was a duty since the poor were considered to be the special representatives of Christ. The good ruler was characterised as the protector of the poor and a large abbey such as Cluny could devote as much as one-third of its income to the relief of poverty (Mollat 1986). In what was held to be a reciprocal relationship, the existence of the poor provided a stimulus to the rich to practise virtue and the giving of alms was seen as a means of ensuring the donor's own personal salvation. Alms-giving implied a contract: the recipient of mate-rial assistance was bound, in return, to pray for the benefactor and in doing so fulfilled a valued spiritual function.

From the late middle-ages onwards, however, poverty began to lose its idealised and sanctified status and came under increasing attack. This was due in part to the contradiction between the Franciscan ideal and the actual wealth of the mendicant orders (Beier 1985). By the beginning of the sixteenth century, social commentators were urging the secular author-ities to legislate against begging (Grell and Cunningham 1997). It became increasingly respectable to condemn the able-bodied poor and increas-ingly legitimate to refuse alms. As a result of their increasing numbers and their alleged insolence and depravity, they were accused of negating their contractual relationship with the rich. In 1516, John Major, a Scottish theologian teaching at the university of Paris, expressed this changing perspective when he declared that it 'would be praiseworthy and lawful' to suppress begging (Ashley 1906: 341).

The redefinition of poverty also owes something to renaissance humanist studies, which celebrated worldly activity and success and were founded on the belief that the individual was capable of moral and social improvement. Humanist perspectives created a space for the idea of moral and social rehabilitation (Hickey 1997). Accordingly, poverty came to be seen, not so much as an inevitable outcome of the human condition, but rather as a manifestation of individual, social and moral failure and, while this deficiency deserved to be condemned, it was also susceptible to remediation. This conceptual shift provided the foundation for a perspective that became commonplace: firstly, that the difficulties of the poor had their origin in some personal flaw or deficiency of character and, secondly, that governing authorities had a duty to intervene in order to remedy the situation.

During the sixteenth century, much of the hostility to the wandering poor was moral and political rather than economic. In moral terms, to be unemployed and masterless came to be regarded as being particularly reprehensible, 'the very mother of all vice' (Beier 1985: 5). It has been argued that the appearance of a Protestant work ethic was a significant influence in changing attitudes to poverty: to labour in one's calling, to be diligent, thrifty and successful were taken to represent the outward signs of salvation (Weber 1930). However, these attitudes were not confined to Protestants nor to countries under Protestant control; unemployment and its correlate, begging, were condemned equally by Catholic commentators and authorities (Gemerek 1994). In highlighting a moral basis for the regulation of the poor, however, economic factors should not be overlooked. Soly argues that the Dutch and Flemish towns where measures to regulate the poor were most rapidly introduced were major centres of industry. Therefore, the new policy 'offered not only the opportunity to discipline the destitute and to punish the indolent: it could also be used as an instrument to enforce low-paid work' (1997: 90).

In political terms, the post-reformation period saw the emergence of the modern nation state. During this period, governments began to extend their authority into many different areas of social life and the laws promulgated against the poor were an expression of this capability. Legislation for the regulation of the poor was justified, therefore, not only on grounds of moral necessity but also on the basis of political security.

During the early decades of the sixteenth century, as secular authorities across Western Europe enacted measures to suppress vagrancy and begging (Piven and Cloward 1972), fears of social breakdown and disorder at the hands of 'the inferior multitude' became a recurring source of anxiety among the social and political elites (Kamen 1984: 172; Woolf 1986: 63; Sharpe 1995: 193). The greatest threat to England, according to Thomas Hobbes, was 'that dissolute condition of masterless men' (1996: 122).

Particular political contexts sharpened the perception of risk. In the unstable colonial context of late sixteenth-century Ireland, vagrancy acquired additional connotations of danger and lawlessness (Fitzgerald 1994). Regular outbreaks of warfare not only exacerbated the extent of poverty and the likelihood of impairment but also added the suspicion of military experience to the many other disreputable characteristics of the poor. The masterless men of Tudor and Stuart England were akin to the idle swordsmen and woodkerne of Ireland during the same period. Though the tasks of organising public charity and repressing begging were seen primarily as the responsibility of local and municipal authorities, within the broader framework of the state, efforts were made to co-ordinate local measures through general legislation. Charles V issued a centralising edict in the Netherlands in 1531 and in England the Elizabethan Poor Law of 1601 attempted to impose uniformity on the piecemeal and localised regulations of preceding decades (Adams 1990).

## AN IDEOLOGY OF EXCLUSION

In the most general sense, human societies have frequently employed ideologies and practices through which certain kinds of people are marginalised or excluded such as, for example, those in early Irish society surrounding the exclusion from kingship of individuals with a physical impairment (Kelly 1988), or those involving the confinement of lepers in medieval society (Foucault 1971; Lee 1996). However, in post-Reformation Europe, the concepts, institutions and procedures associated with exclusion – particularly those that related to the homeless and masterless poor – underwent a profound change and became qualitatively different (Adams 1990; Beier 1985; Fitzgerald 1994; Gemerek 1994; Slack 1988).

What was distinctive about exclusion in Western Europe during the early modern period? Firstly, it acquired more elaborate organisational and administrative characteristics: exclusion became part of the apparatus of government in the management and regulation of the poor. For the first time, local and piecemeal initiatives began to be consolidated within national and more centralised frameworks. Secondly, this period saw the creation of a conceptual repertoire and of institutional procedures, organised around exclusion and confinement and directed at 'the poor ... of both sexes, of all ages and from all localities, of whatever breeding and birth, in whatever state they may be, able-bodied or invalid, sick or convalescent, curable or incurable' (Foucault 1971: 39). These new forms of segregation and exclusion, targeting the poor, created a set of tried and serviceable responses that could be deployed in the regulation of other social groups. Thirdly, distinctive disciplinary technologies – labelling, segregation, confinement and rehabilitation – made their first appearance during this period. These technologies are inextricably linked with modern forms of exclusion and continue to occupy a prominent position in today's institutional and conceptual landscape (Foucault 1971; 1977). Finally, exclusion in the early modern period was distinctive because its purpose was neither merely to exclude per se, nor to proclaim any kind of final or irrevocable state of segregation. Instead, in its early modern form, exclusion incorporated a notion of individual and social engineering and articulated a distinctive perspective on human perfectibility and the possibility of rehabilitation. Exclusion was seen to be necessary but temporary; it created a setting in which a regime of normalisation could be implemented.

It is difficult to assess the extent to which an ideology of exclusion directly affected people with perceived impairment during this period. We have noted the disabling legal restrictions attached to inheritance and to making contracts and wills. However, there were no formal mechanisms for distinguishing between people with perceived impairment and the general population for purposes of segregation or institutionalisation. Neither were there any attempts made to establish particular categories or degrees of impairment for such purposes. Classification of this kind had to wait for the diagnostic and administrative interventions promoted by scientific medicine and health administration (see Chapters 3 and 4). In general, exclusion from mainstream society would have arisen for people with perceived impairment to the extent that they were among the poor, which, as we have argued, was highly probable. As was the case for other poor people, they were more likely to be given relief if they were located in their own town or parish, but punished if they stood accused, like Jane Sellars, of 'wandering abroad' or being 'repeat offenders'. Their *bona fides* were likely to be questioned: was the impairment real or merely a stratagem 'to induce the opulent and industrious to be charitable' (Dobbs 1729: 45–6)? Thus, they were perhaps subject to even greater scrutiny and suspicion than other poor people. On the other hand, there is also evidence that people with perceived impairments were considered to be among the impotent poor and thus were likely to be among those who were given relief or permission to beg (Fownes 1725; Lis and Soly 1979; Nicholas 1997). Similarly, the impotent poor were less likely to be punished for idleness and, therefore, less likely to be institutionalised; at this particular time segregation and punishment were directed mainly at those who were accused of 'wandering abroad' or of being repeat offenders (see below, 'Institutional Structures').

The main point here, however, concerns the issue of exclusion, not the exclusion of people with perceived impairment per se. In the early modern period, an ideology of exclusion shaped social and political responses to the poor, the primary objective of which was the removal of beggars from public view (Munck 1990). Of course impairment and poverty were linked but people with perceived impairments were caught up in these responses because they were poor, not because they were impaired. When it became technically feasible, through medicalisation and institutionalisation, especially during the nineteenth century, the ideology of exclusion was extended to people with perceived impairments. It was at this later stage that exclusion was premised on impairment rather than on poverty.

Exclusion premised on poverty is in many ways similar to exclusion based on impairment. The establishment of discourses of expertise in both fields is a classic feature of both. In relation to poverty (see below, 'Expert Voices'), those claiming expertise assumed the authority to define the problem, to set boundaries for its analysis and resolution and, in doing so, to create new relations of power between the experts and the subjects of their analysis. Although alternative, insider perspectives and explanations of poverty were articulated, these were largely silenced by the authority of the experts. Such dominance was easily sustained through a mutually beneficial collaboration between the experts and the various arms of government. Later, similar relations of domination applied in the field of disability (Bannerman Foster 1987; Oliver 1990).

The individualisation of difficulties stemming from poverty also prefigured the individualisation of disability. Both were constructed as

problems caused by the assumed deficiencies and deficits of the individual. And both were defined in pathological terms. The poor were identified as an unseemly and unhygenic presence in the social body (Kamen
2000) and their 'deformed' condition (Hill 1974: 181; Nicholas 1997:
255) demanded that they be removed from public view. Moreover, the
institutional response that emerged in relation to poverty provided a
model for the establishment of an institutional response to disability. This
response took two forms. One was the enclosed site – the house of correction. The other was the voluntary organisation, such as religious confraternities of the poor, which expressed a rhetoric of charity but which
also had significant supervisory and regulatory functions. Thus, in the
response to poverty in early modern society in Western Europe, we find
an ideological and institutional framework of exclusion that is recognis-
ably modern, one that eventually was extended beyond the poor into other
areas of social life, most particularly into the field of disability.

## EXPERT VOICES

The new perspective on poverty in the early modern period was grounded
in a discourse of expertise. Prominent humanist scholars were preoccupied by the issue and their concerns led to the growth of a substantial body
of theoretical literature in which the nature and causes of poverty were
analysed and proposals were made for its resolution (Gemerek 1994; Grell
1997). Their theories and recommendations effectively transformed the
private troubles of homelessness and unemployment into public issues of
vagrancy and begging. This work also fostered the development of a symbiotic relationship between the experts themselves and the secular and
religious administrative authorities. In the process, authoritative voices
were established in relation to poverty. The boundaries were set as to how
poverty should be defined as a problem, the kind of policies that should
be introduced, and how these policies should be implemented.

   Several key propositions run through the writings of theorists such as
Erasmus, Thomas More, and especially Juan Luis Vives, as to the nature
and causes of poverty, the relationship between the poor and civil society,
and the responsibility of the secular authorities to take appropriate action
(Ashley 1906; Gemerek 1994). A central theme in their work was the fear
that idleness bred social disorder: the idle poor 'stir up Rumours, raise up
Tales ... [and] move people to uproars and Tumults' (Kamen 1984: 172).

Humanist writers expressed a fairly unanimous view that society should not tolerate vagrancy and that the distribution of alms should be controlled; they recommended forced labour for so-called false beggars and that only the deserving poor should be relieved. Some experts drew up schemes that were then implemented by the authorities. In one early modern version of zero tolerance, Juan de Medina claimed that his plan to abolish begging in Valladolid had been so successful that, in contrast to former times, there was now hardly anyone to hang or flog for robbery (cited in Kamen 1984).

The most substantial work on the subject was Vives' treatise, published in 1526, and dedicated to the magistrates of Bruges (Ashley 1906). It was quickly translated into Spanish, French and Italian and became popular all over Europe because it provided secular authorities with both ideological justification and practical suggestions for the development and implementation of new policies. The treatise explained the technicalities of census taking, suggested various methods of categorisation and outlined measures, principally forced labour, for the control and rehabilitation of beggars. Like all politically astute experts, however, Vives did not include among his proposals any that would offend significantly powerful interests, in this case the interests of the Church (Gemerek 1994: 191).

In turn, the civil authorities looked to the social theorists to legitimate their policies. In 1524–5 the magistrates of Ypres took a census of the poor, banned public begging, created a central administration responsible for relief, and appointed special officials to oversee the distribution of alms to the deserving poor (Ashley 1906). The local mendicant orders opposed the new measures and declared them heretical. Fearful of accusations of this nature, the magistrates appealed to the theologians of Paris to resolve the conflict. The verdict of the Sorbonne favoured the magistrates: the measures were held to be severe but just, and not in conflict with Christian teaching. In much the same way, the edict of Charles V on the poor of the Netherlands was issued only after an initial study of previous legislation and doctrinal arguments had been carried out by experts (Soly 1997).

Another important theme in the work of the experts was the psychological distance they created between themselves and the population they problematised. While the experts stressed the importance of work, those who did the work were occasionally treated as objects of scorn. The intellectual elitism of Erasmus, for example, 'involved a large measure of contempt for artisans and their activities' (Gemerek 1994: 186). A considerable lexicon of abuse was employed to describe the undeserving poor in the literature and legislation of the period (Hill 1974; Petersen 1997). Not only did they stand accused of embodying the most reprehensible personal vices, they were also held to be responsible for the most heinous crimes.

Not all of their contemporaries, however, concurred fully with the views expressed by theorists such as Vives, or distanced themselves from the difficulties of the poor. Thomas More, for example, while condemning idleness and recommending forced labour as a punishment for vagrants, recognised that unemployment could stem as much from changed economic circumstances and injustice as from wilful sloth (Ashley 1906; Gemerek 1994). Some critics, however, opposed the new perspective on poverty as heretical and as an infringement of the Church's traditional prerogatives. The most vehement opposition came from the mendicant orders whose revenues and way of life were seriously threatened by the new policies being suggested by writers such as Vivres.

Other criticism, however, showed a more direct awareness of the realities of life for the poor. In a treatise on beggars, a Dominican, Domingo de Soto, defended the traditional doctrine of charity and the Christian duty to help the poor (Geremek 1994). Although he did not deny the need to combat vagrancy as a threat to public order, de Soto insisted that there was no reason to persecute the poor who wandered about the countryside seeking alms simply to survive. He acknowledged that poor people sometimes used dishonest means to evoke compassion, but this was done out of necessity. He also argued that sickness or infirmity were not the only grounds for distinguishing the worthy poor from the others; the loss of tools or the lack of training were equally valid reasons for being unable to work. Therefore, he opposed the policy of categorising beggars as false or genuine because it was morally risky.

The views and opinions of the people most directly affected by the new policies – the poor themselves – are among those least likely to have entered the historical record. It is clear that poor people could envisage a social order very different from the one in which they found themselves. We most often catch a glimpse of an alternative vision only when it was being refuted by those who presumed themselves to be superior (Hill 1974). The poor declared that 'all being of one mould, there is no reason that some should have so much and others so little'; they considered that 'if the feet knew their strength as well as ... their oppression, they would not bear as they do'; and, according to their betters, they were looking for 'a general equality, most dangerous to the society of man'. Sentiments such as these from 'fellows without shirts' alarmed the authorities and generated fear among the social and political elites (Hill 1974). In French cities, the arrest of beggars often provoked riots among the poor and skirmishes with the police (Geremek 1994) and special edicts prescribed penalties for interference with officers arresting beggars (Adams 1990). The uncertainty of life and the repressive actions brought out feelings of social solidarity among the poor: those who were working today could find themselves begging for a living tomorrow.

## CATEGORISING ANOMALOUS INDIVIDUALS

Humanist scholars emphasised the necessity of census taking and categorisation in the political and social management of poverty, two activities that later became ubiquitous in the control and regulation of disabled people (Oliver 1992; 2002). In relation to the poor, the most important distinction was that presumed to exist between the deserving and the undeserving poor. As early as the twelfth century, Church writers had begun to distinguish between honest and dishonest beggars, a differentiation that appeared sporadically in legislation from the 1300s (Grell and Cunningham 1997). During the early modern period, the demarcation was made more explicit and systematic and was reflected in an unprecedented consensus among both religious and secular authorities. The demarcation was further strengthened by legislation to prohibit begging and private alms-giving altogether and to centralise the distribution of poor relief.

Although the primary distinction was between the deserving and the undeserving poor, the new dispensation on poverty in fact created a third category. The old, the sick, the infirm and the very young – the impotent poor – were considered to be the real deserving poor. A second group, the so-called shamefaced poor, who were considered neither insolent nor proud and who had become impoverished through unemployment or misfortune, were thought to be somewhat less worthy than the first group but still deserving of relief (Geremek 1994; Norberg 1984). The third group, the delinquent poor, consisted of those 'rogues, vagabonds and sturdy beggars ... by means whereof daily happeneth horrible murders, thefts, and other great outrages, to the high displeasure of Almighty God, and to the great annoyance of the common weal' (14 Elizabeth, cap. 5).

In contrast with these categories was the undefined category of the normal, composed of civil men and women. During the early modern period there was a growing preoccupation with ideas of civility and the refinement of manners (Elias 1994; Ingram 1996). The respectable, well-ordered society that was being socially constructed implied a reformation of behaviour and morals. The lives of the wandering and afflicted poor offended against respectability and the norms of public comportment and good manners. Values such as independence of family, social position and influence were deemed by the elites to be central to the orderly functioning of society. To be poor was to be deficient in such normal attributes. It was to be *sans état*, without a social station, or *sans aveu*, without any ties of responsibility within the community (Adams 1990: 17–8). Respectable society required that the poor recognise and accept these deficiencies and compensate for them by displaying attitudes of meekness, gratitude and deference (Woolf 1986). As Elias (1994) has suggested, the emergence of the modern state with its monopoly on violence necessitated greater degrees of individual self-control. In this context, the poor deserved to be suppressed not only because they were suspected of being responsible for a crime wave of thefts and murders; their mere public presence constituted a criminal offence because it was a visible manifestation of the absence of self-discipline.

## THE INDIVIDUAL PATHOLOGY OF THE POOR

When professional expertise is applied to a perceived problem it tends to generate administrative and technical responses (Skrtic 1995). If the route to an administrative solution entails categorisation, the route to a technical solution demands that the problem be individualised. In its analysis of poverty, early modern expert opinion concluded that the source of the problem was to be found in individual deficiency. The poor were poor because of their inherent incapacity and indolence: their 'criminal laziness is the source of all their vices' (cited in Norberg 1984: 90) and their poverty was perceived to stem 'from waywardness and pure sloth, through not wishing to work or toil to earn their bread or living' (cited in Kamen 1984: 170); they would 'rather hazard their lives than work' (cited in Sharpe 1995: 192) and should be sent to houses of correction 'till they are broken from their idle course of life, and willing to betake themselves to some honest calling' (Steele 1910: 515). Figures from among the poor provided raw material for the creation of powerful and menacing social stereotypes, especially when these characterisations were linked to perceived impairment and disease. The language used to describe such threatening figures was charged with imagery of pathology and contamination. At the beginning of the seventeenth century, the municipal authorities in Dublin, for example, stated that the city 'doth abounde with great numbers of sturdie beggars, younge and olde ... to the great danger of breeding infections and other contagious diseases' (Gilbert 1892: 220–1). As far as the political and social elites were concerned, the poor had to be isolated from the normal population 'as one might clear a fire lane in the forest, or as one might quarantine healthy individuals suspected of being carriers of an epidemic disease' (Adams 1990: 27).

Notions of social and physical contamination became significant elements in the discourse surrounding the poor. Humanist writers compared the effects of civil decay on the body politic with the effects of contagion on the physical body. They argued that the removal of the poor, particularly the vagrant poor, from society was necessary for the preservation not only of morality and political stability but also of social hygiene. In warning of the dangers of physical, social and moral infection from vagrancy, commentaries of the period expressed a palpable disgust and revulsion. Vives argued that, at large in the community, the vagrant poor 'assail the nostrils [and] the mouth' and spread disease and infection (quoted in Beier 1985: 6). When the faithful were at prayer 'they push through the congregation, deformed by sores, exuding an unbearable smell from their bodies' (Vives, quoted in Kamen 1984: 167). According to Francis Bacon they were 'a burthen, an eye-sore, a scandal and a seed of peril and tumult in a state' (Spedding, Ellis and Heath 1868: 252).

The regulation of the poor became a matter of social hygiene as well as of political security. Poverty, perceived impairment and disease were linked together as matters of concern for the body politic. It was no accident that municipal by-laws against beggars and vagabonds were often issued alongside ordinances for cleaning the streets (Slack 1988: 115; Robins 1995: 27–8). One of the most extreme examples of social cleansing occurred near Limerick in 1606 and involved the summary execution of two disabled people:

> [O]ne Downing, who had been a lieutenant in the late wars ... having obtained a commission from my lord President of Mounster, to execute by martial law vagabonds and masterless men, and such as had borne arms in the late war, it happened that an idiot fool ... with

another of the same quality, came straggling into the village where Downing dwelt; he, meeting with them on a Sunday morning, took them and immediately hanged them both ... (Russell and Prendergast 1872: 470)[1]

Thus, the ideology and practices that came to bear on the poor in the early modern period included a conspicuous element of social cleansing; anomalies in the body politic constituted an offence to the senses and carried the danger of contamination. Similar ideologies were to surface again in nineteenth and twentieth century responses to perceived impairment (see below, Chapter 5; Hunt 1966; Hevey 1992).

## INSTITUTIONAL PRACTICES

In the field of disability, most research and analysis has focused on practices in the public and civil rather than the private sphere of society since information and records are far more likely to have been kept in public institutions and social organisations than in families. Nevertheless, it is important to remember that even after the institutional and organisational expansion of the nineteenth century, the family remained an important locus of provision for disabled people. In relation to mental illness, for example, Bartlett and Wright point out that 'the asylum did not *replace* the family as the central locus of care' (1999: 4, italics in original) and, although such informal responses were often disapproved of, families continued to provide care to a significant degree. Moreover, the regional and national distribution of public institutions was often unsystematic or non-existent. For example, before the establishment of institutions such as the voluntary hospitals and infirmaries during the second half of the eighteenth century and the workhouses in the 1830s, Ireland lacked any public system of poor relief. Until then, the great majority of the poor, including disabled people, looked to their families and communities for support.

In the public and civil domains, segregation and exclusion affected different categories of the poor in different ways. The most common practices included restrictions on movement, identification procedures, and the regulation of public charity. Among the most widespread measures introduced by municipal authorities in Western Europe were regulations to control the movement of the wandering poor. Almost every town that drew up ordinances against begging included a regulation to exclude or expel so-called alien beggars. In Dublin in 1568, one of the duties of the bellman was to expel such beggars from the city (Gilbert 1891). Passports were used to control and supervise the movement of people. These documents permitted individuals, who might otherwise stand accused of vagrancy, to travel unmolested and entitled the holders to ask for lodgings and relief (Beier 1985).

Where public begging was not outlawed completely, the local poor might be issued with special licenses or were given special identification badges. In Rouen in the 1540s the poor were ordered to wear a yellow cross on the sleeve. Cities and towns drew up lists or arranged for a register of beggars to be kept. In 1548 in Grenoble, special officials appointed by the municipal council prepared lists of the poor on a street by street basis (Geremek 1994). Similar badging and registration activities were undertaken in Dublin and other Irish towns (Fitzgerald 1994; Lennon 1999). It was common for urban authorities to introduce measures to enable surprise searches to be made and to investigate poor- and sick-houses to determine whether or not residents were among the deserving poor (Nicholls 1856; Gilbert 1891; Slack 1988).

Municipal and state authorities also aimed to eradicate older, pre-existing responses to poverty by attempting to centralise the distribution of relief and to eliminate individual charity. In 1535, the Parlement of Paris adopted a series of measures against the poor, one of which stipulated that no residents, whatever their status, should give alms in the street or in a church, on pain of a fine (Geremek 1994). In England an Act of 1530–1 provided for the suppression of unauthorised charity: any person giving 'harbour, money, or lodging, to any beggars, being strong and able to work' was subject to 'such a fine as the justices at their sessions shall direct'. Five years later, another Act directed that 'no person … shall give any money in alms, otherwise than to the common boxes and common gatherings', that is, the centralised forms of relief approved under the Act (Nicholls 1854: 118, 121).

Other measures to regulate the poor incorporated the notion of rehabilitation, the intention being to change the moral character of the individual, by force if necessary. Before the medicalisation of social policy (see Chapter 3), the prevailing view among the experts was that the rehabilitation of idle and disorderly persons could be accomplished by physical punishment. The most common punishment for first offences was to be put in the stocks, whipped or forced to work on the municipal fortifications or drains. For further offences more draconian punishments were handed down, ranging from branding and ear-boring to indentured labour in the galleys, transportation or even execution. Such harsh measures were justified in the public interest and authorities failing to take action were accused of a dereliction of duty. In his treatise on poverty, Vives, the leading proponent of secular responsibility, argued that it was the duty of political rulers to intervene because it was harmful to the public interest if a large section of the population was idle (Ashley 1906). If the poor had to be severely punished, it was, in the long run, for their own good too, and if they had to be removed from the streets it was because they were more susceptible than others to the evils of the world and the temptations of the devil (Norberg 1985).

In addition to these legislative and punitive measures, two further institutional initiatives were established. These initiatives were revolutionary and, in the longer term, were to have a profound influence on social policy in the field of disability. Although they deployed similar disciplinary techniques and had similar goals – the regulation of the poor through surveillance – they were structurally and functionally distinct. In the public domain, there were the enclosed sites, institutions of stone and mortar, specially built for the physical segregation and confinement of the poor. In the civil domain there were the social organisations that penetrated the lives of the poor and that set out to mediate and regulate all charitable transactions between those who received and those who gave relief.

## INSTITUTIONAL STRUCTURES

Kathryn Norberg describes the segregation of paupers in Grenoble from the general community and their confinement in a special institution as follows:

> On August 25, 1712, an event occurred in Grenoble which marked an important transition. It began on the Place Grenette where an unspecified number of paupers dined before the assembled inhabitants of the city. After eating, the paupers formed a line and marched through the streets to the Hospital General. There they exchanged their rags for new clothes in a gesture symbolic of their transformation from free individuals to inmates of the Hospital General. Finally, the gates of the *maison de force* closed behind them ... (1985: 81)

The Hospital General was not a medical institution. It was a semi-judicial entity, established for the confinement of an undifferentiated 'population ... without resources, without social moorings, a class rejected or rendered mobile by new economic developments' and its function was to implement a regimen aimed at the elimination of begging, mendicancy and vagrancy (Foucault 1971: 48). The event in Grenoble encapsulates the institutional consequences of the discourse surrounding the poor that had originated in the early modern period and that had become established across Western Europe.

During the early modern period debate among social theorists and governing elites began to crystallise around the notion of a special centre or institution for detaining and reforming the poor. Different regimens would be imposed on different categories of the poor: punishment of the idle, training for children, and relief for the deserving. Geremek (1994) describes the establishment of one of the earliest of these institutions in Lyons in 1534. Food riots and uprisings in the city prompted the formation of a pressure group, consisting of prominent humanists and dignitaries, which insisted on the need for a permanent institution to deal with the problem of the poor. As a result, a permanent *Aumône Générale* was established, modelled on the Paris Bureau of the Poor. Public begging was banned. Relief in the form of bread, and sometimes money, was distributed through the *Aumône* only to the resident, deserving poor. Orphans and foundlings from the institution were apprenticed to a trade or sent into domestic service. The recommended punishment for vagrants and recalcitrant beggars was forced labour for which they would be given food but would not be paid. The *Aumône* was given judicial and police powers and had its own prison for beggars.

The establishment of similar institutions throughout Europe began from the second half of the sixteenth century onwards (Gemerek 1994). In them, the theoretical principles of the new perspectives on poverty were put into practice. Known in Britain and Ireland as houses of correction or bridewells, they were perhaps the most revolutionary of the responses developed to regulate the poor (Beier 1985). They were revolutionary because their purpose was to produce an internal change in the individual, a transformation of character to be achieved through enforced labour, corporal punishment and a regime of discipline. While the economic viability of houses of correction was always an important consideration and while the institutions were expected to be self-supporting through the labour of those who were incarcerated, the moral war against idleness was considered to be of even greater significance.

In addition to coercion through corporal punishment, the house of correction could deploy two other important disciplinary mechanisms – timetables which set out the daily activities, and documentary records which contained details of individuals who were incarcerated (Foucault 1977; Beier 1985). These 'techniques of surveillance' are central to the operation of a disciplinary system. In such a system, 'power … is exercised by surveillance … by observation … by comparative measures that have the 'norm' as reference …' and because its goal is to produce more submissive, more efficient and more productive bodies, surveillance applied to 'the patient more than the healthy man, the madman and the delinquent more than the normal and the non-delinquent' (Foucault 1977: 193). Surveillance was the means by which deviant bodies might be corrected. Thus, the introduction of timetables and records into the house of correction created 'observatories' in order 'to render visible those who are inside …, to transform individuals …, to provide a hold on their conduct, to carry the effects of power right to them, to make it possible to know them, to alter them' (Foucault 1977: 171–2).

Policy proposals and legislation relating to the house of correction tended to emphasise its penal nature and its function as a site where idle and lazy vagabonds would be compelled to learn the habits of industry. It was, however, also seen as a place where children would be trained in 'honest callings and occupations' and 'decrepit, aged, sick, infirm and impotent persons' would be given relief (Royall, 1999: 13). In Dublin in 1631, for example, the city authorities recorded that 'Nicholas Arnold, late porter to the Maior of this cittie, who through weakness of infirmitie is not able to undergoe the said place, shall have his lodginge in the House of Correction, or in the hospitall of Saint John's, dureing his life' (Gilbert 1892: 256).

While houses of correction were perhaps the most visible institutional structures in the new approach to poverty, the work of religious and quasi-religious organisations became equally significant. Charitable foundations had a long history of providing poor relief. In the early modern period, however, these organisations acquired a new orientation and a new set of functions. Many religious congregations, for example, developed much closer working relationships with the secular authorities and the work that they did became more secularised. Many accepted the prevailing ideology

of centralising the distribution of charity, controlling vagrancy and eliminating idleness, and some became directly involved in establishing and
running institutions of confinement. As Gemerek (1994: 208–9) shows,
some of the earliest attempts to centralise the distribution of relief to the
poor were organised by the Catholic Church in Italy, often in collaboration with the secular authorities. In the context of the Counter-
Reformation a different attitude to poverty developed in the Church as it
began to adopt a more direct and systematic role in the organisation of
charity. According to the new dispensation it was argued that beggars
upset the divine order and constituted a source of impiety and scandal.

In England a compulsory poor rate was levied on each parish and
relief was distributed to the deserving poor through official parish bodies.
In France, too, although there was no direct taxation for the poor, charity
became more centralised; through the sixteenth and seventeenth centuries
organisations such as confraternities (Norberg 1985; Woolf 1986) and
*bureaux de charité* (Hufton 1974) increasingly mediated the distribution
of relief between donors and recipients. Congregations such as the
Company of the Holy Sacrament were involved both in the establishment
of vast institutions for the incarceration of the poor as well as in the creation of centralised parish based social organisations for the systematic
distribution of relief. Although confinement was the centrepiece of their
programme, through their weekly visits the Company 'penetrated right
into the homes of the poor' (Norberg 1985: 27).

The core principles of the charitable foundations were similar to those
of the houses of correction – the arrest and punishment of the idle poor,
the prohibition of individual acts of charity, the promotion of a work ethic
through enforced labour, and the organisation of approved forms of alms
distribution. Thus, while a physical regulation of the poor was implemented through houses of correction, confraternities and similar organisations deployed regulatory and surveillance techniques in the wider
social body (Hufton 1974). These two types of institutional structures prefigured developments that eventually reached their full flowering in the
nineteenth century. The house of correction was the prototype for the
development of enclosed institutions that segregated and confined a variety of problem populations – workhouses, asylums, special educational
institutions. The confraternities can be seen as the forerunners, firstly, of
a whole range of voluntary organisations that were established for philanthropic reasons and, secondly, of those professional associations – of

social workers and health visitors, for example (Tomlinson 1996) – whose members worked with particular problem populations. These organisations and associations often retained the religious or quasi-religious missionary character of their precursors.

## IDEOLOGY, PRACTICES AND STRUCTURES IN IRELAND

For the governing authorities in Ireland, idleness and sedition went hand in hand. The unstable political situation and the colonisers' perception of the Irish as innately slothful and dangerous gave an added urgency to the regulation of the poor. Town corporations were influenced by the same ideology of identification, segregation and exclusion of the poor as their English and continental counterparts. Measures proposed for regulating the poor included the separation of the deserving and the undeserving, the expulsion of 'strange' or 'foreign' beggars, the listing, licensing and badging of the resident poor, the regulation of alms-gathering, and the punishment of rogues, vagabonds and sturdy beggars (Gilbert 1891; 1892; Fitzgerald 1994; Lennon 1999; Ryan 2001). Explicit connections were also made between the poor and the dangers of disease and contamination. Thus, the emergence in Ireland of a conceptual framework regarding the poor closely followed the common pattern in Western Europe.

Municipal authorities in Ireland also proposed the same kind of institutional structures. During the 1590s and early 1600s, concerned citizens of Dublin petitioned the corporation for assistance in building a house of correction 'for putting idle persons to work' (Gilbert 1891: 390, 420). However, these efforts did not lead to any concrete scheme (Fitzgerald 1994).[2] Concerns continued to be expressed until the parliament of 1634–5 passed an 'Act for the erecting of Houses of Correction and for the punishment of Rogues Vagabonds sturdy Beggars and other lewd and idle persons' (Nicholls 1856: 28).[3] The Act proposed that a house of correction be established in every county, set out guidelines for its management, and provided a detailed list of those who would be liable 'to be examined of their wandering idle life, and punished accordingly, or otherwise sent to the house of correction and there set to labour and work' (Nicholls 1856: 29).

Compared with practice in England and continental Europe, however, the actual implementation of policy in Ireland was a different matter. In Ireland there was considerable tension between the desire of political and social elites to regulate problem populations and their willingness to meet the costs of so doing. The Act of 1634–5 stipulated a substantial network of institutions, but efforts to implement the legislation were sporadic and short-lived and very few houses of correction were actually built. Property owners in Ireland consistently opposed the imposition of a compulsory poor law rate to underwrite either the cost of a centralised parish based poor law system of the kind that existed in England or the cost of erecting and maintaining houses of correction (Dickson 1988; Fitzgerald 1994). Until the nineteenth century, responses were of the crisis management variety that peaked in times of warfare, crop failure and food shortages. Local authorities relied mainly on the exclusion or expulsion of the foreign poor, effectively shifting responsibility to another jurisdiction, the ultimate banishment being transportation overseas (Fitzgerald 1994).

In Western Europe, the regulation of relations between the poor and society in the early modern period meant that public sphere activities encroached substantially into the civil and private domains. In Ireland, there was theoretical support for these developments. In reality, however, the relative absence of statutory support, the lack of institutional structures and the weakness of the administrative machinery meant that older patterns of relations and practices were likely to be maintained, especially outside the major towns (Fitzgerald 1994; Lennon 1999; Ryan 2001). In the countryside, attitudes to the poor continued to reflect more traditional models of charity although even here there is evidence of a new insistence on discriminating between deserving and undeserving recipients of charity (O'Ciosáin 1998). Thus, in continental Europe and in Britain in the early modern period, disability, insofar as it was incorporated into responses to the impotent poor, emerged as a public issue. By comparison, in Ireland, disability relations remained a largely private matter.

## Conclusion

The political, social and cultural responses to the poor in early modern Western Europe contain the essential ideological and institutional ingredients that prefigure the treatment of other problem populations, especially people with perceived impairment. At the core of these responses was exclusion. Although exclusion was not specifically aimed at people with perceived impairments, it did affect them in a number of indirect ways. As part of the general body of the poor, they were subject to ideologies and practices that set out to justify exclusion. Firstly, the new policy, legislative and institutional measures transformed poverty from a private into a public issue and, by identifying it as a social problem, brought it over a new threshold of public visibility (Foucault 1977: 184). Secondly, poverty became subject to a new discourse of power and knowledge in which the material difficulties experienced by people who were poor were interpreted as the products of their own individual deficits and deficiencies. Thirdly, the house of correction was constituted as a site where problem people were segregated from the mainstream population. While the impotent poor were less likely to be confined than sturdy beggars in the early modern period, the house of correction pointed towards an institutionalising future.

More specifically in relation to disability, because people with perceived impairment were designated as being among the deserving poor, they were thereby subject to relatively greater scrutiny. Arthur Dobbs, an influential figure in early eighteenth century Ireland was, as we have already noted, particularly suspicious of the impotent poor. According to Dobbs, they used

> several arts and strategems ... to induce the opulent and industrious to be charitable to them. They appear in various forms, mostly affected, or brought upon them by particular management; as blind, lame, dumb, distorted, with running sores, pretended fits, and other disorders. They frequently pretend loss by fire, or to have numerous families lying sick. They exercise the greatest barbarities upon children, either their own or those they pick up, by blinding them, or breaking and disjointing their limbs when they are young, to make them objects of compassion and charity ... [They, therefore,] ... ought to be deemed equally cheats with the others. (1729: 45–6)

In addition, perceived impairment was particularly susceptible to the social cleansing measures proposed by social theorists and municipal authorities and to a strengthening of the conceptual and practical associations between impairment and dependency.

In general terms, houses of correction were never considered to be a success, even in countries where they had been established in significant numbers (Adams 1990; Beier 1985; Geremek 1994). Observers everywhere criticised the distortion of what they called the founding principles, the corruption of management, and the failure to make any appreciable progress in rehabilitating those who were confined. Incarceration and enforced labour over an extended period of time entailed considerable expense and there were high levels of recidivism (Gemerek 1994). Moreover, since they were limited to the major cities, only a small proportion of the poor came within the ambit of houses of correction (Kamen 2000). In Britain and Ireland, the function of the house of correction changed over time. Originating as institutions for regulating and disciplining the poor and created as part of a poor law system, by the end of the seventeenth century they were being used as gaols for the punishment of minor offenders (Whiting 1979).

In spite of the limitations and failures of houses of correction, the ideology of a segregationist and rehabilitative institution for the reform of the poor remained a centrepiece of social policy. Efforts continued to be directed, not so much at creating a fresh initiative, but more at attempting to rationalise and make more efficient the existing institutional models and practices. New institutions such as the houses of industry of the eighteenth century and the workhouses of the nineteenth century were, to all intents and purposes, reincarnations of the house of correction. The central objectives remained the same: to clear the streets of the mendicant, to provide some relief for the deserving poor, and to punish the idle.

The house of correction provided a prototype for the many and varied special institutions that eventually filled the landscape of Western Europe, including Ireland – hospitals, houses of industry, asylums, industrial schools, Magdalen launderies, orphanages, prisons, reformatories, special schools and workhouses. The ideology that underpinned these special institutions was already present in the house of correction. It was designed for a problem population whose condition was perceived to be at odds with the norms of society. It demanded that this population be set apart from the community and it prescribed a regime of treatment through which the individual was expected to be reformed.

The houses of industry,[4] which were provided for under Acts of 1771–2 (11 and 12 George III cap. 30), represented the most immediate successors of the houses of correction in Ireland. Introducing more elaborate dividing practices, the new institutions were to be divided into four parts – one for 'poor helpless men', another for 'poor helpless women', a third for men 'able to labour and committed as vagabonds and sturdy beggars', and the fourth for 'idle strolling and disorderly women ... found fit for labour'. Corporations established under the Act were empowered to grant badges and licenses to beg to the helpless poor who had resided for one year in their respective counties, cities or towns. Also, they were 'authorised to seize every strolling vagrant capable of labour who hath no place of abode, and doth not live by his or her labour or industry … and compel them to work' (Nicholls 1856: 53). Individuals caught begging without a licence or badge were to be committed to the stocks and persistent offenders were threatened with confinement and a public whipping.

Since the implementation of these provisions depended partly on local taxation and partly on voluntary subscriptions, 'in very few instances only were the provisions contained in these Acts carried into operation' (Nicholls 1856: 58). What the provisions do show, however, is that the underlying ideology surrounding the establishment of institutions for the poor had changed little since the sixteenth century. In fact, some commentators urged the workhouses to adopt the draconian forms of punishment reminiscent of those found in the early houses of correction. Dobbs suggested that persistent idlers should be confined in a pumphouse 'where being chained by the foot, they must either pump or be drowned' (1729: 51).

With the growth of state power and the expansion of trade, it became apparent that the regulation of the poor was an economic as well as a moral and political matter. The perception that a ready pool of cheap labour conferred advantages in international markets suggested that more exacting forms of evaluation were required to separate the deserving from the undeserving poor. In this context, the emergence of medicine as a *science politique* (Adams 1990: viii) generated a new set of ideologies and institutions with a particular focus on the human body and led to more rational and methodical approaches to the appraisal of problem populations, especially in relation to sickness and impairment.

## NOTES

1. Downing was subsequently indicted for murder, found guilty, but was reprieved by the Lord Deputy. A discussion of the background and context of these events can be found in Edwards, David (ed.) (2004), *Regions and Rulers in Ireland 1100–1650*, Dublin: Four Courts Press, 237–265.
2. The first official and explicit proposal for such an institution in Ireland appears to have been made in a proclamation of 1625 (Steele 1910) and around this time the authorities in Dublin may have built or leased a building as a house of correction (Gilbert 1892).

3.   The Act is quite specific about who was liable to be incarcerated and pun-
     ished and goes on to provide a detailed list: 'all persons calling them-
     selves scholars going about begging; all idle persons going about ... either
     begging or using any subtle craft, or unlawful games or plays, or feign-
     ing themselves to have knowledge in physiognomy palmistry or other
     like crafty science, or pretending that they can tell destinies, fortunes, or
     such other like phantastical imaginations; all persons that be or utter
     themselves to be proctors, procurers, patent gatherers, or collectors for
     gaols, prisons or hospitals; all fencers, bear-wards, common players of
     interludes and minstrels wandering abroad; all jugglers, wandering per-
     sons, and common labourers being able in body, using loytering, and
     refusing to work for such reasonable wages as is taxed and commonly
     given, and not having living otherwise to maintain themselves; all per-
     sons delivered out of gaols that beg for their fees ... all such as wander
     abroad, pretending loss by fire or otherwise; all such as wandering pre-
     tend themselves to be Egyptians, or wander in the habit form or attire of
     counterfeit Egyptians – shall be taken adjudged and deemed rogues,
     vagabonds and sturdy beggars' (Nicholls 1856: 29–30).

4.   An Act of 1703 (2 Anne cap. 19) represented an earlier attempt to revive
     the 'founding principles' of the house of correction. The Act provided for
     the establishment of a workhouse in Dublin 'for regulating and setting to
     work all vagabonds and beggars which shall come within the city or lib-
     erties'. The governors and directors of the workhouse were empowered
     'to apprehend any idle vagrants and beggars' and 'to inflict reasonable
     punishment or correction, from time to time, on all persons within the
     workhouse who shall not conform to the established regulations.' A sec-
     ond workhouse was established in Cork in 1735 where 'beggars and
     other idle vagabonds' were to be confined and 'put to hard labour'
     (9 George II cap. 25).

# 3

# The 'Body Natural' and the 'Body Politick': Medical Science and Medical Administration

[Itard] started by applying electricity to the ears of some pupils, since an Italian surgeon had recently found that a frog's leg would contract if touched with charged metal. Itard thought there was some analogy between the paralysis of the hearing organ and the paralysis of a limb. He also placed leeches on the necks of some of the pupils in the hope that local bleeding would help somehow. Six students had their eardrums pierced, but the operation was painful and fruitless, and he desisted. Not soon enough for Christian Dietz, who died following this treatment. At first, however, his ears discharged some foreign matter and he reportedly recovered some hearing and with it some speech, which led Itard to think the deaf ear might be blocked up rather than paralysed.

It was known that the postmaster at Versailles, M. Guyot, had cured his own hearing loss by inserting a probe in his Eustachian tube, which leads from the throat to the ear, and 'flushing out the lymphatic excrement'. The method had been tried by physicians and abandoned as impracticable and ineffective. Itard made improvements or rather, he had them made by pupils working in the carpentry shop; for example, a metal band was added to hold the probe still despite the patient's agitated movements. Then, over a period of eleven months, one hundred [and] twenty pupils, almost every last one in the school save for some two dozen who would not be subdued, were subjected to the treatment. Let me tell you what it was like. The band was wrapped around my forehead so that a clamp hung in front of my mouth. A long silver probe was pushed into my

47

nose and turned and worked back and forth until it penetrated my Eustachian tube; the pain was intense and I am not ashamed to say that I cried ...

What was accomplished? Why, nothing at all. Not one pupil derived any benefit ...

In desperation Itard tried fracturing the skull of a few pupils, striking the area just behind the ear with a hammer. With a dozen pupils he applied a white hot metal button behind the ear ...

It was all a miserable failure ... We were clearly not Itard's brothers but his raw materials.

Harlan Lane (1984), *When the Mind Hears*, 132–4

## Introduction

Jean-Marc Itard was appointed resident physician at the National Institution for Deaf-Mutes in Paris in 1800. His first experimental efforts were directed at Victor, 'the wild boy of Aveyron', who was placed in the school in the same year (Winzer 1993: 65). However, after several relatively unsuccessful years of attempting to teach speech and other practical skills to Victor, he turned his attentions to the pupils of the National Institution (Lane 1984). The object of his new experiments was to identify the source of the lesion, the paralysis, or the blockage that he believed might be the cause of deafness and, by doing so, establish a rational guide to treatment which would make deaf pupils more like hearing pupils, more 'normal'. Although Itard had already carried out dissections on pupils who had died and had discovered nothing except 'that the ears of the deaf are free from visible lesions' (Lane 1984: 132), he nevertheless decided to proceed with his experiments. The clinical detachment and self-confidence with which Itard approached this task illustrates the extent to which the bodies of deaf pupils, by the beginning of the nineteenth century, had been constituted as anomalous objects to be known, made docile, 'transformed and improved' (Foucault 1977: 136).

It would be wrong to assume that Itard's model of deafness was the only possible or available one. Jean Massieu, a Deaf teacher in the National Institution, had put to Itard an alternative understanding of deafness (Lane 1984: 135). Massieu explained that a Deaf community existed, that it had a distinctive language, sign language, and that for Deaf people deafness was more a question of educational opportunities than a matter of disease or blocked ears. However, it was Itard's definition of deafness as an infirmity that prevailed. It was Itard who contributed the entry on deafness to the major medical dictionary of the period, in which he described Deaf people as 'civilized men on the outside, barbaric and igno- rant as a savage on the inside; indeed, the savage is superior if he has a spoken language, however limited' (Lane 1984: 135). In this set of power- knowledge relations, Itard the physician was the recognised expert. It was he who defined the problem, set the boundaries as to how it should be investigated, and mobilised the normalising practices that were an integral aspect of the medical response.

The National Institution itself was more than a school. It served as a laboratory for the production of a body of knowledge about deafness, deaf children and what were thought to be their special needs. It was a site for subjects who were simultaneously the objects of scientific research and of disciplinary power (Foucault 1977). Itard's experiments illustrate the pre- eminence of medicine among the human sciences in this power-knowl- edge network. The emergence of medicine as a human science made it possible for the physician to exercise judgements and diagnoses of nor- mality and abnormality in individuals and, if intervention was deemed necessary, to propose 'appropriate procedures to achieve a rehabilitation or restoration of and to the norm' (Smart 1985: 93). With gathering impe- tus, from the eighteenth century onwards, society in Western Europe became more medicalised and greater numbers of specially trained and certified practitioners, whose expertise was based on scientific medicine, began to exercise greater authority over individuals and over national pop- ulations (Cook 1997; Kelly 1999; Porter 1997). In this process, people with illnesses and impairments were brought into a new field of knowl- edge and power (Foucault 1977).

In this chapter I discuss the concepts and practices that provided the foundation for a medical model of disability. In particular, I focus on the manner in which scientific medicine and health administration established criteria of definition for the 'body natural' and the 'body politick' (preface to Petty 1691), and on the development of associated clinical, technocratic and quantifying practices. I examine the emergence of the physician as the pre-eminent authority on individual and social anomaly. I explore how institutions, especially the first modern hospitals, functioned as observa- tories where human clinical material was made available for investigation and experimentation, as laboratories where physicians acquired the skills and experience necessary to achieve recognition and acceptance as experts, and as channels through which the distribution of charity could be controlled and supervised. All of these areas constituted interrelated and interdependent elements in a process of change in which individuals began to be assigned to particular categories and to particular institutions on the basis of illness or perceived impairment.

## INDIVIDUAL AND SOCIAL BODIES

Foucault (1979) envisaged two dimensions along which a new modality of power, which he called bio-power, began to be exercised over human life. One dimension, of which Itard's experiments in the Paris institution are examples, was constituted around a systematic investigation and intervention in relation to the individual body in order to optimise its capabilities and increase its usefulness. This is the domain of scientific medicine with its focus on individual states of health, illness or impairment and their associated clinical and therapeutic practices (Porter, R. 1995; 1997; Porter, D. 1999). The second dimension is exemplified in the existence of the Paris institution itself, an institution specifically designed for a deaf population. In a general sense, this dimension involved the management of national populations; more specifically, it involved the regulation of subsets within the social body that appeared to weaken the strength, wealth and productivity of the state (Foucault 1980). This 'medical police' (Rosen 1974: 120), 'social medicine' (Adams 1990: 173) or 'science of health administration' (Porter 1999: 52) required the gathering of concrete, specific and measurable knowledge about the economic, social and physiological conditions of the aggregate body and the implementation of national policies that would ensure a productive and disciplined population. Obviously, a science of health administration will draw on theory and practice in scientific medicine, and vice versa.

Ideologies and practices in scientific medicine and health administration had powerful and interrelated roles in generating normalising regimes for both individuals and populations. By constructing normative types such as, for example, 'the patient' and types of types, such as 'classes of patients', these two disciplines made it possible to link individual case histories with categories of cases (Owen 1999: 598). In this way, specific individuals could be assigned to, and ranked within specific categories. The disciplines of medicine and health administration replaced the earlier heterogeneous and haphazard patterns of identification, segregation and confinement with more scientifically refined dividing practices (Dreyfus and Rabinow 1982).

In addition, as new specialist institutions and organisations were established, there was an accompanying reformulation of the discourse on charity (Powell 1992; Cassell 1997; Geary 2004). The rhetoric surrounding the house of correction had emphasised its penal nature and the central part that physical punishment should play in its programmes of correction. In contrast, the rhetoric surrounding the emerging, more specialised institutions stressed their progressive, reforming and caring nature. Institutions such as public infirmaries and voluntary hospitals, for example, became channels for the distribution of approved forms of charity, and the sick poor and the afflicted were identified and promoted as uniquely deserving populations (Cassell 1997; Waddington 2000; Geary 2004).

Ideologies and practices grounded in scientific medicine, health administration and charity are among the most familiar and prominent features of current responses to disability. A medical model of disability constitutes the most powerful and pervasive modern influence in defining and responding to impairment (Oliver 1990; French 1994; Barnes 1996; Barnes and Mercer 2003). Most research, legislation and policy development in relation to disability is underpinned by a medical paradigm that emphasises measurement, quantification and categorisation (Oliver 1992; 1996). Moreover, cultural representations of disability are dominated by images of disabled people as pathetic and tragic figures in need of help, as objects of pity or sources of inspiration deserving of charity (Morris 1991; Barnes 1992; Shapiro 1993; Shakespeare 1996).

Until the eighteenth century, people with illnesses or impairments had been seen as part of a larger, heterogeneous problem population whose common denominator was poverty: they were poor people who happened to be sick or impaired (Foucault 1980; Jones 1996). The techniques of scientific medicine and the science of health administration provided 'a finer grid of observation of the population' which brought about the progressive dismantling of this population (Foucault 1980: 169). In this process, the 'sick poor' (sick people who happened to be poor), especially during the second half of the eighteenth century, were transformed into the 'poor sick' (sick people who deserved charity). Medical criteria were increasingly used to create new classifications and to propose distinctive institutional and therapeutic responses. Thus, by the end of the eighteenth century in Ireland, the first modern hospitals – for the sick poor – were well established (Kelly 1999) and shortly afterwards the first modern institutions for people with impairments – schools for 'deaf and dumb children of the poor', for example – made their appearance (McDonnell 1979).

A new focus of attention on the body and its capacities is evident when we compare Tudor and Stuart legislation concerned with problem populations with that of the Georgian period. A 1537 Act (33 Henry VIII cap. 15) made only a general distinction between 'aged, poor, and impotent persons compelled to live by alms' and those defined as 'vagabonds and mighty strong beggars'. In contrast, the 1765 Infirmaries Act (5 George III cap. 20) brought a new degree of classification to the impotent poor when it set out to provide 'receptacles in the several counties of this kingdom ... for the poor who are infirm and diseased ...' Similarly, an Act of 1772 (11 and 12 George III cap. 30) stated specifically that it was 'necessary to give countenance to those poor who shall be found disabled by ... infirmities'. Through this visibility, the body became the focus of a 'medical gaze' (Foucault 1976: 29), which interpreted and classified any anomalies and prescribed appropriate treatments.

## The 'Body Natural' and the 'Body Politick'

During the sixteenth century, the primary tenor of the discourse on the idle poor was moral rather than economic. By the eighteenth century, however, the intense moral condemnation of idleness was reinforced by an ideology that stressed the economic and psychological implications of idleness and, more specifically, by a growing perception of the poor as an unexploited economic resource. Discourses on vagrancy and idleness began to highlight the notion of work as a civic obligation (Adams 1990: 30): by depriving the state of their labour, the idle poor reduced the potential of the state to create wealth and, thereby, conceded a competitive edge to its economic rivals. The condemnation of the idle poor now added an accusation of treason to the already familiar one of scandal.

As we have noted, indiscriminate charity was believed to be harmful to the fabric of a society in which the prototypical deviant was the idle beggar. As charity became more centred on the deserving poor, it was thought to be necessary 'to prevent the necessitous poor, capable of labour, from procuring subsistence without useful industry' (Report of the

Association for the Suppression of Mendicity 1819: 23). To dispense charity judiciously, it would not only be necessary to separate the impotent or respectable poor from the undeserving poor, but also to find ways of inducting the impotent poor into the labour force. These processes of differentiation brought about a new preoccupation with the human body and its classification and created a context for the emergence of the physician as the arbiter of the boundary between fitness and impotence.

The preoccupation with physiological characteristics of populations and of individual bodies, was directly related to the rise of mercantilist economics. A fundamental tenet of mercantilism was the definition of labour as the fundamental source of the wealth of the state (Himmelfarb 1984; Rosen 1974). In the mercantilist state, economics and utility demanded a large reservoir of healthy, cheap labour and taught that disease and ill-health damaged both the individual body and the body politic. Sick workers made inefficient employees and a healthy population was required to create both an effective labour force for the production of taxable goods and the maintenance of a competent standing army. The mercantilist perspective on the relationship between idleness and the economy is well captured by Arthur Dobbs, the surveyor-general of Ireland. Dobbs calculated that there were '34,425 strolling Beggars in the Kingdom; of which there are not 1 in 10 real Objects [of compassion] ... So that we may suppose 30,000 of them able to work; and computing their Labour ... the whole Number would amount to £142,000 annually, which is just so much lost to the Kingdom in the way of Trade' (1729: 46–7).

These considerations of the macro-relationship between populations and the economy were supplemented by new interpretations of the micro-relationship between work and the individual. One of the main ideological principles in the new *dépôts de mendicité* of eighteenth-century France, for example, was the notion of enforced work as a civilizing or therapeutic activity, rather than a punishment. This new approach was founded on the belief that willful idleness was a form of illness or disease and that, within an appropriate institutional framework, individuals could be 'led to discover that the effort of disciplined labour was associated with the material and psychic rewards of "ease"' (Adams 1990: 255). In 1818, the founders of the Dublin Mendicity Institution expressed similar views about the civilising and moralising effects of work when they claimed that '[b]y it alone can the unruly passions, the idle and immoral habits of adults be restrained' (Report of the Association for the Suppression of

Mendicity 1819: 15). Work, then, was being positively connected with ideas of good citizenship and social health and negatively with ideas of dependency and worthlessness.

The key elements of the new discourses and practices surrounding the relationship between individual physical well-being and national economic health were united in the person and work of Sir William Petty. Petty, a statistician, economist, physician, and anatomist, was appointed physician general to the army in Ireland in 1652. In the preface to his *Political Anatomy of Ireland* (1691) he refers to the relationship between the 'Body Natural' and the 'Body Politick' and to 'the Arts of preserving both in Health and Strength'. His political arithmetic set out to show that there were economic advantages to be gained through administrative intervention and investment in the health of the labour force. In calculating the labour value of a population, for example, Petty argued 'that 100,000 persons dying of the Plague, above the ordinary number, is near 7 millions loss to the Kingdom; and consequently how well might 70,000 l. have been bestowed in preventing this Centuple loss' (1691: 8). He also estimated the number of individual lives and the amount of wealth that might be secured if the number of medical practitioners was increased (Porter 1999: 50). In Petty's political arithmetic, medicine and its practitioners were the critical mediating factors between individual and aggregate health, and the health of the economy.

Historians of medicine point to distinctive political, economic and cultural patterns in the emergence of modern medical theory and practice in different countries in Western Europe (Conrad *et al.* 1995; Loudon 1997; Porter 1999; Risse 1996). Differences in the impact of the Enlightenment, in the relationship between medicine and the State, in the institutional structures of medicine, in medical training and education, and in the organisation of a medical profession, led to considerable national and regional variation. In spite of these differences, however, the eventual outcomes were remarkably consistent across national boundaries. Firstly, medicine achieved a dominant position in the human sciences; secondly, the modern hospital played a central role in the establishment of scientific medicine and of a medical profession; and, finally, scientific medicine became the decisive discipline, and the physician the mediating authority, in the identification, assessment and treatment of individual and social anomalies. Together, these features constituted the defining characteristics of what became known as Western medicine (Conrad *et al.* 1995; Loudon

1997; Porter 1999) and provided the conceptual and practical foundations for creating a medical model of disability.

## POLITICAL ARITHMETIC: SCIENTIFIC MEDICINE

From the middle of the seventeenth century, three developments, incorporating both theory and practice, were central to the establishment of scientific medicine in Western Europe (Cook 1997; Porter 1997). Firstly, there was a growing conviction that medical truth could be found by investigating the chemical and material structures of the human body. This perspective was linked to distinctive clinical practices that included observation, physical examination, experimentation and dissection. Secondly, new procedures for the formal training, certification and regulation of medical practitioners began to be established. The formation of a medical profession required the articulation of distinctive social practices, including the creation of a rhetoric of progress and of care surrounding medicine and its practitioners as well as the gradual exclusion and devaluation of lay approaches in the medical market. Thirdly, the early modern hospitals of the eighteenth and nineteenth centuries helped to create and, in turn, were creations of, scientific medicine. The hospitals provided the means and the opportunity to acquire clinical skills and professional expertise; they were also the institutional sites where clinical and professional practices could be exercised and promoted.

For observation, physical examination, experimentation and dissection to take place it was necessary to have a ready supply of raw material. The early modern hospital foundations for the sick poor and other relatively powerless groups provided the bodies required for this purpose (Jones and Malcolm 1999; Loudon 1997; Murphy-Lawless 1998; Porter 1997; Powell 1992). In Paris, for example, the huge public hospitals with their 20,000 beds offered virtually unlimited access to the sick poor who 'became commodified as clinical material' (Porter 1997: 308). In Dublin, poor women in the lying-in hospitals created a captive population for the training of male mid-wives and students were provided with opportunities to practise obstetric operations and to use new instruments (Murphy-Lawless 1998). In Edinburgh, the success of the medical school owed much to its links with the town infirmary: there, instructive cases were selected to serve as teaching material for clinical lectures (Porter 1995). Patients in the new military and naval hospitals, being under military orders, were subject to experimental treatments without concern for what today would be called ethical issues (Jones 1989; Tröhler and Prüll 1997). Prisoners, slaves and orphaned children were also selected for testing new treatments (Porter 1997; 1999), the first known attempt to inoculate against smallpox in Ireland being made on prisoners in Cork in 1721 (Kelly 1999).

Although the precise nature of scientific medicine was hotly disputed, by the end of the eighteenth century the issue was being settled in favour of pathological anatomy, most characteristically practised in Paris in the aftermath of the Revolution (Porter 1997). The ease with which it was possible to obtain clinical, and especially dissection, experience in the Paris hospitals attracted hundreds of medical students from abroad and this in turn reinforced a movement towards pathological anatomy that was already under way in other Western European countries (Fleetwood 1983; Richardson 1987; Risse 1996). The central procedure in pathological anatomy was the autopsy, during which an attempt was made to identify and correlate the underlying pathological signs with the symptoms that had already been observed. Its advocates were convinced that pathological anatomy created the basis, not only of all medical knowledge, but also of all medical treatment (Cook 1997; Porter 1997). Throughout the eighteenth century, as clinical teaching in hospitals became more common, the demand for bodies increased and the number of dissections rose dramatically in spite of legal restrictions and considerable popular antipathy (Cook 1997; Porter 1995; 1995a; Richardson 1987).

The dominance of pathological anatomy in medicine oriented practitioners towards an interpretative paradigm that explained clinical differences in terms of pathological anomalies. Illness, disease and impairment were easily conflated within the same pathological model and, while this model might prove valuable in the investigation of disease and illness and in the development of therapeutic responses, this was not so in relation to impairment (Barnes and Mercer 1996). In Itard's experiments we have seen how deafness was defined as a pathological condition which seemed to demand clinical intervention, and how an alternative, Deaf perspective, drawing on language and community rather than on illness and disease, was swept aside. As many recent critical studies in the field of disability demonstrate, a medical perspective has universally pathologised impairment and, in doing so, has masked the political, social and economic inequalities that, in fact, create disability (Abberley 1987; Oliver 1990; French 1994; Barnes 1996; Barnes and Mercer 2003).

The conviction that pathological anatomy was based on reason and science made it virtually unassailable. It generated a 'see much, do much,' hands-on approach in medical practice (Tröhler and Prüll 1987). It fostered aggressive forms of intervention in which the individuality of the patient all but vanished under the all-powerful medical gaze, and left only the pathological condition. Critics warned of the dangers of by-passing the patient and declared that in the face of such clinical detachment, '[t]he sick person has become a thing' (cited in Porter 1997: 311). Patients became 'letters, numbers, symptoms, fragmented into body parts. What matters is the disease process that is thought to have killed them; that is what is named in vivid detail' (Murphy-Lawless 1998: 50). The experiences of deaf pupils at the National Institution for the Deaf in Paris in the early years of the nineteenth century reflected this tendency towards clinical abstraction.

Moreover, the growing practice of dissection displaced many traditional and deep-seated forms of deference towards the body. In her analysis of the Anatomy Act 1832, which made available for dissection the unclaimed bodies of those who died in the workhouse, Ruth Richardson notes that 'dissection requires in its practitioners the effective suspension or suppression of many normal physical and emotional responses to the willful mutilation of the body of another human being' (1987: 30). Richardson goes on to observe that the acquisition of such 'clinical detachment can be seen as a historical process both in the lives of individual clinicians and, over a much longer period, in the history of medicine itself'(1987: 31). But whatever the terror of the destitute before they died, it could at least be argued that during dissection they did not suffer any actual pain. Richardson, however, argues that the detachment acquired in connection with the dissection of corpses became embedded in inhumane and sometimes brutal attitudes towards the bodies of the poor who had to undergo medical treatment.

The construction of difference as individual pathology, combined with the practice of scientific detachment, created a basis for many questionable interventions in relation to perceived impairment. The experiments on the deaf pupils of the Paris institution required a detachment that permitted Itard to force them to undergo harrowing experiences and then to discount their pain and suffering, presumably in the interests of some higher scientific goal. In more recent times, Oliver has argued that the same kind of detachment underlies certain interventions in the lives of disabled children, regardless of 'the costs involved in terms of pain, coercion, loss of child-hood, disruption of family life, acceptance of alternative ways of doing things, and so on' (1990: 56). It also underlies the implantation of young deaf children with 'highly experimental [cochlear] devices of questionable therapeutic value' and 'without informed consent' (Lane 1993: 231).

Scientific medicine silenced and disempowered those who came under its authority. Itard's successor as resident physician in the Paris school, Prosper Ménière, made explicit the nature of the relationship that should exist between the expert and the anomalous subject: 'The deaf believe that they are our equals in all respects. We should be generous and not destroy that illusion. But whatever they believe, deafness is an infir-mity, and we should repair it whether the person who has it is disturbed by it or not' (cited in Lane 1984: 134). Social class, gender and perceived impairment determined whether patients became patrons of medical prac-titioners or whether they became clinical material to be used in observa-tion, teaching, experimentation and research (Murphy-Lawless 1998; Richardson 1987). Rich, literate patients have left abundant individual accounts of their experiences; the experiences of the rest have been trans-formed into data, written up by doctors or administrators in standardised formats and exist only as cases in institutional records (Digby 1997). Murphy-Lawless refers to the way that obstetric medicine has silenced women: 'There were thousands of pages of clinical records from lying-in hospitals but few published first-hand accounts of hospitalised childbirth from women themselves ... up to the emergence of the childbirth move-ment in the 1960s' (1998: 31). In a comparable manner, disabled people have been silenced by the human sciences. Thousands of texts from the fields of medicine, psychology, psychiatry and education, reflect clinical or pathological interpretations of disability. Of these, only a tiny propor-tion consists of alternative accounts by disabled people themselves (Oliver 1992; Borsay 2002). Such a discrepancy indicates the enormous extent to which professional perspectives have dominated their respective fields and thereby functioned as disabling factors (Hoffmeister 1996; Saunders 1997).

The silencing of recipients of medical treatment, the creation of supe-rior voices and the exclusion of lay perspectives were all part of a con-scious effort to confirm the authority of scientific medicine and to extend it into new areas of social life (Lewis 1997; Murphy-Lawless 1998; Pelling 1997). The hospital foundations of the eighteenth and nineteenth centuries provided the necessary institutional context for the development and implementation of these social practices (Powell 1992; Risse 1996; Cassell 1997; Loudon 1997; Porter 1997; Murphy-Lawless 1998; Jones and Malcolm 1999). Essentially, what was involved was the establishment of a medical profession.

## PROFESSIONALISING MEDICINE: SOCIAL AND INSTITUTIONAL PRACTICES

Because of its claims to superior kinds of technical and intellectual expertise, the idea of a profession is closely connected with education and training. With regard to an emerging medical profession, university medical schools, private anatomy schools and hospitals all could offer education and training. Of these, the hospital was the lynchpin institution in that it created the space where observation, teaching, research and treatment could all be conducted and co-ordinated (Freidson 1963; Nettleton 1995; Porter 1995; 1995a; 1999; Risse 1996; Tröhler and Prüll 1997). It is worth looking at the modern hospital as a locus for training, not only because of its role in the professionalisation of medicine but also because it provided a model for a particular type of education and training that came to dominate the field of disability. It permitted captive social groups to be exploited for training purposes, a practice that was justified on the grounds that this was ultimately for the benefit of the individuals concerned. In addition, the conduct of training and research was legitimated by the status of the hospital as a charitable foundation and by its aura of altruistic endeavour.

Two kinds of hospital foundation stimulated the emergence of a medical profession in Ireland. The Infirmaries Act of 1765 stated that the provision of infirmaries 'in the several counties of this kingdom ... for the poor, who are infirm and diseased, would be a means of restoring the health and preserving the lives of many of His Majesty's subjects, of promoting labour and industry, and of encouraging the manufacturers of this kingdom' (5 George III cap. 20, 1765). This Act provided public subsidies for several existing hospitals and empowered local authorities to erect infirmaries in each county that would be supported by a combination of private and public funding. Although many of the infirmaries were later criticised for the poor quality of medical care and hygiene they provided (Howard 1789), they did mark an important first step in facilitating the spread of scientific medicine and of 'professional medical men' through-out the country (Cassell 1997). In attempting to ensure that the infirmaries were staffed by qualified personnel, the Act stipulated that the credentials of appointees had to be approved by the surgeon general and by surgical staffs at Steevens' and Mercer's hospitals in Dublin (Kelly 1999). After 1796, appointees were required to hold a license from the College of Surgeons (Cassell 1997).

The second kind of foundation was the voluntary hospital. Voluntary hospitals were at first supported entirely through charitable subscriptions and were 'frequently the initiatives of medical entrepreneurs who sought profes-sional and social advancement as well as material gain' (Powell 1992: 15). The first voluntary hospital in Ireland or Britain, the Charitable Infirmary, was established by six surgeons in Dublin in 1718 and was quickly followed by others.[1] The voluntary hospitals were, from the beginning, institutions for the conduct of medical training and research (Fleetwood 1983; Coakley 1988; Harrison 1995; Tröhler and Prüll 1997). They provided a base for the commencement of a career in medicine, for making a scientific name, and for achieving public recognition (Porter 1995a). The point was not lost on contemporary critics: '[E]very thing is left to the care of people intent on gain … Everything appeared to be conducted for the accommodation of medical men and their pupils, who came to make experiments on the poor, for the benefit of the rich' (Wollstonecraft 1798: 118).

Every hospital had one or more honorary positions to be filled. Through the hospital, ambitious individuals could also expect to gain access to powerful patrons and wealthy private patients (Porter 1995a; Risse 1996). The rapid rate at which the new voluntary hospitals appeared and expanded in Dublin indicated how relatively successful they were as business enterprises (Kelly 1999). Students paid for the opportunity to walk the wards, view the patients, treat the sick and attend lectures on anatomy, pharmacy, surgery and practical medicine (Porter 1995a). The income for the first year of the Royal City of Dublin Hospital, which was established in 1831 by six doctors associated with the Royal College of Surgeons, came mainly from the fees of students who were taught in the hospital. By making the treatment of accidents a speciality, this hospital was particularly attractive for students who wished to pursue a career in the British army or navy (Coakley 1995). By 1800, doctors had acquired a pre-eminent position in Dublin society (McGeachie 1999), and during the nineteenth century the growing status of doctors as professionals was confirmed when they become the decisive figures in hospital management and administration (Tröhler and Prüll 1997).

Hospitals enabled doctors to transform their relationship with patients (Fissell 1991). Before the appearance of the early modern hospital, doctors were not thought to hold a monopoly of medical expertise (Porter 1995a). When people became ill they might make their own diagnosis and seek the advice of friends, family members, the squire, the parson or the lay healer. Because doctors came from a lower social class relative to many of their patients, they were expected to show deference and confirm the diagnosis the patient had already arrived at (Porter 1997). Even after the establishment of voluntary hospitals, middle- and upper-class patients continued to expect to be visited at home by the doctor (Digby 1997). One early nineteenth century text advised that doctors should prescribe any medicines favoured by their wealthy fee-paying patients, if their patients so wished, but that poor charity patients being treated free in hospitals should not be so indulged (cited in Porter 1995a). In the longer term, however, through the hospital, control shifted from the patient to the doctor, and diagnosis and treatment based in the institution became the norm (Jewson 1976; Fissell 1991).

The institutional structures and social practices surrounding the emergence of a medical profession are significant because they created a model and a methodology for induction into what Skrtic (1995) calls the social professions, that is, where professional formation is grounded in the social sciences. As we have seen, the hospital constituted an institutional space where trainees could be exposed to the applied knowledge of the profession and where they could acquire the appropriate skills and attitudes under the guidance of experienced practitioners. The idea of practical placement or internship, where trainees could get hands-on experience, became a central element of induction into the social professions (Skrtic 1995). The emerging medical profession also established a particular kind of professional-client relationship in which the latter had to accept a subordinate role. Two elements were central to this process – the creation of a body of professional knowledge and the establishment of professional autonomy. Because of their specialised knowledge, professionals were deemed to know what was best for their clients and all decisions as to the efficacy of this knowledge were made by professionals themselves.

For the sick poor, however, hospitals were places to be feared: fear of being used as clinical material for observation and teaching, of becoming trial subjects of new procedures and experiments, of undergoing surgery

without anaesthesia or antisepsis, of dying from hospital infection, or of dissection (Digby 1997; Porter 1997; Richardson 1987).[2] Yet, the poor entered
hospitals in increasing numbers (Digby 1997). During the second decade of
its existence, the numbers of poor women giving birth in the Dublin Lying-
in Hospital doubled, and nearly doubled again over the next twenty years,
even though both infant and maternal mortality rates remained very high
(Kelly 1999). For the poor, the primary attraction of the hospital was charity
rather than medical care (Geary 2004). In the absence of an Irish poor law
the medical charities were among the few avenues to public relief for the
poor. As one contemporary medical practitioner put it: 'The medical charities are in fact the *poor law* of Ireland' (Phelan 1835: 9, italics in original).

## MEDICAL CHARITY: PHILANTHROPY OR DISCIPLINE?

The rhetoric of care and benevolence surrounding the establishment of
medical charities – the principal form of which was the early modern
hospital – was a powerful one. Early modern hospitals could refer back to
a much older and explicitly Christian tradition of the hospital as a centre of
material and spiritual welfare rather than as a medical institution for the
poor (Jones 1989). Because the hospital could claim to be a response to a
deserving population, the founders invariably highlighted the benefits that
their institution could bring to the sick poor and the afflicted. Thus, the
Charitable Infirmary was founded in Dublin in 1718 to alleviate 'the miserable conditions of the sick poor in the city' and once established it catered
for 'great numbers of the maimed, wounded and diseased poor' (cited in
O'Brien 1987: 2–3). Similarly, the Dublin Lying-in Hospital was established in 1745 to alleviate 'the Misery of poor women of the city of Dublin,
at the time of their lying-in … in cold garrets … or in damp cellars … destitute of attendance, medicines, and often of proper food by which hundreds perished with their little infants' (cited in Campbell Ross 1986: 14).

One recent study argues that the real significance of eighteenth century medical charities in Ireland was their provision of comprehensive and
relatively generous relief (Cassell 1997: 17). Hospitals, especially voluntary hospitals, came to be regarded as uniquely philanthropic institutions
(see, for example, Campbell Ross 1986; Browne 1995; Coakley 1995).
Most histories of these foundations accept this perspective and are content
to repeat the altruistic rhetoric of the founders (Malcolm and Jones 1999).
Even the more self-consciously critical accounts find it relatively difficult

to look beyond notions of scientific progress and philanthropy (O'Gráda 1995; Kelly 1999; McGeachie 1999). It would be unreasonable to deny outright the existence of benevolent motives on the part of the founders and supporters of early modern hospitals, or to claim that there was no humanitarian dimension to their work. It seems reasonable to believe that, in every period, individuals are moved to try to alleviate suffering. On the other hand the philanthropic impulse which, it is suggested, brought about so many hospital foundations (Jones 1989; Porter 1999; Waddington 2000), was often contingent on the individual, professional and social benefits that could be gained by donors and by medical practitioners.

By dispensing charity through institutions such as hospitals, social and political elites could acquire social recognition and prestige and con-firm existing ties of deference and paternalism (McDonnell 1979; Porter 1995a; Waddington 2000). Religious revival and spiritual reform move-ments emphasised how contributions to hospitals could fulfill the moral responsibilities of wealth and leisure and, for those with deep religious convictions, such enlightened charity constituted 'a form of fire insurance for the afterlife' (Waddington 2000: 27). At the same time, hospitals appealed to ideas of national efficiency, of being institutions which pre-vented the spread of disease and which reduced the time lost through sick-ness by expeditiously returning patients to work (Geary 2004). Thus, the hospital could guarantee value for money and, at the same time, present an effective and rational medium for dispensing relief (Waddington 2000). Furthermore, it was argued that hospital development contributed to social progress and the advancement of science (Loudon 1997; Porter 1997; Waddington 2000). The identification of social groups such as the sick, the very young, and people with impairment as uniquely deserving of charity was copper-fastened when the charitable support of the public was supplemented by parliamentary grants (Kelly 1999).

Financial support for the regulation of public health was, of course, of practical benefit and enlightened self-interest to the donors themselves. The hospitalisation of the poor was certainly in their interest since, during epi-demics, the wealthy were even more at risk than the poor (Cassell 1997; Crawford 1999), and the costs involved in caring for the poor could be considered 'as a kind of life insurance to the rich who are in health' (cited in Geary 2004: 193). Some of the early voluntary hospitals in Ireland were founded for the specific purpose of preventing the spread of conta-gion (Kelly 1999) and, like houses of industry, some had an explicit social hygiene remit in that they were expected 'to remove from view patients whose diseases render them offensive' (Burke 1993: 41–2).

In many respects, the ideology of charity in relation to disability is derived from the hospital model. Like disability charity today (Drake 1996), the hospital depoliticised the contexts in which it offered its services. It justified its work in terms of goodwill rather than entitlements and claimed to be a distinctively philanthropic institution. Similarly, the recipients of its services were always constructed as deserving, and sometimes as inspiring, tragic or pitiful figures. Hospitals provided a channel for the distribution of an approved form of charity that was outside the influence of those who received it. In the hospital, funds were transformed into particular kinds of services, over which recipients had little control, and the altruistic context in which these were offered made it very difficult to criticise or reject them. If they did question or challenge what was being offered, supplicants ran the risk of having to do without, since the hospital was often the only source of relief. The whole process brought moral, professional and even economic gains for those who ran the hospital as well as moral and practical benefits to those who supported it. A similar ideology of worthy social investment is used to encourage modern charitable giving, when it is claimed that contributions will be used to underwrite disability-related research, training and education.

It is important, however, to recognise that, while altruistic motives may have played some part in the development and expansion of a hospital sector, other very powerful social, political and economic forces were at work. Theorists such as Foucault (1976) argue that hospitals had regulatory and disciplinary functions that were much more significant than their role as centres of care.[3] Hospitals incorporated many of the regulatory and coercive functions of contemporary prisons and houses of industry (Jones 1996; Tröhler and Prüll 1997). The daily lives of patients were tightly regulated and were kept under close surveillance (Burke 1993). On being admitted to hospitals, patients had to comply with the authoritarian discipline or be dismissed, regardless of their state of health (Tröhler and Prüll 1997). Hospitals demanded obedience (Porter 1995a) and strict submission 'to the Rules and Orders of the House' (cited in Campbell Ross 1986: 35). The Royal Hospital, for example, stipulated that patients had to wear hospital clothing at all times, even when they left the hospital grounds, and many patients were punished for disobeying this regulation (Burke 1993). Punishment incurred a reduction in diet, complete confinement in the institution – some patients were permitted to leave the premises at stipulated times – or even dismissal.

Hospitals were selective in their admissions policies (Porter 1989). The main criteria for admission were economic and social rather than medical and, for a long time, poor people with what were deemed to be morally condemnable or incurable illnesses were excluded. Such patients were considered to be undeserving, or it was thought unlikely that they could be restored to the labour force. Thus, governors of the Royal Hospital Donnybrook objected to individuals being transferred from the House of Industry since they 'were necessarily of the lowest description, they brought with them all the vicious and immoral practices of early habits and soon introduced among the established patients of the house, who were selected from decent classes of society, their own habits and propensities' (cited in Burke 1993: 13).

Some hospitals had a very specific regulatory function. A primary function of the Royal Hospital for Incurables, for example, was to remove from the streets 'those miserable objects who were offensive to the sight' (Burke 1993: 5). The hospital later drew up 'a list of such objects as appear from their deformity as unfit to be exposed to public viewing' (Burke 1993: 42). Freeing the public 'from those disagreeable sights' was clearly important to the governors since certain listed individuals were not permitted to leave the premises under pain of being forced to leave the hospital altogether. To keep 'wretched objects' off 'the Public Streets' the governors planned to construct 'a proper walk ... at the hospital' so that 'there would no longer exist any necessity for permitting them to go abroad' (Burke 1993: 42, 45). For the governors, seclusion from the public view was so important that they went so far as to consider how individuals on the restricted list might be suitably indemnified for their confinement (Burke 1993). The notion of segregation and confinement out of sight echoes the earlier objections to the public presence of beggars, and prefigures the wholesale segregation and confinement of thousands of adults and children in institutions in Ireland during the nineteenth and twentieth centuries.

With its sponsorship of the poor, with operating paradigms of progress, care and rehabilitation, and with its promotion of activities designed to gain the financial and moral support of political and social elites, the early modern hospital provided an institutional model for the many new charitable and philanthropic foundations that were to be established during the nineteenth and twentieth centuries. Firstly, it provided an enclosed site for the segregation of a social group deemed to present a threat to the well-being of the social body. The accompanying rhetoric, however, dwelt heavily on the claim that segregation and confinement were for the patient's own good. Secondly, the hospital created a base for the development and practice of a form of scientific medicine which was based on pathology, which interpreted human anomalies in terms of pathology, and in which the 'sick person is transformed into a pathological site' (Porter 1997: 311). The ideology and practice underlying this medical model of the individual was, as we shall see in Chapter 4, transferred to, and articulated in, other institutions. Thirdly, the hospital functioned as an observatory for the collection of clinical data and facilitated the exploitation of the sick poor for the training of medical professionals. Practices of this kind were to become standard in institutions where on-site professional training was provided in disciplines such as education, psychology and psychiatry. Fourthly, the hospital constituted a site that enabled medical practitioners to acquire professional authority and expertise. It provided a springboard for the domination of other institutional sites – asylums and special schools, for example – in which medical professionals had a vested interest (McDonnell 1992).

## POLITICAL ARITHMETIC: THE SCIENCE OF HEALTH ADMINISTRATION

As we have seen, the primary goal of scientific medicine was the identification, explanation and treatment of individual pathological conditions. The goal of the science of health administration, or medical police as it was called in some countries, was the identification, explanation and treatment of what were perceived to be pathological conditions in the social body (Porter 1999; Rosen 1974). The science of health administration combined enumeration and classification with the clinical practices of scientific medicine in order to bring 'life and its mechanisms into the realm of explicit calculations' (Foucault 1979: 143). Fundamentally, it was about setting quantitative standards or norms, at an aggregate level, in relation to matters such as the regulation of public health, sanitation and the control of disease (Porter 1997), and at an individual level in relation to personal physiology, hygiene and nutrition (Adams 1990).

The science of health administration made it possible to identify subsets in the general population 'in order to make them the focus of attention of a medical social apparatus' and to employ statistical techniques for 'abstracting the characteristics of ... [such a] population subset in mathematical form' (Murphy-Lawless 1998: 159). In this context, statistical techniques were first applied in relation to what were perceived as deviancies – suicide, crime, vagrancy, madness, prostitution and disease (Hacking 1990). The underlying notion was that enumeration and classification were crucial elements in the attempt to control and transform deviant social groups. The combination of quantitative and clinical practices created the foundation for more elaborate and systematic differentiation between normal and pathological social states (Porter 1999).

The operation of more sophisticated dividing practices in eighteenth century Western Europe is reflected in the number and variety of new, especially medical, institutions that were established (Finzsch and Jütte 1996; Loudon 1997). Although dividing practices in Ireland had not achieved the degree of refinement favoured by John Howard (1789) in his survey of Irish institutions, things were moving in that direction. The new medical foundations ranged from simple, one-roomed dispensaries to large multi-purpose general hospitals (Cassell 1997: 1). In addition, many specialist institutions began to appear – lunatic asylums, lying-in hospitals, foundling hospitals, fever hospitals, hospitals for venereal diseases, as well as military hospitals (Howard 1789; Kelly 1999).

The more traditional institutions of confinement were also affected by the science of health administration. The Dublin House of Industry, for example, set up in 1773 as a house of industry for the idle poor, incorporated a hospital, an asylum for children, penitentiaries for women and young offenders, as well as cells for lunatics (Reynolds 1992). In 1786, its directors stated that the present buildings were 'utterly unfit for the purposes of properly separating and classing the Poor' and petitioned the Irish House of Commons '... to grant them a Building adapted to the Discrimination of the different Classes of Paupers'. In their petition, the directors categorised the occupants of the institution on 25 December 1785 as follows:

659 Infirm and Incurable
 83 Lunatic
 24 Blind
102 In the hospital
488 Employed at Manufactures, and in the servile Work of the House

(Journal of the House of Commons 1786: 31)

Thus, newly constituted subsets of the population were now being brought above 'the threshold of description … [t]o be looked at, observed, described in detail' (Foucault 1977: 191).

While various categories of the sick poor were among the first to become the objects of 'a new technology of power and a new political anatomy of the body' (Foucault 1977: 193), towards the end of the eighteenth century people with perceived impairments began to be separated from both mainstream society and from the able-bodied poor. They also began to be assigned to new and distinctive institutions and made subject to special programmes of rehabilitation. The first schools for deaf children of the poor appeared in Western Europe during the last quarter of the eighteenth century (Fischer and Lane 1993; Winzer 1993) and the first known example in Ireland opened in 1816 (McDonnell 1979). Schools for blind children of the poor were established in France and Britain during the 1780s and 1790s and new forms of provision for people with mental illness also appeared around the same time (Winzer 1993).

The science of health administration also influenced practices within the institutions themselves (Adams 1990; Porter 1999). In his analysis of French social policy in the age of the enlightenment, Adams (1990) argues that new medical and statistical models were deployed in analysing and 'treating' poverty and vagrancy. According to mercantilist ideology, the health of the body politic depended on the size, strength and low cost of the workforce and, to achieve this, the idle poor must be compelled to work, by punitive confinement if necessary. Social medicine, however, claimed that the successful exploitation of the labour of the poor would not be accomplished by 'chains and blows' alone; punitive regimes had manifestly failed to achieve such a transformation (Adams 1990). What social medicine proposed was a more deliberate approach based on science and reason. Accordingly, the source of the problem was not the defective morality of the idle poor, rather it was their defective rationality. In this analysis, their rehabilitation would require a process of corrective intervention by experts in social medicine in which 'conjecture might be refined by the accumulation of empirical data' (Adams 1990: 232).

Just as in hospitals where the sick poor became 'demonstration material' in the development of the clinical techniques of scientific medicine (Porter 1997: 290), the science of health administration also required experimental populations to provide data for an accurate diagnosis of social pathologies. Consequently, those held in institutions of confinement became objects of systematic observation, examination and measurement in the development of new professional and scientific standards in social medicine. As Adams (1990: 255–6) demonstrates, the *dépôts de mendicité* of eighteenth century France became 'hospitals of vice' where the social pathology of the inmates could be studied case by case, and where corrective clinical and therapeutic measures could be tested. Regulations introduced into the *dépôts* in 1776 constituted good examples of these practices. Officials were authorised to transfer the sick, the aged and the infirm from the *dépôts* to hospitals; new arrivals in the *dépôts* were to be bathed and have their clothes disinfected and washed; inmates with infectious diseases were to be segregated from the rest; and standard levels of provisioning, which included details of diet, clothing and medical remedies, were introduced (Adams 1990). The new regulations synthesised prevailing medical expertise and doctors were conferred with authority to supervise and inspect institutional practices and to set out new standards in health and hygiene.

Similar rational and scientific perspectives are evident in Howard's survey of Irish institutions (1789), which he visited in 1787 and 1788. Throughout his report, Howard evaluates levels of diet and nutrition, details of institutional furnishing and design, practices of hygiene and cleanliness, as well as prevailing modes of segregation in the institutions. His assessments clearly imply notions of 'average' or 'standard' individual requirements as well as 'acceptable' institutional norms in provisioning, administration, and the appropriate classification of people. He refers, for example, to the presence in Dublin's Newgate prison 'of several boys, from nine to twelve years, confined with the most daring offenders' (1789: 79); he criticises the absence of soap in the Foundling Hospital in Dublin and notes that there are 'no fixed hours for meals' (1789: 82); in the County Infirmary in Wicklow the diet is 'a sixpenny loaf every four days and three pints of milk every day ... a very proper diet for the general class of patients admitted into the Infirmaries in this country ... [but] the diet (especially for recovering patients) is scanty' (1789: 84).

To underline his remarks, Howard regularly makes international comparisons or points to existing legal requirements. Comparing them with St Patrick's Hospital for Lunatics in Dublin, for example, he prefers 'the *Dol-huis* at Amsterdam and the Hospital at Constantinople, where rooms open into corridors and gardens rather than to dark passages'. He looks forward to the completion of a new military infirmary adjacent to the

Phoenix Park where there will be a water supply 'for baths in a receiving room for washing the patients on their admission, similar to practice ... at Plymouth and Gosport' (1789: 84). He 'carefully weighed the twopenny loaves of both the prisons [Kilkenny County and City Gaols] ... and found the weight on June 9 1787, one pound and three ounces. By the last assize, on the 23rd of the preceding month, the weight ought to have been one pound ten ounces and two drams' (1789: 85). This rational approach, dealing with the concrete details of nutrition, furnishing, design and hygiene, created a practical foundation for the institutional expansion that would take place over the following century.

## DESERVING OR EXPENDABLE POPULATIONS?

The appearance of social policies shaped by science and reason demonstrated a new pragmatism in the analysis of individual and social anomalies and marked a significant departure from the past. However, alongside these reforming trends there existed other ideologies and practices that contradicted the humanitarian rhetoric of scientific and social medicine and that, in the future, would significantly influence the relationship between disability and society. In the interests of a disciplined society, the more humanitarian aspects of social medicine continued to be accompanied by external coercion and punishment. Even if the scandal of inhumane treatment in the older institutions was condemned, the penal regimes that characterised them were graduated rather than abolished altogether (Adams 1990). Inside the new institutions the more finely calibrated and temporary punishments of purgatory replaced the generalised, all-encompassing punishment of hell (Adams 1990); corporal punishment was 'held ready ... should the patient refuse to obey' (Winzer 1993: 64).

During the eighteenth century, the young, the aged, the sick, and people with perceived impairments – those who were usually counted among the deserving poor – were drawn into a tightening net encompassing work, discipline, dependency and relief. Nowhere was this more clearly demonstrated than in Jeremy Bentham's proposal for the establishment of a National Charity Company, to be privately owned but licensed and partly subsidised by the state (Himmelfarb 1984: 79–80). The company would be given 'undivided authority' over the 'whole body of the burdensome poor' whom it would have the power to seek out and force into the institution. Every individual, whatever his or her condition, would be put to labour and made to yield a profit. Although Bentham's scheme did not attract much explicit support, it did reflect a widespread belief that the relationship between poverty, relief and work might be regulated in a manner that would tame seditious and disorderly propensities among the poor, and foster industry and discipline (Porter 2000). It would also extract an economic return even from those who, traditionally, were thought to deserve relief without the requirement of work. The subsequent expansion of special educational provision came to rest on this very argument: industrial training for deaf children, for example, 'in agricultural, gardening, mechanical and household occupations' (Orpen 1836: 54) would reduce the burden on the public purse and ensure that its recipients 'would not be allowed to eat the bread of idleness' (National Institution for the Education of the Deaf and Dumb Children of the Poor in Ireland 1820: 18).

Doubts, however, were expressed as to the efficacy of even these minimal levels of utilitarian charity. Some claimed that poverty was indispensable to society since without it there would be no incentive to labour and therefore no industry; low wages encouraged virtue and hunger taught 'decency and civility, obedience and subjection' (Porter 2000: 381). Others expressed a darker view of the burdensome poor as worthless and expendable. In this context, Richardson identifies the emergence of an 'appalling heartlessness towards the poor' in which the clinical detachment which applied in the dissection of the dead was, through the New Poor Law, extended to the living (1987: 268). Although another century would pass before proponents of this view would advocate eugenic measures to eliminate so-called defective stocks altogether (see Chapter 5), towards the end of the eighteenth century they were content to argue for the complete abolition of relief so that famine and disease could fulfill their 'natural' functions (Porter 2000). What constitutes a 'worthwhile life', how decisions about such a life are made, and even more importantly, who makes these decisions, continue to be immediate and current questions and, literally, are of life and death concern to disabled people (see, for example, Blume 2000; Scally 2002).

In other respects, the operation of dividing practices and the appearance of new disciplinary institutions activated what Foucault (1980) calls the productive aspects of power. The establishment of schools for deaf children provides a good example of this. While the schools were founded as explicitly regulatory institutions, they soon became more than that: their existence created a space where new Deaf communities came into being and where future members of those communities forged a common identity and experience (McDonnell 1994; Saunders 1997). Attendance at a school for the deaf became a key factor in becoming a member of a Deaf community, in acquiring sign language, and in transmitting Deaf cultural values. Paradoxically, the schools that set out to assimilate deaf children into hearing society were at the same time the places where resistance to that very idea was most radically constituted (McDonnell and Saunders 1993). The strength of the modern disability movement is, in a similar way, grounded in the extensive institutionalisation of disabled people that characterised so much of the twentieth century (Davis 1993; Finklestein 1991).

## Conclusion

The most dominant and pervasive modern responses to disability are shaped to a very large degree by the ideologies and practices of scientific medicine and a science of health administration. These can be traced to the social mathematics of the eighteenth century in which the health of the national population at individual and aggregate levels was linked to the economic well-being of the state. Medicine, articulated in these two distinct but related forms, emerged as the dominant human science in the management of this relationship. Both forms of medical practice were preoccupied with anomaly: scientific medicine created its knowledge base through the investigation of individual pathology, and the science of health administration deployed quantitative data and a medical paradigm in its analysis of perceived deviance in the social body.

The early modern period in Western Europe was a critical transitional period in the relationship between disability and society. During this period, new institutional, administrative and conceptual developments had created the potential to segregate, in the most general way, particular social groups from mainstream society. The application of medical and statistical techniques enabled finer and more complex distinctions to be made between subsets of the population and, by the end of the eighteenth century, not only were particular subsets being directed to specific institutions but new purpose-built institutions were being established for specific groups. More significantly, clinical and statistical techniques facilitated the creation of ideas of normality with reference to individual bodies, of social norms with reference to subsets of the population and of normal standards of provisioning within the institutions. The institutional regulation of people with regard to the specifics of age, disease, sickness or impairment could now claim to be justified on the basis of medical science.

The deployment of quantitative measurements and clinical techniques also led to the introduction of the notion of standards in the operation of institutions. Standardised procedures, usually based on prevailing medical practices, began to be introduced for the induction of inmates, for the segregation of certain individuals and groups, for the design of programmes of treatment and intervention, and for setting levels of diet, hygiene, sanitation and other institutional utilities (Adams 1990). While all institutions continued to share some general features, specific institutions now began to develop specific regimes of treatment with regard to the particular problem population that they catered for.

The emergence of scientific medicine and scientific health administration as dominant forms of knowledge and practice enabled doctors to become the accepted experts in the regulation of these individualised and public domains. Through a professional base which developed during the eighteenth century, doctors acquired the capacity to speak with authority about the individual and the social body and consequently to police the border between the normal and the pathological. A new set of relationships developed between medical professionals and the state. Doctors demanded and gradually acquired the power, for example, to regulate and inspect a wide range of institutions (Dublin Directory 1825; Phelan 1835; McDonnell 1979; Stone 1985). As a result, the medical profession emerged as a powerful interest group associated with the expansion of the ideological apparatus of government (Althusser 1971; Foucault 1980; Rosen 1974). Medical practitioners became mediators, not only between national populations and the state, but also between individuals and the agencies that provided services. They advised governments and local authorities, devised policies and frequently were given the authority to administer those policies (Cook 1997; Woods 1998).

Finally, the employment of a social mathematics to determine standard practices paved the way for the emergence of notions of individual and social norms. A concept of the norm also implies a concept

of deviation or pathology. Thus, techniques based on statistical measurement combined with clinical practices to create a powerful and
influential conceptual framework for defining problem people, for categorising them accordingly, and for legitimating aggressive forms of
intervention in their lives, whether or not these were the kinds of interventions they desired. These ideologies and practices inevitably led
towards a greater degree of institutional specialisation.

NOTES

1. The Charitable Infirmary (later, Jervis Street Hospital) was followed by
   Steevens' Hospital in 1733, Mercer's Hospital in 1734, the Royal
   Hospital for Incurables in 1744, the Meath Hospital in 1753, St. Patrick's
   Hospital for the Insane in 1757, and Sir Patrick Dun's Hospital in 1792
   (Kelly 1999). The first hospital in Ireland or Britain founded specifically
   for lying-in women was the Dublin Lying-in Hospital (later, the
   Rotunda), established in 1745 (Campbell Ross 1986).
2. Around 1780, John Howard found the hospitals of Europe to be 'hotbeds
   of infection' and near contemporaries of Howard coined the term 'hospi-
   talism ... a general morbid condition of the building, or of its atmosphere,
   productive of disease'. Hospital mortality in surgery was estimated 'to be
   three to five times higher than in private cases' (cited in Porter 1997:
   375). Nor was the point lost on the patients themselves. Elinor Proudfoot,
   'about twenty', was admitted to Mercer's Hospital with 'an acute pain in
   the hip' where she was 'bled, purged and blistered'; when 'the symptoms
   increased' and after suffering 'a loss of the Limb ... she left the Hospital
   for fear of dissection' (cited in Lyons 1991: 44). Lying-in hospitals were
   known to have very high mortality rates. Women entering the
   Krankenhaus in Vienna begged 'in terror' not to be sent to the First
   Division which was 'devoted exclusively to the instruction of
   accoucheurs' and was known to have the highest death rate (Murphy-
   Lawless 1998: 144).
3. In some instances, hospitals evolved from houses of correction or similar
   institutions (Tröhler and Prüll 1997). Developments in France, where the
   key institution for the regulation of the poor in the seventeenth century
   was the *hôpital général*, provide a good example of an evolution of this
   kind. In its early form, the *hôpital général* was not a medical establishment in the modern sense; it was a semi-juridical institution intended for
   the regulation and confinement of the poor, which included the very
   young, the aged, the chronically ill, people with impairments, as well as

those who were deemed to be unwilling to work (Foucault 1971: 39). By the late eighteenth century, however, the *hôpital général* was being transformed into a largely medical institution (Norberg 1985: 181). As a result, the characteristic population of the *hôpital général* changed: the proportion of healthy entrants steadily declined while the number of those with contagious diseases, fevers and other ailments increased; surgeons were appointed and special medical wards established.

# 4

# A Great Confinement: Institutionalisation in Nineteenth Century Ireland

'Form A' – the Family Return – [was] left at every house to be filled in by the head of each family dwelling therein ... 'Form B' – named the House and Building Return – was filled in by the enumerator from personal observation and inquiry ...

On 'Form C', designated the Sick Return, we procured an account of the name, age, sex, relationship to the head of family, occupation, disease from which suffering, and how long affected, of each person in every family who laboured under sickness on the night of Sunday, the 30th of March, 1851. We also obtained a return on 'Form D' of persons afflicted with insanity or idiocy on that night. Special forms were prepared on which to enumerate the inmates of public institutions. These were:- 'Form E' which embraced three Tables – the 1st, for the inhabitants of workhouses; the 2nd, for the sick inmates; and the 3rd, for those who had died in these institutions since the 6th of June, 1841. 'Form F' containing two Tables – one for a return on the persons under treatment in hospitals; the other for the deaths in hospitals from the 6th of June, 1841 to the 30th of March, 1851. 'Form G' containing an account of persons resident in schools and colleges; and 'Form H' of the military in barracks. 'Form I', 1st Table embraced persons under treatment in lunatic asylums and gaols; and 'Form I', 2nd Table, those who had died in these institutions from the 6th of June, 1841 to the 30th of March, 1851. On 'Form K' were given the persons confined in prisons and bridewells on the night of the Census. On 'Form L' the pupils attending schools were enumerated; on 'Form O' the emigrants from Ireland from the 1st of May,

1851 to the 31st of December, 1851 were returned ... and on 'Form P' was obtained a return of the inquests held from the 6th of June, 1841 to the 30th of March, 1851 ...

Part III [of the Census] was published on the 30th of March, 1854 and gave an account of the 'status of Disease' in Ireland. It contained the results of the first attempt to ascertain on a single day of the year, the entire number of persons in this country suffering from sickness, and the diseases of a temporary or permanent nature by which they were affected. From this Report may now be known the numbers of the Deaf and Dumb; of the blind; of the lunatic and idiotic; of the lame and decrepit; and of the sick in the workhouses, hospitals, prisons and asylums – together with the diseases under which those who were returned to us as sick were labouring on the night of the 30th of March, 1851.

Census of Ireland 1851, General Report, v–vii

... [T]he general return of the diseased may be divided into two classes, one for persons afflicted with Permanent maladies and the other for those whose afflictions are of a more Temporary nature. Among the former may be classed the Deaf and Dumb, the Blind, the Lunatic, Idiotic, Paralytic, and Epileptic, as also the Lame and Decrepit; while under the latter head may be placed all those labouring the ordinary acute and chronic maladies to which the inhabitants of this country are liable ...

Census of Ireland 1851, Part III:
Report on the Status of Disease, 1

## INTRODUCTION

In administrative and statistical terms, the 1851 Census of Ireland is a comprehensive and sophisticated document. It is evident from the range and detail of the enumeration forms that the dividing practices of a science of health administration were well-established in Ireland by the middle of the nineteenth century. New administrative categories had been created for people with 'diseases of a ... permanent nature' – what today would be termed impairments or disabilities – and, although the terminology may have changed, many of these categories have remained in use down to the present time. In addition, the census reports explicitly located impairment along with illness within a discourse of medicine and, while conceptual distinctions were made between impairments and illnesses, the former being defined as 'permanent' and the latter as 'temporary', both conditions were regarded as 'diseases'. As far as the census commissioners were concerned, impairment was a medical matter.

The commissioners regarded their work as being more than a mere compilation of statistics. Their Report on the Status of Disease was, they felt, a ground-breaking social survey: 'we hope we are opening up a field of investigation which will hereafter prove a source of lasting benefit to science, and may, we trust, be a means of directing attention to the afflicted classes whose position it exhibits' (Census of Ireland 1851, Part III: 39). The report contained an extensive discussion and analysis of the medical, administrative and institutional dimensions of 'permanent and temporary disease' in Ireland and included several pages of individual case histories. The commissioners also saw their work as creating a necessary foundation for rational policy making, arguing that 'one of the chief objects in making statistical inquiries into the condition of the diseased, the destitute, or the helpless, is that they may be either relieved of their infirmities, provided with suitable asylums, or afforded the means of supplying their own necessities ...' (Census of Ireland 1851, Part III: 26).

Exclusion, medicalisation and institutionalisation are among the principal ideologies underlying the creation of disability as a social and ideological phenomenon (Oliver 1990; Barnes and Mercer 2003). It is difficult to determine exactly when people with perceived impairments began to be defined as a distinct social group in Ireland or at what specific point in time the 'personal trouble' of impairment became the 'public issue' of disability (Borsay 1986). As we have seen, by the middle of the eighteenth century, exclusionary and medical discourses were already shaping public responses to the sick poor. Refinements of these approaches were evident in the 1841 census, which enumerated 'lunatics, idiots and epileptics in asylums and jails' but not in the general population (Census of Ireland 1841, General Report: lvi–lvii). However, the reports on the census of 1851 marked both a quantitative and qualitative development in the identification of impairment as a public policy issue. In effect, by individualising impairment through which each individual became a case, by classifying impairment into types, by defining cases and types in medical terms, and by highlighting institutionalisation as a response to the anomalous populations so defined, the reports confirmed the emergence in Ireland of disability as a social construct. In sum, the 1851 census showed the extent to which medicalisation, segregation and institutionalisation were already being perceived as appropriate public responses to people with perceived impairments.

Developments in relation to disability are frequently discussed as unique phenomena, largely abstracted from mainstream political and social movements; if disability is at all discussed in a broader context, it tends to be regarded as an appendix to humanitarian advances in medicine, education or welfare. The aim of this chapter is to trace the emergence of a social construct of disability in the context of increasing levels of administrative intervention, medicalisation and institutionalisation, with particular reference to Ireland. In this chapter I argue that the administrative, medical and institutional discourses that came to bear on perceived impairment were part of a more general transformation in the governance of nineteenth century Ireland. I also argue that institutionalisation became the dominant ideological response to people with 'permanent diseases' and I show that confinement in institutions was practised, not only in relation to people with perceived impairments, but was also the experience of several other categories of anomalous people within the national population. People with perceived impairments constituted only one of several sub-populations deemed to be in need of institutional regulation and rehabilitation.

## Suitable Cases for Treatment

The number and variety of institutions of confinement established in Ireland during the early decades of the nineteenth century was extraordinary (McDonnell 1996a). According to Foucault (1971, Chapter 2), the signs of a great institutional confinement are to be found a century earlier all over Western Europe, in the *hôpital généraux* of France, the *zuchthäusern* of German-speaking countries, and in the new workhouses of England. In Ireland, as we have seen, similar kinds of disciplinary institutions had been discussed and thought necessary but, for a variety of reasons, one of which was the fact that Ireland did not have the equivalent of an English Poor Law, the material realisation of these proposals was sporadic and haphazard. But when institutional development and expansion did commence at a national level and in a co-ordinated way in Ireland, it was concentrated within a relatively short period of time and involved a whole range of new institutional initiatives, some of which appeared well before similar systems were established in Britain or indeed in continental Europe.

Between 1817 and 1821 the legislative basis for a lunatic asylum system was put in place, legislation that made Ireland the first country in Western Europe to have a public system of asylums (Finnane 1981; Reuber 1999). The first phase of this development ended in 1835 with ten district asylums established in different parts of the country (Finnane 1981) and by 1837, with over 1,600 occupants, these institutions were already overcrowded (Robins 1986). The fever epidemics of 1816–1819 led to legislation which provided for the building of fever hospitals, the setting up of local health boards and the appointment of public health officers (Crawford 1999). By 1845 over a hundred fever hospitals had been constructed (McDowell 1994). The establishment of more than 600 dispensaries between 1805 and 1840 brought institutionalised medicine into local communities (Lyons 1973). Thus, in terms of policies and structures, 'Ireland had one of the most advanced health services in Europe in the first half of the nineteenth century' (MacDonagh 1977: 37).

This government willingness to experiment (Lyons 1973) is equally evident in the creation of two further institutional systems – national schools and workhouses. In 1831, the first steps were taken in the introduction of mass public primary schooling, antedating 'by almost four decades the establishment of a similar system in England, a country well advanced along the path of industrial and urban change' (Akenson 1970: 521). The Irish national school system expanded rapidly: in 1835 there were 1,106 schools with an enrolment of 107,042 pupils; by 1850 the number of schools had grown to 4,547, with over half a million pupils on the rolls (198, 276). The Poor Law Act, passed in 1838, proposed a national system of workhouses in Ireland, similar to those already established in England under the Poor Law Amendment Act of 1834. Although 'the application of the New Poor Law to Ireland was an exception to the general rule that Irish administrative experiments were made independently of, and frequently in advance of, what was happening in Britain' (Lyons 1973: 78), the workhouses represented a radical change: firstly, in that they were the first manifestation of a comprehensive poor law in Ireland and, secondly, in that they replaced local, ad hoc provisions with an institutional structure that was centralised and systematic. As with the national schools, expansion of the workhouse system was rapid: in 1841 there were 5,468 people in four

workhouses but by 1845 this had grown to 42,068 people in 123 institutions (Freeman 1989).

The disciplinary ideology underlying the operation of schools and
workhouses was even more pronounced in its application in the Irish
penal system (Carroll-Burke 2000). New and more detailed codes of practice, introduced in a Prisons' Act of 1810 and consolidated and extended
in a further Act of 1826, demonstrated a steady shift towards the individualisation of punishment. The new regulations proposed a more rigorous
segregation of offenders: of male from female prisoners; of debtors from
felons; of felons from petty criminals; and of offenders from those await-
ing trial (Carroll-Burke 2000; MacDonagh 1989; McDowell 1989). The
creation of a unique Irish Convict System in 1853 signalled the introduction of a more radical individualised correctional programme. The system
was based on 'discipline, intelligence and surveillance' – the classification
of prisoners in terms of moral progress, the use of labour as part of the
strategy of correction, the recording of detailed personal files, and a
continuing surveillance over discharged offenders (Carroll-Burke 2000:
231–2).

The operation of institutions of confinement depends on the presence
of supporting administrative structures. The most important move in this
context was the establishment of a trained, national and centralised police
force which in 1836 amounted to approximately 10,000 officers and men
distributed throughout the country (MacDonagh 1989). The force was
placed under a unified command,

> with an autonomous national inspectorate to enforce, as the original
> recommendation put it, 'one uniform system of rules and regulations
> for the entire Irish police establishment', and with a single large
> training depot in Dublin to serve the whole body. Thus, Ireland came
> to possess a coherent, stratified, paramilitary police at a time when
> the lonely untrained village constable was still the instrument of law
> enforcement over most of rural England. (MacDonagh 1989: 214)

The new police force provided the authorities with an efficient and
flexible instrument, rare in the Europe of the time, not only for enforcing
law and order but also for extending the administrative reach of the state.
The duties of the constabulary brought it into regular contact with local
people and facilitated access to the most remote districts. The force found

itself spearheading efforts to cultivate acceptable public behaviour and was charged with enforcing an increasing volume of legislation designed to regulate a whole range of activities, from keeping a dog to begging (Crossman 1996). It was also the principal agency for compiling statistical returns. The census commissioners acknowledged that the accuracy and reliability of their reports depended on the co-operation of the constabulary and attributed the success of their work to its 'zeal and diligence' (Census of Ireland 1851, General Report: vii).

The constabulary became the direct link between communities and the new institutions. The constable's manual instructed him to know the 'individual character' of local inhabitants (Carroll-Burke 2000: 84) and, if it was the doctor who signed a committal form or a medical certificate (Finnane 1981; McDonnell 1979), it was the constable who knew the individual and details of the family circumstances. In relation to mental illness, for example, the police conducted investigations of the kind that today might be carried out by social workers. This might be an inquiry whether a family was able to maintain a mentally ill person or would agree to the transfer of a family member from one institution to another; or it might involve investigating allegations of neglect or ill-treatment (Finnane 1981). From time to time between 1845 and 1877, the police were requested to take a census of 'lunatics, idiots, imbeciles and epileptics' not in institutions and thus they acquired a 'comprehensive knowledge of all insane persons in the community' (Finnane 1981: 106). Constables were also key figures in the actual process leading to confinement. It was they who brought the committed person to the asylum, though often under duress and often accompanied by allegations of maltreatment (Finnane 1981; Robins 1986).

The institutionalisation of Irish society can be seen in the context of two important processes which are explored in the next two sections. Firstly, many historians have detected a paradigm shift in the political administration of Ireland in the early decades of the nineteenth century (Lyons 1973; Connolly 1989; 1989a; Hoppen 1989; McDonagh 1989; McDowell 1994). This was a shift from repressive towards more ideologically based measures (Althusser 1971) in response to what were regarded as alarming and worsening political, social and economic conditions. The second process involved the emergence of a more bureaucratic style of administration which 'represented a new departure that was truly radical in the nineteenth century context' (Lyons 1973: 77), and in which the interests of the state were seen to be above and beyond the narrower concerns of particular political or sectarian groups (MacDonagh 1977).

## REGULATING IRISH SOCIETY

From the point of view of successive British administrations, Ireland presented enduring problems of governance. The close of the eighteenth century was marked by open rebellion and the early decades of the nineteenth century by a high level of popular discontent, often accompanied by violent protest (Crossman 1996). Regular and repeated outbreaks of agrarian disorder in particular gave the impression of a country with a permanent law and order crisis. The boom period of the Napoleonic Wars, from 1793 to 1815, was followed by a depression which meant that scarcity, subsistence and survival increasingly determined the conditions of life for the rural Irish poor. The pressures of population, subdivision, falling prices, rising rents and evictions generated an increasing incidence of violence and outrage, to such a degree that '[i]f the level of violence could be measured by the weight of the law arrayed against it, then Ireland surely contained one of the most violent countrysides in Europe' (Scally 1995: 95). In pre-famine Ireland the most characteristic expression of the law was coercion, typically exercised through the proclamation of disturbed districts, the suspension of *habeus corpus*, the introduction of martial law and the imposition of sunset-to-sunrise curfews (Connolly 1989*a*).

In addition to political instability, Ireland was perceived to be a country with serious social and economic problems (Kinealy 1994, Chapter 1). Particular concern was expressed about its rapidly growing population, its over-dependence on one crop, the potato, and the extreme levels of poverty among a large proportion of the population. Despite a considerable degree of social and economic diversity, the received wisdom in government circles was of a country becoming ever more impoverished, whose 'surplus' population constituted not only an economic liability, but was also a threat to wages and moral standards in mainland Britain (Kinealy 1994). In the period 1800–1840, more than a hundred royal commissions and special committees of enquiry were set up to report on conditions in Ireland (O'Connor 1995). One of the most important of these, the Whateley Commission, appointed in 1833, conducted the most comprehensive enquiry ever undertaken in either Britain or Ireland into the condition of the poorer classes (Kinealy 1994). On the basis of the information gathered in these investigations, many political economists, who otherwise might have opposed any kind of state sponsored poor relief, conceded that state intervention was necessary in Ireland (Powell 1992, Chapter 2).

The Act of Union, uniting Ireland and Great Britain, replaced indirect with direct rule from London, and came into effect on 1 January 1801. Although the repressive powers granted to the Irish authorities during the 1798 rebellion were maintained into the early years of the Union, the new administration also seemed anxious to introduce policies of 'general conciliation' (Connolly 1989: 9). The institutional systems that were established during this period involved the introduction of ideologically oriented measures to accompany rather than to replace the traditional coercive responses to political and social crises: schools were required to create 'peaceable subjects and good members of society' (cited in Kelly 1978: 41); workhouses to discipline the 'idle and disorderly conduct, and the ... proneness to outrage ... of the Irish peasant' (Nicholls 1856: 163); a centralised constabulary with the capacity, on the one hand, to put down armed rebellion, and on the other to undertake routine surveillance (Finnane 1981: 106); and a range of specific institutions of confinement for particular groups within the general body of the poor in Ireland – the lunatic, the sick, the impaired, and the uneducated poor.

## ADMINISTRATIVE EXPERTISE

The organisation of national populations into different social categories presupposes specialised administrative and statistical expertise. Statistics provide the raw material that makes it possible to isolate anomalies in the social body, to establish normative measures, and to organise spaces where therapeutic or corrective measures can be deployed to control such anomalies (Rabinow 1984). Stone (1985) has highlighted the function of administration in the social construction of disability. Clearly, administrative practices were crucial in transforming disability from a private trouble into a public issue in Ireland. Less attention, however, has been given to the fact that, at least in Ireland, disabled people were only one constituent of a range of problem populations coming under the administrative gaze and that the construction of disability was just one element in a wider project of governance.

The extent to which information gathering was undertaken in Ireland during the early decades of the nineteenth century was unprecedented. Over a relatively short period of time, vast amounts of data became available on population distribution, land valuation, crime, levels of poverty, incidence of disease, rates of mortality and other social matters (O'Gráda 1989). Royal commissions and special committees of enquiry conducted numerous investigations into the condition of the Irish poor (Nicholls 1856, Chapter 2). A national census of the population was first attempted in 1811 and was conducted every ten years thereafter, although it was not until 1841 that relatively thorough and accurate returns were achieved (McDowell 1994). A comprehensive ordnance survey of the entire country began in 1825 and between 1833 and 1846 a complete series of six-inch maps were published (Andrews 1975; Freeman 1989). The survey provided the foundation for a more stable administrative framework that, in turn, made it possible to achieve more precise census enumerations, a more scientific land valuation and a more reliable basis for taxation, all of which were important preconditions for the establishment of national institutional systems.

The establishment of institutions, national in scope and more centralised in terms of control and funding, demanded administrative innovation. In calculating the regional requirements for the development of the lunatic asylum system, for example, new administrative districts had to be created which 'represented a startling break with the conventional divisions of local government and ... marked the entry of quantitative "rationalisation" on the administrative scene' (MacDonagh 1989: 210). Equally remarkable was the rapid co-ordination of several spheres of administrative activity, evidenced in the speed with which the workhouse system got under way. This involved dividing the country into new districts or unions, electing poor law guardians, and of course getting the workhouses built (Kinealy 1994).

Ireland, a mainly rural and agricultural society, seemed an unlikely location for the emergence of structures and practices more typically associated with urbanisation and industrial capitalism (Mayer 1983; Philips 1983). In relation to the development of lunatic asylum systems, for example, Scull (1993) points to the contrasting economic conditions that prevailed in Britain and Ireland, although equally extensive systems developed in both countries.[1] However, what is particularly unexpected is the great variety of institutions that were established in Ireland and the rapidity with which this was achieved. Equally surprising is the fact that these institutional innovations entailed considerable and increasing administrative centralisation and public expenditure in the context of, and in spite of, a powerful laissez-faire ideology (Kinealy 1994).

It is important, however, to recognise that there were considerable variations in the centralising capacities and professional competence of the various institutional systems. The poor law commissioners and the commissioners of national education, for example, wielded significant power in their respective fields while the central authority in the area of public health was comparatively more limited. The General Board of Health consisted entirely of unpaid members and, having no statutory basis, could have been abolished as easily as it had been appointed (O'Brien 1999a). Similarly, the influence of the inspectors of lunatics 'ebbed and flowed depending on the indifference, enthusiasm and prejudices of individual inspectors' (Robins 1986: 91). Furthermore, it was not always possible for central authorities to impose policies just as they desired. The commissioners of national education, for example, faced regular opposition from Church authorities and from time to time were forced to make concessions to powerful denominational interests (Akenson 1970, Chapter 5; Coolahan 1981).

It is also important to remember that there was considerable variation in the national scope of the various institutional systems as well as in the status of some of their individual elements. Connaught, the poorest of the provinces, had only 13 per cent of the total number of dispensaries (McDowell 1994) and only two fever hospitals (Phelan 1835). In other parts of the country, some hospitals were of the most rudimentary kind (Phelan 1835). Also, in terms of funding, government assistance was subject to an overall policy of laissez-faire. Thus, grants to medical institutions were normally pitched at the equivalent of what could be obtained through voluntary subscriptions (Robins 1986). Nevertheless, even with these reservations in mind, the administrative and institutional developments which occurred in Ireland during the first half of the nineteenth century are striking when compared, firstly, with the very restricted degree of institutional development that had taken place previously and, secondly, with the timescale for similar developments in Britain and on the continent.

Some historians have suggested that the administrative and institutional changes that occurred during the early decades of the nineteenth century meant in effect that Ireland became 'a field of experiment on a grand scale ... an experiment in political control' (Carroll-Burke 2000: 231; see also Lyons 1973; MacDonagh 1977; 1989). Others have argued that government policy was more a series of ad hoc solutions to exceptional Irish conditions (O'Brien 1999). Both views, however, miss a major point. Conditions in such diverse fields as mental health, education and poverty were perceived to be exceptional in the same kind of way: they were understood to be products of 'impaired' and 'deficient' people. And whether we see the proposed solutions as ad hoc or experimental, they were determined by the same parameters – the identification and enumeration of those anomalous populations, their segregation from mainstream society, and their confinement in institutions where they were made subject to programmes of corrective treatment.

## Individual Impairment and Deficiency

Institutionalisation implies certain assumptions about the nature of the people for whom it is intended. The newly established lunatic asylums, schools, workhouses and hospitals, with their hallmark practices of confinement, surveillance and discipline, shared a common ideological framework. They undertook projects of moral regulation in which the idea of inculcating habits of order, regularity and subordination in particular sectors of the population was a recurring motif (Driver 1993). The institutions identified and brought into their regulatory orbits populations who were defined primarily in terms of impairments and deficits – of citizenship, of ambition, of enlightenment, and of physical and mental integrity. The main aims of the institutions were to repair or defuse these flaws, reform the undisciplined impulses and inclinations that the deficiencies were deemed to produce, and thereby create properly socialised subjects.

The kind of institutional treatment to which the deficient individual was subjected was based on a number of different theoretical positions – relief, remedy, prevention or deterrence. While each institutional system could claim to respond to some extent in terms of all of these criteria, each tended to emphasise its own special rehabilitative orientation. As we have seen, hospitals highlighted their relieving and remedial provision for the sick poor as well as their sanitising role in society. Similar claims surrounded asylum provision for those perceived to be deprived or deficient in reason. The promise of moral treatment in the new asylums incorporated a rhetoric of cure and care (Ingleby 1983) in addition to the necessity of institutionalisation 'for the protection of the community' (Nicholls 1856: 160).

The preventive orientation of the national school system was emphasised. Unlike earlier forms of public education in Ireland, which had set out 'to civilise, anglicise and protestantise' (Kelly 1986: 4–5), the mission of the new system was to socialise and enculturate rather than to proselytise, and to inculcate political and moral rather than denominational values (Coolahan 1988). Its supporters, which included the Protestant establishment, the Catholic hierarchy, and wealthy middle-class professional and business interests, believed that such an education would counteract tendencies towards idleness and sedition among the lower orders. They were convinced that a well-ordered system was needed to replace what they regarded as a haphazard, disorganised and subversive education that was 'more pernicious than ignorance itself' (cited in Kelly 1978: 48). In a similar vein, it was argued that children with perceived impairments 'permitted to grow up in ignorance and poverty, must remain a permanent tax upon their respective Unions'. The census commissioners went on to argue that 'it might be found an eventual economy' to have them sent to specially constituted schools for literary and industrial instruction (Census of Ireland 1851, Part III: 35).

If the schools set out to redress the political, cultural and vocational deficits of the child population, the new workhouses set out to remedy the impaired economic and moral behaviour of the Irish poor. Influential members of the government and leading political economists believed that the relative backwardness of Irish agriculture stemmed, not from resource constraints, such as poor soil quality, high land-labour ratios and an inadequate diet during the 'hungry' summer months, but rather from slovenly farming practices and inherent incompetence and indolence (O'Grada 1989; Kinealy 1994, Chapter 1). The watchword of the workhouse was deterrence because

> the peasantry ... seem to have no pride, no emulation; to be heedless of the present and careless of the future ... If they desired to live better, or to appear better, they might do so; but they seem to have no such ambition ... Mendicancy and indiscriminate alms-giving have produced in Ireland, results similar to what indiscriminate relief produced in England – the like reckless disregard of the future, the like idle and disorderly conduct, and the same proneness to outrage ... which are

now too generally the characteristics of the Irish peasant. (Nicholls
1859: 162–3)

The workhouse and the national school systems constituted compli-
mentary regimes of rehabilitation and both extended their regulatory
orbits beyond the institutions into the wider society. The workhouses
promised to inculcate habits of industry, sobriety, regularity and order in
the present generation; the schools would accomplish similar goals for the
next. Both systems set out to eradicate the abuses that were believed to be
at the root of the respective sets of problems. The workhouses would put
an end to 'desultory habits', 'indiscriminate alms-giving' and the 'evils of
mendicancy' (Nicholls 1856: 163, 182–3). The schools would teach future
citizens 'to be profitable members of society in their humble stations, ful-
fillers of their religious, moral and social duties, obedient to the laws, and
loyal to the government' (cited in Kelly 1978: 42).

Among the first lessons to be learned by new inductees into the institutions were lessons in humiliation and powerlessness:

> The National School curriculum contained a variety of messages but
> perhaps none rang more clearly in the ears of this first generation of
> National School children than the note of shame and subservience
> that was palpable in nearly all aspects of the school regimen. Their
> bodies and clothing were examined for dirt and disease on entering
> each morning. They stood in borrowed shoes if they came without
> their own. Their speech and manners were relentlessly corrected.
> Punishments, like reciting from 'the Black Stool,' also emphasised
> public humiliation as the main disciplinary tool, as did the threat that
> transgressions of the children might be brought on the heads of the
> parents. Foremost, the children's experience was a lesson in power-
> lessness, both their own and their parents. (Scally 1995: 158)

Likewise, the General Order for Regulating the Management of Workhouses
in Ireland stipulated the following admission procedures for paupers:

> As soon as a pauper is admitted, his name and religious persuasion
> shall be duly entered into the register, and [he] shall be placed in the
> probationary ward, and shall there remain until examined by the
> Medical Officer of the workhouse ...

> Before being removed from the probationary ward, the pauper shall be thoroughly cleansed, and shall be clothed in a workhouse dress; and the clothes which he wore at the time of his admission shall be purified, and deposited in a place appropriated for that purpose, with the pauper's name, and a list of the several articles, signed by the Porter, affixed thereto. Such clothes shall be restored to the pauper when he leaves the workhouse ... (Banks 1872: 756–7)

Nineteenth century Ireland constituted a unique context for the emergence of a social construct of disability. Its colonial status generated an administrative perspective that judged the great majority of its inhabitants to be impaired and to be in need of political and cultural rehabilitation. The specialised institutions that developed around perceived impairment per se – special schools and lunatic asylums – were informed by the same disabling definitions and the same rehabilitative theories and practices that characterised the workhouses and national schools. Thus, the segregation and confinement of disabled people was but one element in a much larger programme of institutionalisation.

## DISABILITY AND INSTITUTIONALISATION

The returns of the 1851 census estimated the number of people with perceived impairments in the total population and reported how they were distributed in the various institutions (Table 4.1). The institutions with the

**Table 4.1: Numbers of Disabled People in Institutions in 1851**

|  | National Total | Workhouse | Prison | Educational Institution | Lunatic Asylum | Hospital |
|---|---|---|---|---|---|---|
| Deaf and Dumb | 4747 | 296 | 10 | 232 | 233 | 57 |
| Blind | 7587 | 995 | 0 | 118 | 3 | 303 |
| Lunatic | 5074 | 494 | 273 | 0 | 3234 | 68 |
| Idiot | 4096 | 1129 | 13 | 0 | 202 | 3562 |
| Lame and Decrepit | 4375 | 2342 | 207 | 0 | 0 | 1664 |

*Source*: Census of Ireland 1851 (1854), Part III, Report on the Status of Disease, Dublin: Alexander Thom.

largest number of disabled people were the lunatic asylums and the workhouses. Although 'infirm men and women, idiots and incurable lunatics' had been confined separately in some houses of industry (Nicholls 1856: 84), the asylums were the first public institutions to be specifically established for people who today would be categorised as 'having a disability'. After the Poor Law Act of 1838, however, the workhouse became the main institution 'in the first place [for] such destitute poor Persons as by reason of old Age, Infirmity or Defect, may be unable to support themselves' (1 and 2 Victoria, cap. 56, section 41). Although relief was always at the discretion of the guardians and subject to the orders of the commissioners, only after 'the aged, the infirm, the defective and children … had been provided for were the Guardians at liberty to assist other persons in need' (O'Connor 1995: 69).

Attempts were made to transfer immediately to the workhouses 'the idiotic and harmless lunatics confined in gaols or maintained in the asylums, which would then be enabled to receive more curable cases, and thus extend their usefulness' (Nicholls 1856: 286–7). The poor law commissioners advised a 'gradual absorption by the workhouses of such … unfortunates' rather than 'any forced or immediate transfer of insane or idiotic persons or harmless lunatics' (287). Nonetheless, in the years before the famine, the workhouse had become an institution largely for disabled people. Of the 2,187 people first admitted to the South Dublin Union in 1840, 1,083 were people with perceived impairments, 992 were described as having 'no disorder', while no details were given about the remaining 112. Even when distress became very general in the first months of 1846, only 8,246 people out of a total of 50,717 in the workhouses on 28 March were described as 'able-bodied' (Burke: 1987).

Along with asylums and workhouses, special schools were the most significant institutional foundations for disabled people to appear during the nineteenth century. The first school for deaf children was established in Dublin in 1816 and by 1850 nine such schools had opened in different parts of Ireland (McDonnell 1979). In 1860, seven institutions were providing 'literary and industrial education … for the blind' (Census of Ireland 1881, Part III: 284–5), and in 1869 the 'Stewart Institution for Idiotic and Imbecile Children' was opened (Robins 1986: 165). Being voluntary foundations, special schools differed from asylums and workhouses but were clearly part of the larger movement towards institutionalisation. Their underlying rationale was similar to that governing the state sponsored systems. In the

first place, because they were institutions for the moral and industrial training of children of the poor, special schools were products of similar ideologies of regulation and political economy. Advocates argued that it
made economic sense to have institutions 'for instructing in morality and
religion as well as fitting for some useful occupation, those who would
otherwise remain a burden on society' (Stoker 1863: 458). The census
commissioners expressed similar views in their reports: if the 'uneducated
Deaf and Dumb ... grow up in ignorance and poverty [they] must remain a
permanent tax upon the public purse' (Census of Ireland 1851, Part III: 49;
Census of Ireland 1861, Part III: 10). Schooling was 'calculated to ... rescue them from the evil of dependence, and fit them for some useful exercise in life ...' (Sixth Report of the National Institution 1822: 16).

In the second place, the schools were part of a general process of
administrative classification whereby anomalous populations began to be
directed towards more specialised institutions. As asylums and workhouses became established components of the institutional landscape,
there were calls for a greater degree of differentiation in their populations.
Particular concerns were expressed, for example, about the number of
'idiots and imbeciles' in both institutions, whose presence was deemed by
critics to disrupt the discipline and order of the workhouse and reduce discharge rates in the asylum (Ingleby 1983; Robins 1986; Scull 1993). The
census commissioners advocated

> the propriety of taking some steps towards the education and moral
> improvement of Idiots and Imbeciles, a subject which at present
> engages the attention of the philanthropic both on the Continent and
> in England, where several establishments for the purpose have been
> erected and are supported by the State; and in which the susceptibil-
> ity of this class to a certain amount of education has been demon-
> strated (Census of Ireland 1851, Part III: 49).

Contributors to the Statistical and Social Inquiry Society of Ireland made
the same argument, emphasising the need for public support and the eventual economy of such social investment (Stoker 1863; Pim 1864).

Finally, the special schools were surrounded by a very particular
rhetoric of humanitarian progress and by appeals for charitable support for
the most unfortunate and afflicted individuals in society. In contrast with the
explicitly punitive ideology of the workhouse, the educational institutions

emphasised the philanthropic and reforming nature of their work, their objectives being the moral and economic salvation of the pupils. The National Institution promised to rescue deaf children 'from the depths of more than heathen darkness' (First Report of the National Institution 1817: 13). The school committee thought itself 'entitled to hold up the Institution as one of the most interesting that can claim the support of a benevolent public' (Sixth Report of the National Institution 1822: 16). At the same time it was 'determined to avoid the error sometimes committed by benevolent institutions in exalting the poor, while at school, above that level in accommodation, diet, attendance, comfort, bodily exertion, and manual labour, in which they must pass the remainder of their lives' (Fourth Report of the National Institution 1820: 18).

In spite of the urgings of the census commissioners and other campaigners, public funding for special educational institutions was slow to develop. An amended Poor Law Act of 1843 stated that

> the Guardians of any Union may send any destitute poor deaf and dumb or blind Child under the Age of Eighteen, to any Institution for the Maintenance of the Deaf and Dumb or Blind which may be approved of by the Commissioners, with the Consent of the Parents or Guardian of such Child, and may pay the Expense of its Maintenance there … (6 and 7 Victoria cap. 92, section 14).

However, since the guardians were empowered rather than obliged to do so, they were in no hurry to provide support for pupils. In their 1851 report the census commissioners regretted that so few blind children were educated and that the poor law guardians had not availed of the opportunity to maintain a greater number of blind children in existing institutions. In 1851 only twenty out of a total of seventy-six pupils who were entitled to assistance were supported under the Poor Law in institutions for deaf children and, although by 1881 two thirds of the running costs of the two largest institutions for deaf children were met under the Poor Law, haggling with boards of guardians over payments and admissions became a recurring issue for special schools for most of the nineteenth century (Census of Ireland 1851, Part III; Census of Ireland 1881, Part II; McDonnell 1979, Chapter 5).

Repeated efforts were made to establish separate institutional provision for people who today would be defined as having learning difficulties. In

1843, the Report of the Select Committee on the Lunatic Poor in Ireland stated that the workhouses were unsuitable for so-called idiots and incurables and recommended that provision be made available for them in existing asylums or by constructing separate provincial institutions. A commission of enquiry into the state of the lunatic asylums in Ireland in 1858 made similar recommendations (Robins 1986). However, in the post-famine period, the impetus for institutional expansion that characterised the early decades of the nineteenth century dissipated. When spare accommodation became available in the workhouses after the deaths and emigration of hundreds of thousands of the destitute poor, the treasury and the ratepayers strongly resisted any proposal that involved additional public expenditure (Robins 1986).

Other groups of disabled people attracted the support of voluntary organisations. Special schools for deaf children, for example, continued to expand and by 1877 'the largest Female Deaf-Mute Institute in the United Kingdom was in Cabra; as was also the largest Male Deaf-Mute Institute in the United Kingdom, and the two combined formed the largest Deaf-Mute establishment in the ... world' (St Mary's School for the Deaf 1946: 11). However, apart from the Stewart Institution for Idiotic and Imbecile Children, the educational institutions for the relatively much larger population of children with learning difficulties which had begun to appear on the continent and in Britain (Winzer 1993) were not replicated in Ireland. Here, custodial provision in the workhouse continued to function as the primary institution for people with learning difficulties. Perhaps the strangest absence in this particular institutional field is that of the Catholic Church. But before going on to explore this question, a more general discussion of the relationship between charity and disability is in order.

## ENLIGHTENED REFORM, BENEVOLENCE OR SOCIAL CONTROL?

A popular and long held view has been that disability became a public issue when enlightened reform and humanitarian progress put an end to centuries of cruelty, ignorance and neglect (Burke 1987; Robins 1986; Winzer 1993). However, since Foucault's analysis of the development of disciplinary power in modern societies, and in the light of the more recent critique of the relationship between charitable organisations and disability (Drake 1996; Oliver 1990), it has been difficult to accept such claims at face value. Two questions arise in relation to the connection between these critiques and ideas of enlightened reform and benevolent intervention. Firstly, were humanitarian claims merely forms of rhetoric that were used to mask processes of social control, the 'real' objective of institutionalisation? Secondly, did institutional systems, especially those that emphasised altruism, such as hospitals, asylums and special schools, in fact create more oppressive conditions and experiences than what had existed previously? Was humanitarianism, then, just 'so much incidental music' (Scull 1983: 133)?

The difficulties that Scull (1993) identifies in Foucault's analysis of the encounter between madness and civilization in Western Europe can be applied to the issue of disciplinary institutions in general and the anomalous conditions they were meant to correct. Foucault rejected the belief that the treatment offered in the new institutions could be understood as philanthropic or as a liberation from the cruelty, brutality and ignorance of the pre-enlightenment period; moreover, he argued that the institutions initiated new regimes of moral imprisonment that in fact were more pernicious than the oppressions of the past (Rabinow 1984). In Foucault's view (1977), the main concern of the new disciplinary institutions was not to punish more humanely but to punish better. With respect to madness in the pre-enlightenment period, Scull (1993) argues that, while Foucault on the one hand romanticises the nature of societal attitudes and responses, on the other he over-generalises the extent of the subsequent internment and moral imprisonment that took place across Europe. To be fair, however, Foucault himself stated that he did not set out to write 'the history of all the different institutions, with all their individual differences. I simply intend to map on a series of examples some of the essential techniques that most easily spread from one to another' (Foucault 1977: 139).

The reform movement that occurred in Britain and Ireland during the late eighteenth and early nineteenth centuries was preoccupied with many different social groups, including the poor, the sick, children, and disabled people. The movement consisted of several different strands (Kidd 1999; Luddy 1995; Maxwell 1956; Robins 1980; 1986; Scull 1993). For Thomas Malthus and Joseph Townsend, reform meant a qualified acceptance of voluntary charity (Himmelfarb 1984) but, warned Malthus (1803: 281, 285), 'the impulse of benevolence ... must be regulated' because 'poverty and misery have always increased in proportion to the quantity of indiscriminate charity.' More importantly, this particular version of reform meant the abolition of any kind of state supported poor relief; there was no right to charity and no poor person should expect to be relieved by the state on the grounds that 'if he cannot get subsistence from his parents, on whom he has a just demand, and if society does not want labour, has no claim of right to the smallest portion of food, and in fact, has no business to be where he is' (Malthus 1803: 249).

Among those who did support the idea of some kind of public poor relief, enlightened reform meant different things to different people. Representing a Benthamite strand, George Nicholls argued that the Irish workhouse system would lead to 'a more enlightened benevolence' than the 'indiscriminate almsgiving, which now prevails so generally among all classes in Ireland' (1856: 182–3). This perspective advocated a rational, centralised approach to social issues to replace what its proponents regarded as the profligate, ignorant and inept practices of the past. Their utilitarian principle of the greatest happiness of the greatest number stressed efficiency and expertise, and their humanitarianism, in so far as it can be called that, was conditional on the discipline, sobriety and order of those who received relief. The ultimate sanction in this perspective was the institutional coercion of the workhouse.

A third strand derived its moral underpinnings from religion and the evangelical movement and found expression in an extraordinary range of philanthropic activities (Kidd 1999; Luddy 1995). In relation to Ireland, Luddy (1995) argues that, while some philanthropic organisations were engaged in political action, the primary concern of the great majority was the moral reform of the individual rather than the reform of existing social and economic conditions.[2] It seems reasonable to assume that many acts of individual and collective charity were based on genuinely altruistic motives (Lindsay 1987; Luddy 1995). But even if this was the case, it was next to impossible for even the most radical of reformers to ignore the dominant perceptions of the period – that the poor were responsible for their poverty and that philanthropy with no strings attached was both dangerous and irresponsible (O'Carroll 1987; Luddy 1995). Furthermore, in Ireland the attitudes of the philanthropists towards the poor were conditioned by hierarchical ideas of class and race (Preston 1998). Theirs was the paternalistic benevolence of the middle and upper classes who believed themselves to be the social and moral superiors of a 'dirty ... violent ... thriftless ... politically volatile ... race apart' (cited in Preston 1998: 102–3; see also Luddy 1995; Scull 1993).

Both philanthropists and Benthamites supported institutionalisation as the principal means of reforming the poor. Philanthropic and coercive strands can be seen as complementary rather than opposing approaches to the achievement of this aim. Working together they constituted a social police: benevolent institutions maintained a strong tutelary hold over the poor, while the poor law and the workhouse dealt with idlers (Donajgrodzki 1977). In Ireland as in Britain, although the diversity of charitable causes was extraordinary, there was a preponderance of institutions based on educational, medical, rescue, and poor relief charities (Kidd 1999; Luddy 1995). Some, like the Association for the Suppression of Mendicity in Dublin, founded in 1817, incorporated a typical workhouse ethos (Woods 1993). Many made explicit their intention of helping only the deserving poor who 'through training ... could be made honest though certainly never equal' (Preston 1998: 112).

Scull (1983) argues that the humanitarianism of the reformers should be taken very seriously indeed but that taking it seriously is not the same as taking it at face value. He suggests that the reform movement did reflect an authentic shift in moral consciousness, the outcome of which was the development of a new sensibility regarding anomalous groups and expressed in such diverse but related endeavours as relieving the poor, visiting the sick, schooling the young, and abolishing slavery. Many reformers were genuinely repelled by the degradation and suffering they observed among the poor in general and by the cruelty and neglect they found in existing institutions.[3] There are good grounds, Scull claims, for preferring the manipulation of moral treatment to chains, brutality and fear and, we might add, for welcoming educational opportunities for deaf and blind children where none had existed before.

At the same time, the humanitarianism of the reformers was conditional: those to whom it was offered were expected to show moral improvement (Ignatieff 1983; Porter 1989). It reflected a new framework of class relations between the poor and the professional, commercial and industrial classes. It was part of a deal: in return for what was perceived to be more humane treatment, whether this was relief, schooling, prison reform or moral treatment, the poor were expected to become more industrious, obedient and disciplined. The distribution of relief directly in money or in kind, for example, received far less support than the provision of schools, hospitals or reformatories (Kidd 1999). Thus, the charitable imperative was inextricably linked to social control and was a much

more ambiguous phenomenon than what we think of as disinterested philanthropy or the self-proclaimed benevolence of professionals who were
involved in the institutions (Scull 1993). Humanitarian intervention was
always contingent on the expectation that anomalous individuals would
actively engage in their own transformation and would be grateful to their
sponsors.

The shift in moral sensibilities clearly influenced societal attitudes
and responses, especially to the deserving poor. Thus, in addition to the
administrative and medical perspectives articulated in the reports of the
census commissioners, an ideology of charity exerted a significant influence on the emergence of disability as a specific social issue in the nineteenth century. With extreme levels of destitution among large numbers
of the population and in the absence of a significant framework of public relief, urban centres such as Dublin, where the scale of distress was
greatest, had extensive networks of charitable foundations (Lindsay
1987). In the context of an increasingly influential medical model, the
central elements of this charity discourse – that recipients were tragic,
helpless, dependent and uniquely deserving – easily transferred from
sickness to disability. Moreover, since charitable foundations tended to
focus on the most deserving social groups, this process furthered the differentiation of people with perceived impairments from among the general body of the poor.

The laissez-faire ideology of the times made the charities hypersensi-
tive to charges of fostering dependency or promoting mendicancy. To off-
set this, charitable foundations went to considerable lengths to stress how
prudently the donors' contributions were spent and how deserving were
the causes that they supported. The National Institution for the Education
of Deaf and Dumb Children emphasised that it was 'a school of industry,
in agricultural, gardening, mechanical and household occupations' (Orpen
1836: 54) in which 'the time of all the pupils is nearly equally divided
between study and labour or domestic work ... and any person examining
the quantity of various labours performed ... by the pupils ... will acknowledge that they have not been allowed to eat the bread of idleness' (Fourth
Report of the National Institution 1820: 18). The schools stressed that
their endeavours corresponded with rather than contradicted the tenets of
political economy. Their aim was to enable their pupils 'to take a place in
society, and contribute to their own support instead of being a burden on
others' (Sixth Report of the Stewart Institution 1875: 2; see also Second

Report of the National Institution 1818; Second Report of the Catholic Institution 1848; Census of Ireland 1851, Part III).

An important promotional strategy for the charities, therefore, was to emphasise the economic and social benefits that they conferred on society. Charities could not afford to be radical in any political or cultural sense since they could not offend or challenge the elites on whose patronage they depended. When members of the elite contributed money and served as honorary officers in charitable institutions, both they and the institution stood to gain something: the status of the charity increased while a substantial contribution or position of patronage could legitimate wealth, create a public identity, and even open doors to public life (Kidd 1999). Furthermore, as far as the elites were concerned, support for charitable institutions served more direct hygienic ends: the removal of the impotent and afflicted from the streets reduced 'the discomfort of those who had to witness the public exhibition of human misery with which the inhabitants of this city [are] already too familiar' (cited in Lindsay 1987: 152–3).

Paradoxically, the efforts of charitable institutions to reduce one measure of dependency reproduced it in other forms. The large number of charitable foundations meant that there was considerable competition for revenue and, in order to maintain its share, each agency tended to focus on specific recipient groups – for example, female penitents, aged men, deaf and dumb children, sick and indigent roomkeepers (Lindsay 1987; Shaw 1850) – and to emphasise the particular helplessness, neediness and misfortune of that particular group. The more lurid the descriptions of the tragic circumstances, the higher the contributions that might be expected. Without the National Institution for the Deaf and Dumb, for example, 'the unfortunate individuals among the lower classes, who are separated from commerce with their fellow creatures, by the want of hearing and speech, have been left to neglect, as merely pitiable specimens of hopeless infirmity' (First Report of the National Institution 1817: 6).

The composition, power structure and ideology of charitable organisations made it impossible for them to represent the distinctive interests of disabled people or to challenge the disabling consequences of societal barriers (Drake 1996). In these charity relationships, the recipients were manoeuvred into subordinate roles and were expected to show deference and to appear appropriately deserving. As a result, disabled people were excluded from positions of power in charitable organisations and had little or no authority to influence decisions about policy or the disposition of resources (Oliver 1990; Drake 1994). Moreover, as their involvement in the field of disability expanded, the charities colonised the discursive spaces where ideology, policy and practice concerning disability were determined. The more charities were perceived to represent disabled people, the more they came to mediate the relationship between disability and the state. In Ireland, after the institutional expansion of the early nineteenth century and the retrenchment of the post-famine period, the state left the field of disability to the charities which, by the end of the nineteenth century, were dominated directly and indirectly by the Catholic Church (Luddy 1995).

## DISABILITY AND THE CHURCHES

Over the course of the nineteenth century, the Catholic Church moved from a relatively negligible to a substantial presence in the field of disability. This process paralleled a more general change in the position of the Church in Irish society. Although Church and State authorities might quarrel over the substance and the details of social and educational policy, as the century progressed there was an increasing degree of mutual accommodation between them. Both expressed a desire that the lower orders would learn to obey the civil laws and accept the existing ranks and orders in society (Kelly 1978). In a submission to the Powis Commission on Education, Cardinal Cullen remarked that

> The requirements for the teaching in these National schools ought not be too great ... Too high an education will make the poor oftentimes discontented, and will unsuit them for following the plough, or for using the spade, or for hammering iron or building walls. The poor ought to be educated with a view to the place they hold in society ... [T]he rich ought to get one sort of education and the poor ought to get another sort. Each class ought to be educated for the sphere of life in which they have to move. (1870: 1242)

One of the first opportunities for the Catholic Church to flex its denominational muscles arose in relation to special schooling. Increased activity on the part of Protestant charitable societies was a characteristic feature of the educational scene in Ireland at the beginning of the nineteenth century. Some of the more prominent societies were overtly proselytising agencies which received considerable amounts of public funds to establish schools, buy books and pay teachers (Akenson 1970; Kelly 1978). This evangelising spirit and the promise of enlightenment and salvation through education were key factors in the establishment of the first school for deaf children of the poor in Ireland. It was believed that without education, deaf children of the poor 'were ... suffered to drag on a miserable existence, in a state of mental darkness and spiritual desolation, more awful than even that of the most ignorant of the heathen, and not unfrequently productive of a great degree of outrage and vice' (*The Dublin Penny Journal* 1836: 313).

In the case of deaf children, education was regarded more as a missionary than a proselytising undertaking. The perception of deaf people as pagans rather than as misguided Christians is evident in the title of a book written by Charles Orpen, founder of the National Institution for the Education of the Deaf and Dumb Children of the Poor in Ireland: *The Contrast between Atheism, Paganism and Christianity Illustrated or, the Uneducated Deaf and Dumb as Heathens, Compared with those who have been Instructed in Language and Revelation and Taught by the Holy Spirit as Christians.* The Catholic Institution for the Education of the Deaf and Dumb founded thirty years later, in 1846, was informed by the same kind of missionary zeal:

> There are in Catholic Ireland alone about 4,000 Deaf-mutes doomed to go down into their graves in total ignorance of the existence of a Supreme Being and of man's destiny in this life and in that to come, if not rescued from their sad estate ... [N]o glimmering knowledge of a great Creator, no remote conception of a loving Saviour, no vague idea of their possessing immortal souls have even got entrance into their darkened intellects (Sixteenth Report of the Catholic Institution 1862: 18).

The establishment of the Catholic Institution stemmed from a belief that the Protestant controlled National Institution was engaged in proselytising activities among deaf children. The first annual report of the Catholic Institution claimed that one of its aims was 'to combat a system of proselytism that is ... unprincipled ... comprehensive and effective, extending its operations over the entire country' (First Report of the Catholic Institution

1847: 20). A pastoral letter from Cardinal Cullen on the matter quoted a contemporary newspaper report:

> In the *Saunders News-Letter* containing an account of the annual meeting of the juvenile association at Clermont [the location of the National Institution] (1st April, 1850) the following words are attributed to one of the rev. speakers on the occasion: – 'The Report of the Catholic Institution for the Deaf and Dumb referred to the work of that (Clermont) Institution and charged them with proselytism. He hoped they were liable to that charge and the only thing that grieved him was, that they were not so in a sufficient degree (Hear, hear).' (Twenty-third Report of the Catholic Institution 1869: 14–22)

Cullen raised similar objections to the Stewart Institution for Idiotic and Imbecile Children, which he also regarded as a proselytising agency and he instructed Catholics not to support it in any way (Robins 1986). However, unlike the denominational reaction to the establishment of the National Institution, neither the Catholic Church nor Catholic charities became involved in establishing an alternative to the Stewart Institution. Byrne (1980) suggests two reasons for this. Firstly, in general, through the workhouse and asylum systems, the state authorities were thought to be responsible for provision for people then defined as idiots and imbeciles. Secondly, no special financial inducements were offered to religious bodies that would attract them to undertake this work. Moreover, Ireland lacked an industrial base and a strong, socially active middle-class at that time, factors that underlay movements for the provision of institutions for children with learning difficulties in Britain and the United States, for example.

There are some difficulties with these arguments, however. Deaf and blind people were also confined in state institutions. In 1851 there were almost as many blind people as 'idiots and imbeciles' in workhouses and more deaf people in workhouses than in educational institutions (Census of Ireland 1851, Part III), yet this did not prevent the establishment of Catholic institutions for deaf and blind children. Furthermore, the threat of proselytisation seems to have been a more significant factor in the establishment of schools for deaf children, for example, than the availability of financial supports under the poor law, although these maintenance payments did become more important as the century progressed

(McDonnell 1979). But even the extension of poor law provision in 1878 to the maintenance and instruction of 'idiots and imbeciles ... [in] any hospital or institution for the reception of such persons' (Dept. of Education 1965: 10) did not lead to any new development. Moreover, to point to the absence of a socially active class in Ireland is to overlook the fact that the Catholic Church was involved, directly and indirectly, in a great variety of charitable enterprises in the fields of education, health and welfare throughout the nineteenth century. These included schools, hospitals, asylums, orphanages and penal institutions such as reformatories and industrial schools (Fahey 1987; Barnes 1989; Luddy 1995; O'Sullivan 1998; Raftery and O'Sullivan 1999). During the ninetheenth century, and especially between 1850 and 1900, the Catholic Church spent comparatively large sums on the construction of Church related institutions (Larkin 1967). Therefore, the absence of a Catholic involvement in the comparatively large field of learning difficulty is puzzling.

In attempting to explain this absence we must look beyond philanthropy. In terms of a scale of human worth in nineteenth century Ireland, individuals with learning difficulties were more devalued than any other anomalous group. As early as the 1830s, while investigating the condition of the poorer classes, one assistant commissioner on a visit to the Ballinasloe asylum reported that, instead of building institutions for curable lunatics, the government was, in fact, 'erecting palaces for the permanent accommodation of worthless and slavering idiots' (cited in Robins 1986: 159). At regular intervals throughout the century, the census commissioners, the inspectors of lunatics as well as private individuals continued to press for separate provision for people with learning difficulties. The cheaper alternative was to send the 'chronic and incurable classes' and 'harmless lunatics' to the workhouse as destitute or to convert a gaol or workhouse 'into a low-grade custodial asylum' (Finnane 1981: 71). Ironically, during a period of increasing medicalisation what counted was not altruism but economics and, apart from the Stewart Institution, no special provision was established for people with learning difficulties.

Meanwhile, links between existing institutions and emerging professional self-interests were gathering strength. In his study of asylums in Britain, for example, Scull (1993) detects a connection between an increasing medicalisation and a shift towards a more custodial function over the course of the nineteenth century. He argues that medical control of asylums was accomplished when doctors successfully monopolised moral treatment as 'something only physicians were qualified to dispense' (Scull 1993: 260). Just at the point when this was achieved and the asylum was transformed into an arena for professional practice, 'all the crucial features of moral treatment – those elements which were supposed to distinguish the asylum from the prison ...' decayed and disappeared (277). Scull implies that the primary factor behind the medicalisation of the asylums was professional self-interest and, when asylums became overtly custodial institutions, doctors did a *volte face* on the presumed benefits of moral treatment and adjusted their professional ideology accordingly. Developments in Ireland followed a similar pattern. In Irish asylums moral treatment proved to be short lived, 'in fact, little more than a pleasant illusion' (Robins 1986: 129). An analysis such as Scull's suggests that the role of professionals in the development of institutions for people with perceived impairments needs to be re-examined and the altruism, which is assumed to constitute such a significant element in the professional role, needs to be questioned.

## DISABILITY AND THE EMERGING PROFESSIONS

According to many social scientists, two of the core attributes of a profession are the extent to which its practice is based on theoretical knowledge and expertise and the degree to which the ideal of altruistic service is observed (Johnson 1972). As we have seen, the first comprehensive report of the census commissioners (Census of Ireland 1851, Part III) regarded doctors as the experts in relation to impairment. Their Report on the Status of Disease stated that '[w]here any difficulty arose with respect to the true, the physiological or pathological condition of a case, an examination by a medical man was had recourse to ...' (Census of Ireland 1851, Part III: 4). In the same report almost all the sources quoted in relation to disability are from the field of medicine. The report also includes detailed discussion on the aetiology and pathology of deafness, for example, and contains several descriptions of 'rare and remarkable cases' (17–26). It was taken as given that intervention by medical practitioners in the field of impairment was altruistic. Dr Charles Orpen's account of the establishment of the first known school for deaf children in Ireland provides a good example:

> After having finished my medical and surgical studies, I made, on my way to Dublin in 1814, a tour ... to examine the principal hospitals,

> prisons, manufactories, &c. &c. ... Dr De Lys at Birmingham ... gave
> me the first Report of the Institute for the Deaf and Dumb, then
> recently established there ... I knew that no such school had ever
> existed in Ireland ... Thinking it probable, that in some of the great
> establishments of the poor in Dublin I might find some Deaf and
> Dumb persons, I enquired at the Foundling Hospital, and at the
> Bedford Asylum for Orphans, then attached to the House of Industry,
> and in both I found several; – of course totally uninstructed and igno-
> rant. Out of those in the latter who seemed the most neglected, I took
> one to my own house, by permission of the Governors, with whom I
> was intimate ... (1836: x–xi)

The combination of expertise and altruism associated with the medical profession generated a powerful and sustained medical influence in
the emerging fields of mental health and special education. Within three
years of its establishment, a physician, consulting surgeon and surgeon
had been appointed to the National Institution for the Education of Deaf
and Dumb Children (Third Report of the National Institution 1819: 4). As
we have seen, the voluntary hospitals, the county infirmaries, the fever
hospitals and the local dispensaries created institutional vehicles for the
medicalisation of Irish society. Thus, by virtue of their existence as members of a significant professional group and by virtue of the discursive
connections that doctors and administrators made between illness and
impairment, on the one hand, and impairment and altruistic service on the
other, doctors were well placed to secure dominant roles in policy-making
and practice in asylums and special schools, the two most characteristic
nineteenth century institutions specifically intended for people with perceived impairments (Robins 1986; Potts 1983).

However, doctors were not the only occupational group to incorporate
impairment within their field of expertise. As special schooling expanded,
teachers and administrators, both lay and religious, laid claim to particular knowledge and altruistic motives in their respective fields. Advocates
of special schooling argued that teachers 'not initiated in this peculiar art'
would not be able to surmount the difficulties of instructing the deaf; furthermore, it was 'folly to think that the Deaf and Dumb can ever be taught
fully at common schools' (Orpen 1836: 404, 538). Claims like these did
not go unchallenged. Orpen had occasion to rebut an argument in the
*London Quarterly Review* 'that the belief that the Deaf and Dumb could

only be taught by a peculiar and difficult method of instruction, arose only from Deaf and Dumb Teachers themselves, who invented and propagated the idea from interested motives, and that like some prophecies it produced its own fulfilment' (Sixth Report of the National Institution 1822: 11). In his response, Orpen 'left it to teachers of the various Deaf and Dumb Institutions in the United Kingdoms [sic], to repel the ... charges of mercenary and selfish motives made personally against them ...' (12).

Although the strength of professional presence and control varied according to the specific institutional context, a number of general elements can be detected. Firstly, in practical terms, the process of professionalisation represented a colonisation of institutional services. As professional bodies established their authority, non-professionals were replaced, demoted or excluded altogether from institutions. Having established an influential presence in matters of public health in Ireland, medical practitioners, for example, secured a dominant role in the management of the state's mental health policies. In 1834, Dr John Jacob ridiculed the idea of anyone but a doctor being able to apply appropriate treatment in the asylum. He deplored the policy of placing patients in the care of 'rude and illiterate keepers' whom he contrasted with the educated and intelligent physician (Robins 1986: 94). At first, as each new asylum opened, non-medical managers had been placed in charge but this policy was quickly circumvented in favour of medical management. From 1845, newly appointed managers of public asylums had to hold a medical qualification and by 1860 only one lay public asylum manager remained (Robins 1986).

Similar processes of replacement and exclusion occurred in special schools for deaf children. From the beginning, the schools used a monitorial system (First Report of the National Institution 1817) and deaf student monitors could train to become teachers in the schools. School authorities acknowledged that they derived 'considerable assistance in the management of the school from the aid of the deaf mute pupil teachers' (Eleventh Report of the Catholic Institution 1857: 21). On completion of training, institutions were usually anxious to retain deaf trainees as teachers who became role models for the pupils in the school, and who, because of their signing skills, had a particular 'facility of communicating knowledge' (Fourteenth Report of the Catholic Institution 1860: 24–5). As long as sign language remained the medium of instruction and communication in the schools, Deaf teachers were seen to have a significant, if not an equal, role in the education of deaf children. However, as schools shifted towards 'oral education'[4] during the second half of the nineteenth century, Deaf teachers were excluded and teaching in schools for deaf pupils became an occupation for hearing professionals only (Lane 1984). Although this change was implemented much later in Ireland than in the rest of Western Europe, when it did occur the exclusionary consequences for Deaf 'non-professionals' were exactly the same (McDonnell and Saunders 1993; Saunders 1997).

Increasing professionalisation created progressively greater degrees of social distance between those who administered and worked in the institutions and their clients. This social distancing can be linked to a shift from an ideology of humanitarianism that accompanied the first appearance of institutions for disabled people to an ideology of expertism that accompanied the expansion of the institutions over the course of the nineteenth century (Baynton 1993; Valentine 1993; Winzer 1993). Officers of the institutions – medical superintendents, administrators, teachers – became professionalised through ideology, training, qualifying associations, specialised journals and the use of distinctive technologies (Dear and Wolch 1987; Finnane 1981; Ingleby 1983; Scull 1993). Increasing professionalisation was accompanied by a growing conviction that clients did not know their 'own best interest' (Lane 1984: 413) and by an unwillingness to admit that failures in rehabilitative programmes could be attributed either to professionals themselves or to their programmes of treatment (Robins 1986; Scull 1993). Convinced that they were at the cutting edge of scientific and social progress, it is not surprising that professionals and their associations were among the most vociferous and active members of the eugenics movement – a topic that is explored in more detail in the next chapter.

Expressions of opposition to professional domination were usually dismissed with disdain. Successive national and international congresses on the education of deaf children, for example, fostered professional solidarity and certainty among hearing teachers regarding their views on how it should be organised (Lane 1984: 402–4). At the fourth international congress held in Paris in 1900, a leading Italian educator claimed 'that the deaf, even well instructed, can in no way be put on the same plane with their hearing educators'; another, representing the hearing professional view, asked: 'since when do we consult the patient on the nature of his treatment?' (cited in Lane 1984: 409). And when Deaf communities, with congresses of their own, mounted a challenge to the educational approaches being advocated by hearing professionals, they were firmly rejected. As Lane puts it in relation to the goals and conduct of education and the teaching profession: '[o]f all the conclusions on these issues reached by hearing professionals in Paris, Milan and Brussels, not a single one agreed with the views of the deaf themselves ...' (1984: 405)

In the asylums, the failures of programmes of treatment were put down to the prevalence of 'hopeless cases' (Scull 1993). The close supervision of patients, characteristic of earlier times, was apparently less acceptable to doctors than it had been to the lay superintendents – the retired soldiers or ex-naval officers who had governed the first asylums (Reuber 1999). Direct supervision became the responsibility of nurses and keepers and the medical manager became a visitor to the wards rather than a constant presence. In the 1860s, medical superintendents successfully campaigned to have their residence physically separated from the main building (Reuber 1999). The appearance of architectural and organisational buffers between managers and patients reflected a new social distance as well as a new set of power relations between professional experts and their clients.

Physicians were not the only professionals with vested interests in institutions. Associated with the rhetoric of doing good works, institutions were seen as ideal places for members of religious congregations to pursue a personal vocation. In particular, the new female religious congregations, the Irish Sisters of Charity, the Loreto order and the Sisters of Mercy, provided women with 'a socially acceptable way to engage in purposeful work' (Luddy 1988: 304). For lay people too, working in any area of special needs is associated in the public mind with the idea of an exemplary commitment or vocation. A more immediate motivation for the involvement of lay people in this field was the attraction of white-collar employment. As Binet and Simon observed:

> Ever since public interest has been aroused in the question of schools for defective children, selfish ambition has seen its opportunity. The most frankly selfish reasons conceal themselves behind a mask of philanthropy and whoever dreams of finding a fine situation for himself in the new schools never speaks of children without tears in his eyes ... There is no reason for indignation. Everyone has the right to look after his own interests so long as he does not compromise interests superior to his own. (1914: 10)

Professionals often have a vested interest in greater institutional differentiation. The desire to off-load individuals who present administrative and rehabilitative difficulties is often the underlying rationale for the establishment of new forms of special provision, although the overt argument for change may be couched in terms of it being in the best interests of the individuals concerned. During the nineteenth century, as schooling became a mass activity and as more special schools and other forms of special provision appeared, strategies emerged which facilitated the exclusion of pupils who presented pedagogic and organisational difficulties for teachers in mainstream schools (Thomas 1978; Tomlinson 1982).

As professionals became integrated into institutional systems and as their career and status ties within institutions were strengthened, those who were confined were expected to deport themselves in acceptable ways – to show diligence, to be obedient and to be grateful for what the institution had to offer. Because institutional regimes were harsh and oppressive and because confinement was usually involuntary and often carried out under duress, resistance was always a likely reaction among those who were confined.

## RESISTANCE TO INSTITUTIONALISATION

Resistance to institutionalisation can and did take many different forms. Although property owners in Ireland, for example, wanted greater regulation of the poor they strongly opposed the workhouse system, not on humanitarian grounds, however, but because it meant extra taxation; Church authorities wanted an alternative to the hedge schools but opposed the national school system for denominational reasons. However, the focus here will not be on the institutional mediators (i.e. those agencies which managed, oversaw and administered the institutions on the ground)[5] but rather on those social groups who were or who could be institutionalised. One of the great difficulties in identifying lines of resistance among these groups is the absence of impartial information, since the history of institutions is usually recorded from the point of view of policy makers and power brokers (Digby 1997).

Although we may lack information about the details of resistance in institutions in the past, accounts of resistance in modern institutions illustrate how such strategies can emerge even under conditions of intensive surveillance. When schools for deaf children in Ireland introduced oralist education policies a wide variety of coercive and ideological strategies were employed in an attempt to eliminate the use of sign language among the pupils (McDonnell and Saunders 1993). Consequently, signing became an underground activity:

> We were very vigilant when we signed. We always had to be ready for someone to come along. We had a particular posture which meant 'Be careful!' There were eye movements which said, 'stop signing, someone is coming! ... We used to sign in the toilets. In the dormitory we could open the curtains to let in a little light. We used to sign away for hours. (McDonnell and Saunders 1993: 257)

Signing persisted among the deaf school population and Irish sign language, although it was technically forbidden, continued to be transmitted to new entrants (McDonnell 1996).

Different degrees of resistance were possible among different groups and in different institutions. Adults, for example, are likely to be in a better position to organise and exercise resistance than are children, and people who are well, better than people who are ill. Resistance in the workhouses, for example, could amount to open revolt (Burke 1987; O'Connor 1995) and, clearly, workhouse administrators were prepared for this. A whole section of the General Order for the Management of Workhouses contained guidelines for the punishment of refractory or disorderly paupers (Banks 1872) and each workhouse had a refractory ward for the punishment of those who broke workhouse rules (Burke 1987).

Resistance could also be influenced by the effectiveness and subtlety of the disciplinary power exercised in the institution. Goffman (1968) gives considerable attention to the strategies devised by individuals in mental hospitals to circumvent regulations, though these strategies might be regarded as adjustments rather than challenges to institutional life. The scope for resistance in the lunatic asylums was limited by the hegemony of the medical model of mental illness and the difficulties of preserving any alternative model of mental health free from medical control (Scull 1993). Individuals in other institutions were probably in a more favourable position to mount an opposing or alternative interpretation of their circumstances. As we have seen, the spread of oralist ideology in special schools for deaf children lead to greater discrimination against Deaf people. At the same time, it was possible for Deaf communities to organise resistance to these ideas using an alternative model of deafness based on distinctive linguistic and community values (McDonnell and Saunders 1993; Saunders 1997).

Sometimes the interests of the individual coincided with the interests of the institution (Goffman 1968) and aspects of what the institution had to offer could be turned to personal or collective advantage. The national schools, for example, presented opportunities for children to become literate and numerate at a time when the desire for literacy in the English language seems to have been widespread among parents. On the other hand, attempts by the commissioners to introduce agricultural instruction into the national school system in the 1840s – even when accompanied by financial inducements for the pupils – proved unsuccessful due in large measure to resistance from parents and pupils (Kelly 1978). Special schools for deaf children provide an example of how institutions could produce unforeseen but positive benefits. The schools brought together individuals who otherwise never would have had opportunities to become members of a supportive community nor to acquire sign language. For Laurent Clerc, entering the National Institution for the Deaf in Paris meant leaving the isolation of the countryside to join the 'society of the deaf ... my new family' wherein he 'came out from a cave in which the shadows of meaning had flickered ...' (Lane 1984: 10).

## CONCLUSION

The 1851 Census of Ireland employed the major dividing practices that underlie modern responses to disability – the separation of disabled people from the general body of the poor and their differentiation into specific categories of perceived impairment. The census reports employed a medical model of disability and advocated institutionalisation as the most appropriate form of public intervention. Associated with this ideological position was a discourse of private charity that had two forms. Firstly, charitable organisations were engaged with the state in public-private partnerships of institutionalisation in which institutions were partly, largely or completely supported by voluntary subscriptions. Secondly, charity provided a rhetoric of benevolence which enveloped both public and private responses to disability and facilitated a particular kind of social policing that incorporated both coercive and philanthropic impulses (Donajgrodzki 1977).

All of these features constituted a familiar response to disability in the urbanising and industrialisng capitalist societies of Western Europe

(Armstrong, Belmont and Verillon 2000; Barnes 1996; Oliver 1990; Winzer 1993). Their presence in the very poor, predominantly rural society of nineteenth century Ireland was surprising. Here, the institutionalisation of disabled people formed part of a larger project – the disciplining of Irish society. The language of deficiency and dependence that permeated definitions of disability was applied to the greater part of the population, and institutionalisation was seen as the primary mechanism for removing or moderating these problems.

Institutionalisation represented one of the major transformations in the relationship between disability and society during the nineteenth century. Its advocates were convinced of its potential as a mechanism of normalisation. As it turned out, the number of people who seemed to require institutionalisation continued to increase, greater degrees of segregation were required, and institutions became more specialised and more expensive. At the same time, it appeared that anomalous social groups remained as problematic as ever. The sense of optimism associated with the early institutional initiatives began to dissipate and to bring about a further ideological transformation in the relationship between disability and society. This change reflected a growing perception that impairment was not so much a deficit or dependency that needed to be treated, but rather was the manifestation of a degeneracy that had to be eradicated. This particular ideological transformation is explored in the next chapter.

## NOTES

1. Scull explained the emergence of lunatic asylum system in Britain in terms of a response to the demands of industrial capitalism and the removal of an economically unproductive and socially disruptive population from society. He attributes the establishment of the Irish system to the operation of a British colonial administration (Scull 1993). Malcolm (1999) draws attention to the fact that many of those who were institutionalised in asylums in Ireland in the post-Famine period were typically not 'useless' and 'unwanted' but rather were members of a significant social and economic group in Irish rural society. Agreeing with Finnane (1981), she argues that the asylum system was used by families to discipline 'troublesome' members. This analysis may go some way towards explaining why the system expanded in the post-Famine period but it does not explain why it was established in the first place.

2.  While Luddy's (1995) study focuses on organisations founded by women her conclusion seems to apply to philanthropic organisations in general (Lindsay 1987).
3.  The 61st Report of the Belfast Charitable Society (1832: 5), for example, records an exchange with Charles Orpen, the secretary of the National Institution for the Education of the Deaf and Dumb at Claremont in Dublin. The committee of the Charitable Society claimed that 'the charges for the Clermont pupils appear to be extravagant, when compared with the rigid economy practised in the expenditure of the public money for the use of the Belfast Poor-House.' Orpen had declared that the children in the Belfast Poor-House were '*badly* clothed, and *badly* educated, and that there is hardly a single pupil in the children's school, or infants school, who is not over-run with scrofula ... the most miserable, sickly, squalid, unhappy-looking objects that one can well conceive' (italics in original). On another occasion in his Address to the Public on the State of the Poor of Dublin (1832: 10–11), Orpen declared that he 'could easily fill your whole paper, several days in succession, with details and anecdotes, as to the excessive misery of the poor in Dublin, which I myself witnessed ... such scenes and such cases, which even habituated as I have been for years to all the painful sights of the medical and surgical profession ... still, when I think of them, sometimes literally make me shiver ... The rich can know nothing whatever of the state of the poor, unless they visit them and ... see with their own eyes ... and seeing it, relieve it as far as they can.'
4.  'Oral education' or 'oralism' applies to a particular pedagogic and organisational approach adopted in schools for deaf children. It does not recognise the cultural or linguistic standing of a Deaf community and its primary aim is the assimilation of deaf children into hearing society. Oralist teaching programmes put great emphasis on the acquisition of skills in speech, do not use sign language, and generally forbid its use with and among deaf children (Lane 1993; McDonnell and Saunders 1993).
5.  Here I draw on the idea of mediators as established interest groups and power brokers in institutional services such as education (Drudy and Lynch 1993). 'The mediators of educational services are basically those groups that manage, oversee and administer the services at local level .... The character of state policies ... is ... dependent on the co-operation and compliance of those who administer the services on a day-to-day basis' (Drudy and Lynch 1993: 117).

# 5

# Eugenic Ideology: Segregation and Surgery

| | |
|---|---|
| defectives | inferior stocks |
| degenerate types | the less fit stocks |
| national deterioration | the feebleminded |
| race suicide | the degenerate |
| racial degeneration | useless and inefficient citizens |
| the defective classes | the teeming progeny of the unfit |
| the handicap of heredity | the worthless kind |
| the inferior races | the dependent class |
| the sub-races of mankind | low grade families |
| the lower types | the subnormal |
| the social problem group | the residuum |
| unfit and degenerate persons | the dangerous units |
| defective genes | inferior blood |

## INTRODUCTION

The terminology outlined above does not come from the margins of political and social thought; it is standard usage to be found in mainstream texts in disciplines such as education, psychology, law and medicine from the closing decades of the nineteenth century until the 1930s. It came from the pens of men and women throughout Western society, significant and influential figures in the worlds of science, medicine, politics, religion, the humanities, commerce and the law. Hahn Rafter (1997) draws attention to the profusion, vagueness and chameleon-like qualities of terminology of this kind. At its most basic, it served as a metaphor for otherness, an otherness that was taken to be biologically determined, that threatened the very foundations of society, and that no amount of social intervention could remediate (O'Brien 1999*a*).

The terminology reflects a perspective on human nature and human potential very different from the view that prevailed at the beginning of the nineteenth century in Ireland and in other Western countries. Then, institutional interventions in relation to anomalous populations – whether we attribute such interventions to processes of social control or to more humanitarian attitudes – were governed by a general sense of optimism, a belief that deficiencies could be remedied by the discipline, treatment or training which the relevant institution could bring to bear on the individual. There was a strong belief that experts would soon be in a position to identify and successfully treat the lesions that were responsible for such deficiencies, whether, as *The Asylum Journal of Mental Science* put it, these were 'lesions of intelligence and will' (1854: 137), 'lesion(s) of understanding' (1854*a*: 94), or simply lesions that caused disease. Experts had also argued that progress would be made only through the establishment of more specialised institutions, the exercise of a greater degree of care in the allocation of individuals to particular institutions, and the application of expertise in designing and delivering appropriate forms of treatment within those institutions (*AJMS* 1856: 130–136).

This chapter describes how the shift towards a pessimistic perspective found its most powerful expression in the eugenics movement. Fundamentally, eugenics refers to the belief that the selective breeding practices being applied in the plant and animal kingdoms could also be applied to human beings. Thus, legislative and social programmes could be introduced to foster the birth rate among so-called good stocks and pre-vent it among allegedly degenerate types. This chapter focuses on the implications for disability of eugenic thinking and practices; in particular it explores the disabling effects of expertism (Troyna and Vincent 1996) in eugenic discourse and how what was called mental incapacity became the primary ground for eugenic intervention. Analysis of developments in Ireland is set in the wider context of Western society: eugenics was an active international movement (see, for example, Broberg and Roll-Hansen 1996) and, because there were both similarities and differences in the way that countries responded (Porter 1999*a*; Weindling 1999; Weingart 1999), eugenic activity in any one particular country can only be fully understood in relation to what was happening elsewhere in North America and Western Europe. In this chapter, I first discuss how the shift towards a more pessimistic view of human possibility turned on the question of mental health. I then briefly describe the ideological and social conditions under which eugenics developed in Western society. The subsequent sections are devoted to the other themes of the chapter: the nature and effects of eugenics as a discourse of expertism; the focus on mental incapacity as the primary source of a whole range of social pathologies; and the disabling measures proposed and implemented as a result of eugenic policies. The final section examines the impact of eugenic thinking and practice in Ireland in relation to disability and compares this with responses in other countries. The chapter concludes with a brief examination of how eugenic ideas continue to influence social policy and practice in the field of disability.

## FROM OPTIMISM TO PESSIMISM

Nowhere was the initial sense of optimism better reflected than in the fledgling institutions associated with mental health. The Board of Guardians of the new lunatic asylum at Ballinasloe, for example, believed itself to be responsible for a modern enlightened institution (Walsh 1999). Around the same time the Inspectors of Lunatic Asylums in Ireland observed that

> it would be falling into a great mistake to imagine that even the most miserable objects of mental incapability are beyond the reach of being relieved; for there is no species of disease or affection, from the highest state of maniacal excitement to the very lowest grade of imbecility, that does not admit of cure or alleviation under judicious treatment, such alone as can be obtained in establishments exclusively devoted to the object. (Seventh Report on the District, Criminal and Private Lunatic Asylums in Ireland 1855: 5)

In their report for 1851, the census commissioners for Ireland emphasised the benefits that education in special institutions would bring to 'the Deaf and Dumb' (Census of Ireland 1851, Part III: 26); they also stressed 'the necessity ... for the establishment of some general institution for the pauper blind' (45) and urged that steps should be taken 'towards the education and moral improvement of Idiots and Imbeciles' (49). For the commissioners, special institutions were a social investment that would prevent or reduce the likelihood of these social groups becoming 'a burden on society' (Stoker 1863: 458).

With a view to 'claiming them for humanity' (Ryan and Thomas 1987: 93), schools for idiots and imbeciles began to appear in Western Europe and North America from the 1830s onwards (Ireland 1900: 359). In France in 1846, Seguin published his influential *Traitment Moral, Hygiène, et Éducation des Idiots, et des autres Enfants Arrières*, declaring that 'while waiting for medicine to cure idiots, I have undertaken to see that they participate in the benefits of education' (cited in Ryan and Thomas 1987: 92). In the US during the 1850s, the successes of the newly established special schools were enthusiastically reported and advocates toured the countryside and lobbied public officials and private philanthropists to seek support (Trent 1994). Information and opinion about new developments were exchanged at an international level through publications, visits and correspondence.[1]

Over the second half of the nineteenth century, however, this optimistic vision vanished, again nowhere more completely than in relation to mental health (Ryan and Thomas 1987; Pick 1989; Winzer 1993). The major concern was a perceived increase in the incidence of lunacy and idiocy and its implications for society. In 1881, the census commissioners of Ireland observed that, while there had been a slight decrease in the relative number of 'the Blind' in the general population since 1851 and 'a satisfactory decrease' in the relative number of 'the Deaf and Dumb', the number of 'Lunatics and Idiots' had more than doubled, rising from a ratio of 1 in 657 to 1 in 281 during the same period (Census of Ireland 1881, Part II: 34, 41, 48). In 1898, the Inspectors of Lunatics (48th Report of the Inspectors of Lunatics 1898: 1–4) noted that the asylum population had increased from 3,436 in 1851 to 12,251 in 1898, representing an incidence of 1 in 657 and 1 in 222 respectively in the general population. Leading theological and medical commentators expressed anxiety at the relatively large number of so-called defectives in Ireland (Slater 1911; Cox 1912; Nixon 1912; Boyd Barrett 1913; Dawson 1913). There was an accompanying complaint that the 'ratepayers of today groan under the yolk [sic] of taxation for the care and support of degenerates' (Leeper 1912: 184; see also Barry 1907; Nolan 1912; Dawson 1913).

As we have seen, pessimism about problem populations and the possibility of reform and progress was not new. At the beginning of the nineteenth century Malthus and others had speculated that famine and dis-ease might be allowed to do their worst (Porter 2000). However, at that time the weight of expert opinion supported the idea of institutional inter-vention and believed in its capacity to reform the individual.

The pessimism that took hold from the middle of the century onwards, however, differed from the earlier version in four important respects. Firstly, there was an increasing preoccupation with individual mental states rather than with economic conditions. The perceived relationship between poverty and mental health was, in a sense, reversed. In many countries at the beginning of the nineteenth century, including Ireland, mental illness was seen as part of the general problem of poverty and the development of asylum systems as but one element in the wider field of poor relief. By the end of the century, 'mental defect' had come to be regarded as the root cause rather than just one other aspect of poverty. Secondly, the increasingly pessimistic vision was underpinned by a con-viction that the apparent failure of professional and institutional endeav-ours to effect reform was due to the inherently flawed and fundamentally irredeemable nature of the defective classes. While there was a long tra-dition of blaming individuals for their conditions, the new pessimism located the causes of the problem at the level of biology and germ plasm, defects which were held to be beyond remediation and to threaten the well-being of both the current and future generations (Hahn Rafter 1997). Thirdly, the application of science in the improvement of society was deemed to have had socially negative side effects. It seemed that modern urban conditions acting in conjunction with medical, sanitary and welfare advances actually favoured the selection and survival of 'a low type of humanity' (Searle 1976: 45). Finally, advocates of the view that the prob-lem was biological rather than environmental were no longer content to leave the defective classes to nature or to fend for themselves. Instead, they proposed an even more interventionist role for the state in terms of controlling these 'dangerous units of society' (Gerrard 1912: 36). This pessimistic vision found its most extreme expression in the eugenics movement.

A considerable body of literature has critically explored the emer-gence of eugenic theory and practice in Western societies – in North America (Kevles 1985; McLaren 1990; Radford 1994; Hahn Rafter 1997; O'Brien 1999a), Western Europe (Nye 1984; Weiss 1987; Pick 1989), Northern Europe (Broberg and Roll-Hansen 1996) and Britain (Searle

1976; Barker 1983; King and Hansen 1999). These studies devote particular attention to the intellectual and ideological origins of eugenic discourse and to the specific political, economic, social and cultural conditions that fostered the development of eugenic movements. A number of studies have made cross-national comparisons and connections (Kühl 1994; Miller 1996; Porter 1999; Weindling 1999; Weingart 1999) while occasional studies have set out to make a distinction between positive and negative eugenics (Carlson 2001).

Less critical attention has been given to the view that eugenics was in many important respects a classic discourse of expertism. Its key adherents and advocates were professionals, typically from medicine, but from other disciplines, too; eugenic policies found substantial support in the universities and other academic institutions; eugenics claimed that its findings and proposals were based on scientific research and statistical data; and national eugenic movements were frequently linked to specific academic or research institutes which provided arguments and apparent evidence to justify eugenic policies (Searle 1976; Kevles 1985; McLaren 1990; Broberg and Roll-Hansen 1996; Allen, 1999). Studies of the eugenics movement have also shown how experts from the sciences and social services exerted a powerful influence on policy making and legislation and how these activities enhanced the status of expert authority in society. However, less critical attention has been given to the manner in which expertism operated as a *disabling* discourse, especially in relation to mental health.

Perceived impairments – especially impairments in relation to mental health – were relentlessly, and without notable opposition, used to justify the introduction of eugenic measures. Mental handicap in particular was a core construct in the initial ideological formation of eugenic theory. The story of mental handicap in the modern period, however, is usually told in terms of steady progress and reform, apart from some so-called eugenically inspired lapses (Ryan and Thomas 1987, Chapter 5). In fact, the eugenic measures directed at people with learning difficulties, rather than being atypical lapses, represented an explicit attempt, which claimed to be based on science and professional expertise, to eliminate a devalued problem population. Even under what was referred to as reform eugenics, when theorists began to have second thoughts about the reliability of data on which eugenic arguments were based, people with learning difficulties continued to be perceived as appropriate subjects to be controlled through eugenic interventions (see, for example, Broberg and Tyden 1996).

## THE EMERGENCE OF EUGENICS

Eugenic thinking drew from several different ideological and conceptual sources, one of the most significant of which was evolutionary theory. Although Darwin's account was only one of several hypotheses circulating at the time, it was his theory of natural selection as the principal mechanism of evolution that was the most convincing. He proposed that, in the struggle for survival, those variations in a species that were best adapted to their environments would be most successful and those that lacked such variations were less likely to reproduce and survive. Even before the publication of *Origin of the Species*, the idea of evolution was being applied by social theorists in their analyses of human societies. One of the most prominent of these, Herbert Spencer, argued that societies progressed through the operation of natural laws that involved the survival of the fittest and the elimination of the unfit (Carlson 2001). Darwin's cousin, Francis Galton, who coined the term 'eugenics', made the most explicit connection between evolutionary theory and the idea of social progress and proposed that heredity could be harnessed to a social programme for improving the human species (Kevles 1985). The merging of these two strands of thought, that is, the application of a biological idea of evolution to the development of human societies, gave rise to social Darwinism which, with its hierarchies of race, gender, class and perceived ability, became one of the main pillars of eugenic thinking.

If evolutionary theory held out the prospect of progress and improvement, it also implied regression and decline. The converse of evolutionary theory was degeneration theory which proved to have an even more profound influence on eugenic thinking (Nye 1984; Gilman and Chamberlain 1985; Pick 1989; Hansen 1996; Carlson 2001). In its earliest form, the theory implied that degeneration presented no particular threat to social progress since it carried within itself the seeds of its own destruction. In one of the earliest versions (Morel 1857),[2] degeneration was described as a progressive pathology that could pass from one generation to the next and ultimately led to sterility and death. In later accounts, however, degeneration acquired a more ominous relationship with evolution. By the 1880s it was being described not 'as a subsidiary stream veering off from the river of progress and leading nowhere, but a major current threatening to carry all before it' (Pick 1989: 209).

Early theorists looked to the complex interactions of environmental conditions and hereditary factors as the principal agents of social degeneration (Pick 1989). As the nineteenth century progressed, however, and as degeneration was accorded a more prominent and threatening presence in society, heredity came to be regarded as the dominant mechanism of transmission. Bolstered by Lombroso's theory of the 'born criminal',[3] by the 1870s the hereditarian perspective had eclipsed all others (Carlson 2001; Hahn Rafter 1997; Pick 1989). As a result, heredity eventually came to preside over an 'empire of pathologies' (Pick 1989: 50) and was regarded as the central cause of a vast array of defective physical conditions, moral tendencies and social habits. Degeneration theory sustained the belief that social pathologies were attributable to biological defects found in particular social groups and passed on by individuals who were assumed to be either defective themselves or unknowing carriers.

The merging of evolutionary, degeneration and hereditarian theories created eugenic templates for evaluating cultural, social and individual worth. In international terms, it seemed that white, industrial and scientific society represented the most advanced stage of evolution while non-white, non-Western, or peasant societies represented examples of worlds that had been left behind or were in decay. In national terms, the professional elites placed themselves in the evolutionary vanguard, while poor, delinquent, and disabled groups were stigmatised with the mark of degeneracy. Pick (1989) argues that distinctive political, social, economic and cultural conditions underpinned the emergence of such views in different Western European countries but, in spite of these differences, there were several important features that crossed national and regional boundaries.

Eugenics came to prominence during a period of widespread social upheaval associated with population growth, industrialisation and urbanisation. Rich (1977), for example, estimates that in Europe during the second half of the nineteenth century, more than 300 million people – about 85 per cent of the entire population – were on the move, 70 per cent in internal urbanisation movements and the remainder in emigration to the other continents. Dislocation on such a scale led to the concentration of millions of people in conditions that 'could only intensify the massive squalor, overcrowding, misery, and disease of city life' (Pick 1989: 53). Furthermore, large quantities of detailed statistical information about urban poverty, crime and disease were becoming available for the first time and new social surveys, such as those of Booth and Rowntree in Britain, painted grim descriptions of urban life and brought them to public attention. The introduction of school medical inspection (Boyd Barrett 1913) revealed that large numbers of children suffered from medical problems of one kind or another. In Britain, the Inspector-General of recruitment at the outbreak of the Boer War reported that large numbers of men had been rejected as physically unfit (Searle 1976). Thus, statistics not only revealed the magnitude of social problems in detail but also appeared to show that the situation was getting progressively worse (Kevles 1985).

Urbanisation made it possible for workers to organise and campaign more effectively in pursuit of social and political reform and, from the 1850s, the urban proletariat became increasingly aware of how its interests diverged from those of the middle classes (Rich 1977). Workers turned to more radical economic and political organisations – trade unions and socialist parties – to promote their interests and Pick (1989) argues that in the last quarter of the nineteenth century, the ideology of degeneration functioned as a powerful counter-theory to mass democracy and socialism. Moreover, during this period the feminist movement assumed a significant and permanent form in Western society in its struggle for equal legal, economic, social and political rights for women (Rich 1977). Most alarming for the eugenically minded were reports of relatively higher levels of fertility among the urban, proletarian and non-white immigrant poor compared with a falling birth rate among the educated middle classes (Searle 1976). The demand by middle-class women for a greater role in public and professional life, therefore, became a major concern for the early eugenic movement whose supporters thought it would inevitably lead to reduced birth rates among the better stocks (Kevles 1985).

In the context of prevailing beliefs about evolution, degeneration and heredity, these powerful forces for change led to fear for the stability of society in two respects. On the one hand, they led to increased anxiety and insecurity within Western countries, especially among the white, male, professional middle classes. It seemed that the privileges that the middle classes had wrested from the aristocracy during the nineteenth century were now being threatened not only by a radical working class but also by increasing numbers of 'the unfit'. In Britain and Germany, for example, the primary threat was thought to stem from 'lower class degenerates' (Searle 1976; Weiss 1987). In other countries the main threat was thought to come from outside rather than inside the state. In terms of the assumed superiority of the culture of the West, non-white peoples were 'variously designated as backward, degenerate, uncivilized and retarded' (Said 1978: 207). In North America, the particular focus of middle-class anger and anxiety was directed at 'the lower races' as millions of immigrants from Southern and Eastern Europe and from Asia settled in the United States and Canada (Kevles 1985; McLaren 1990). The eugenics movement offered a seductive explanation as to the sources of major social problems, provided a vehicle for the articulation of associated fears and anxieties, and proposed solutions that fitted comfortably into the world view of the professional middle classes.

The eugenic movement attracted the support of numerous and leading members of the medical, scientific and literary establishments, professional figures 'of weight, gravity and established reputation' (Searle 1976: 11). Its membership included people of very diverse, even opposing social and political views: progressives and conservatives, from the political left and the political right, from feminist organisations as well as from groups who opposed the idea of higher education and independent careers for women. Although the attitudes of the professional middle classes towards the commercial and business worlds and towards the landed upper classes were ambivalent, the full force of their rage was directed against the lower orders, sometimes identified as the mass of unskilled workers, but usually more narrowly defined as a sub-proletariat of the dependent, the deviant and the deficient (MacKenzie 1981; Searle 1976).

## EUGENICS AS A DISCOURSE OF EXPERTISM

Professional expertise not only discounts lay perspectives (Rose 1996) but also resists perspectives from within if they challenge the dominant orthodoxy in any fundamental way (Kuhn 1962). Towards the end of the nineteenth century, the professional middle class saw itself as a social and cultural elite, representing a high point in evolution and civilization. As far as educated professionals were concerned, they conducted the really important work of the world but received inadequate recognition and reward in return. They were convinced of their own biological and intellectual superiority and regarded eugenic theories as providing scientific proof of this superiority. For the founding figures of eugenics such as Francis Galton, Karl Pearson and Charles Davenport, the professional class was the repository of ability and civic virtue and was the centrepiece in their programme for the creation of a eugenic utopia (Kevles 1985). The attitude of Wilhelm Schallmayer, co-founder of German eugenics, expresses this perception unequivocally: the biologically fit were those from the educated middle class, the same socio-economic group as that occupied by Schallmayer himself (Weiss 1987). In 1920, William Tait, professor of psychology at McGill University, called for rule by experts who would lay the foundation for a more stern and more virile society (McLaren 1990). The world envisaged by the experts would be based on technocratic principles that would boost national efficiency through the rational management of human reproduction among various groups and classes (Weiss 1987). Weingart (1999) argues convincingly that the relative independence of eugenic thinking from political ideology was based on the conviction that experts, especially those in the medical profession, had the authority to decide what was in the best interests both of society in general and of those individuals who were most likely to be affected by eugenic measures.

Eugenicists who professed socialist politics – Karl Pearson and the Fabians, for example – argued for a new kind of society, not egalitarian, but stratified in terms of education and culture rather than in terms of wealth. While socialist eugenicists rejected the poverty, squalor and complacency of nineteenth century Europe, this did not imply any identification with the working class or the poor. For them, head-work was more important than hand-work. The proposed state socialism of groups such as the Fabians, with its emphasis on technocratic reform, represented a route to power for middle-class, professional experts. They rejected the inefficiency of laissez-faire capitalism in favour of an elite socialism of planners, managers and administrators. While the working classes of the great cities were despised for their 'grey, proletarian mediocrity', they were also feared for their insurrectionary potential (Weiss 1987: 5, 12–3). The political manoeuvering of a rising professional middle class represented a strategy for displacing the land and property owning bourgeoisie from positions of power. At the same time it sought to harness and contain revolutionary pressures in the working class through a process of gradual reform; it was the duty of the expert to restrain radical forces and steer them into non-threatening channels (Kevles 1985).

This is the perspective that informed the welfare state eugenics of Scandinavia where in the 1920s and 1930s eugenic measures were promoted by professional and administrative authorities as elements in the rational management of state resources (Broberg and Roll-Hansen 1996). Social democrats were among those who campaigned most energetically for the introduction of eugenic policies, a project that reflected their ambition to eradicate all that was perceived to be 'old, dirty and diseased' and to create 'a sound and healthy people free from defective genes' (Broberg and Tyden 1996: 136). Societies, however, did not have to be engaged in social engineering or to have undergone significant industrialisation for professionals to claim a role in the eugenic management of problem populations. In Ireland, for example, it was argued that the state had a right to 'protect itself if … the feeble-minded present a threat' (Davis 1929: 54). Additionally, as in most Western countries, the professional responsibility for identifying any such threat was thought to rest with the medical profession. Thus, 'medical men' were thought to be best placed to discriminate between the fit and the unfit, to determine the fact of 'unfitness in cases of lunacy and criminality' and, if necessary, to 'eliminate the unfit' (MacDermott 1910: 339).

Although a heightened sense of social and intellectual superiority characterised the professions, there were some critics. In 1922, H.S. Patton, an economist at the University of Alberta, complained about the reign of professional experts who were seeking to control every aspect of human life: 'Whether, indeed, we shall be born at all or not', he claimed, 'is becoming a matter of eugenic research and scientific birth control' (cited in McLaren 1990: 27). Josiah Wedgewood attacked the eugenically inspired Feeble-minded Persons (Control) Bill of 1912 as an attempt at 'government by specialists' (cited in MacKenzie 1981: 47). In a review of de Gobineau's *The Inequality of Human Races*, Alfred O'Rahilly (1916: 138), who later became the president of University College Cork, observed that 'de Gobineau's Aryan is as unreal and as unscientific as Lombroso's criminal.' O'Rahilly went on to argue that 'before attributing to some mysterious and inherent inequality of race the diversities of character and capacity of humankind, we should first exhaust the possible influence of physical, social and economic environment' (140). From the last decades of the nineteenth until the middle of the twentieth century, however, experts of all kinds from the natural and the social sciences equated human worth with schooling and professional training, and they felt both qualified and entitled to judge who should, or should not, be allowed to reproduce (Kevles 1985; McLaren 1990; Searle 1976; Weiss 1987).

Eugenics claimed to be a discipline based on science and, as such, it endeavoured to establish links with the academic world. In Britain, the Galton Laboratory for National Eugenics, formerly the Eugenics Records Office, was incorporated into University College London in 1911 under Karl Pearson (Kevles 1985). In the US, a Eugenics Record Office was established at Cold Spring Harbour in 1910 under Charles Davenport. The Norweigan and Swedish governments provided the eugenics movement with institutional and academic bases at the University of Oslo in 1916 and at Uppsala in 1922 (Roll-Hansen 1996; Broberg and Tyden 1996). In 1922, the Danish government provided a grant to introduce teaching and research in race hygiene at Copenhagen University, a precursor of the Institute of Human Genetics which was eventually established in the university in 1938 (Hansen 1996). These institutions set down the academic and scientific benchmarks for eugenic discourse in their respective countries and provided institutional centres for the exchange of ideas and information (Broberg and Tyden 1996; Hietala 1996). At a national level, they conducted research, gathered data, published articles and were the principle sources of authoritative information on eugenics (Kevles 1985).

The particular emphasis on the use of statistics and the development of statistical techniques, especially in the Galton Laboratory and at Cold Spring Harbour, created an aura of scientific objectivity and gave the impression that these institutions were in pursuit of science rather than the promotion of a political agenda (MacKenzie 1981). However, both Davenport and Pearson were deeply prejudiced in their attitudes to class and race differences and the work carried out in the institutions under their direction 'concealed assumptions which [had] no factual basis behind an impressive facade of flawless algebra' (Kevles 1985: 139). Scientific data, as long as it was interpreted only by experts schooled in the importance of heredity, served as a guide for social action. Eugenic research was more about confirming what experts already claimed to know, than about discovering any new truth. It was particularly desirable, as Davenport put it, to 'collect facts supporting the conclusion that the offspring of two imbecile parents are all imbecile' (cited in Zenderland 1998: 157). For the most part, eugenic researchers were convinced they knew what the truth was and their efforts were directed at finding evidence to support this conviction. For example, in making subjective assessments of the mental capacity of their interviewees for Goddard's study, *The Kallikak Family*, fieldworkers knowingly violated both the letter and the spirit of Binet's guidelines for the use of the mental tests he had designed (Zenderland 1998: 160–1). In the deliberations of the Brock Committee (1934), which investigated proposals for the introduction of sterilisation in Britain, experts sympathetic to eugenics attempted to construct stronger arguments for sterilisation than were warranted by scientific evidence (King and Hansen 1999).

Once eugenic institutes were established it was a short step to the exploitation of populations of people with perceived impairment for research purposes.[4] Not only could the institutes select the particular topics for investigation and determine the direction of any study, the academic credentials of their members facilitated access to important medical, institutional and other records. A primary objective of the Norwegian Institute for Genetics at the University of Oslo, for example, was the collection of genetic data among the isolated populations in remote valleys to provide guidelines for the development of eugenic policies (Roll-Hansen 1996). In Finland, preparations for eugenic legislation included gathering information about 'degenerate families', the details of which were then used in public speeches and reported extensively in the press in order to generate support for the proposed measures (Hietala 1996: 220–1). Individuals admitted into Danish institutions for mental illnesses and learning impairments were required by law to fill out questionnaires for the Institute of Human Genetics (Hansen 1996). Special schools and other institutions provided captive populations for testing new research instruments. The children in the Vineland Training School for Feeble-Minded Boys and Girls provided its Director Henry Goddard with the population he needed to experiment with Binet's new mental tests (Zenderland 1998).

That individuals who were the subjects of eugenically oriented measures might want to contribute to the development of policy, be informed about the purpose and conduct of research, or resist the procedures they were expected to undergo, was ignored. Instead, they were lied to or told nothing (Gould 1987; Broberg and Tydén 1996). Fieldworkers collecting data for Goddard's *The Kallikak Family*, for example, were careful to disguise the real purpose of their visits, which was to establish the family pedigrees of parents and not, as families were led to believe, to discuss 'the progress of their children' or gather information about 'the family's involvement in the American civil war' (Zenderland 1998: 159–60). More serious issues arose in relation to eugenic practices being carried out without the knowledge or consent of the individuals concerned, such as in the case of sterilisation. According to Swedish law, sterilisation was not compulsory except for individuals defined as being 'legally incompetent', in effect, those with a mental age of 'a person twelve years old or younger' (Broberg and Tydén 1996: 114–5). At the same time the authorities were well aware that, if individuals who were classified in this way were fully informed about the procedures being planned for them, they might reject such procedures. One of the key figures in the Swedish eugenics movement argued that

> the individual should not be allowed to decide the matter for himself. Very many of those who should be sterilized are feeble-minded or mentally ill and are therefore not even able to understand what it is all about, or cannot at least, judge the reasons. Most of the time they would not want the operation at all; nor would they agree to one. (cited in Broberg and Tydén 1996: 115)

Similarly, the Swedish Board of Health, which evaluated applications for sterilisation, recommended that if resistance arose at an early stage it should be ignored and that bureaucratic and professional pressure should be used to gain compliance (Broberg and Tydén 1996). Ryan and Thomas make the similar point that, although sterilisation was never legalised in Britain, 'many such operations were carried out under various forms of coercion' (1987: 109).

An important aspect of eugenic expertism was its rhetoric of progress, efficiency and benevolence. Advocates of sterilisation, especially in Scandinavia, spoke of it in terms of social progress (Broberg and Tydén 1996; Hietala 1996; Roll-Hansen 1996). In order to create a modern industrial welfare state, social engineers argued that sterilisation was both necessary and inevitable and some proposed 'quite ruthless sterilization policies' for people with learning difficulties (cited in Broberg and Tydén 1996: 104). It was widely believed that the preventive impact of such policies would reduce considerably the costs of institutionalisation. Experts insisted that, regardless of individual wishes or objections, eugenic measures were ultimately for the good of society and of the individual. Sterilisation would reduce the need for confinement of people with mental illness and learning difficulties and thus contribute to their well-being and liberation (Kevles 1985; Trent 1994).

Those who supported large-scale incarceration pointed to examples of 'colonies ... for every class of defectives' that pleased 'relatives, friends and the public' and where '[t]hey are all happy' (Gerrard 1912: 33, 35). From this standpoint, enforced institutionalisation was, in fact, held to be humane because it offered protection, training and other presumed benefits. Helen MacMurchy, a leading Canadian eugenicist, argued that special institutions would 'give the mental defective all the chances he needs to develop his gifts and all the protection he needs to keep away from him evils and temptations that he never will be grown up enough to resist, and that society cannot afford to let him fall victim to' (cited in McLaren 1990: 39). Although it appeared costly, advocates of segregation argued that it would be efficient and economic in the long run; it would ultimately pay for itself because even greater expense would be faced if the feeble-minded were allowed to remain in society. As it was, their education in public schools was considered to be a waste of time, effort and money; it was claimed that their dissolute lives resulted in illegitimacy and the spread of venereal disease; they burdened public expenditure and obstructed the efficiency of hospitals, industrial schools and reformatories (Kevles 1985; McLaren 1990; Hahn Rafter 1997).

Eugenic discourse not only silenced the so-called unfit; it left no room for promoting alternative responses to social problems. Eugenic theory proposed that, since degenerate characteristics were inherited, they were impervious to environmental influences. Social reforms, therefore, were not simply a waste of resources; they were positively harmful. Karl Pearson asserted that measures such as the minimum wage, the eight-hour working day, free medical advice or reductions in infant mortality only encouraged an increase in unemployables, degenerates, and physical and moral weaklings (Kevles 1985). Francis Galton believed that modern humanitarian institutions and civilisation were protecting the weak, the stupid and the unfit (Weiss 1987); charities for incapables, therefore, were more a curse than a blessing. Eugenicists regarded decreases in child mortality rates with foreboding because greater numbers of defective stocks were being artificially kept alive (Searle 1976); natural selection was being suspended through the effects of charity, medical science and sanitary reform. The preface to one German eugenics journal of 1930 encapsulates this perspective:

> Civilisation has eliminated natural selection. Public welfare and social
> assistance contribute ... to the preservation and further reproduction
> of hereditarily diseased individuals. A crushing and ever-growing

burden of useless individuals unworthy of life are maintained and taken care of in institutions at the expense of the healthy ...' (cited in Weiss 1987: 151–2)

Eugenicists claimed that any attempt to meet the costs of degeneracy imposed an unwarranted financial burden on the efficient members of society (Searle 1976; McLaren 1990). They argued that poor social conditions could not be blamed since the vast army of dependants had shown no sign of decreasing despite the fact that the environment was being continuously improved and at great expense. Thus, the elimination of defective stocks made economic sense: lower taxation would follow, which in turn would encourage middle-class couples to have larger families. In condemning reforms that created opportunities for some degree of social mobility, eugenicists were in fact arguing for the preservation of the status quo. It was comforting to believe that many of the major problems of society could be attributed to faulty genes rather than to the unjust social and economic structures of society (McLaren 1990).

## DISABLING 'THE UNFIT'

The fact that eugenics was a discourse of expertism was not the only crucial issue. A related and equally important matter was the status of the individuals over whom the experts exercised their power and authority and who were the objects of their diagnostic gaze. One of the main conclusions that can be drawn from recent studies of eugenic movements is that individuals deemed to be mentally defective became the most devalued people in Western society. In this context, the historical studies themselves give cause for concern with regard to the following question: is it possible to speak of moderate eugenic programmes in view of the biases, particularly those concerning mental capacity, gender, race, and class, that underpinned all eugenic practices?

In relation to the notion of moderate eugenics, some historians have identified two distinct but overlapping waves of eugenic activity: the first lasted into the 1920s and has been referred to as 'mainline' eugenics; the second has been called 'reform' eugenics and was characteristic of the 1930s and 1940s (Searle 1979; Kevles 1985; Roll-Hansen 1996). The so-called reformers criticised the earlier version of eugenics for its social and racial biases and for over-estimating the role of heredity and under-estimating the role of environmental factors in the production of social problems. Although they rejected the poor research methodologies and simplistic hereditarian conclusions of mainline eugenics, reform eugenicists remained convinced that biology counted and that the stability and progress of society 'depended upon the gifted capable minority who might prevail' over the 'dull', the 'underdeveloped' and the 'weak' (Kevles 1985: 192). The most successful period in terms of eugenic legislation was during the reform period when it became possible to sterilise more and more people without their consent (Kevles 1985). In the US in the 1930s, for example, when it is claimed that the eugenics movement was on the wane 'sterilization was actually practised – as distinct from mere legislation – in a greater number of states than before' (Roll-Hansen 1996: 154) and the national rate increased more than five-fold (Kevles 1985).

More significant still was the fact that during both phases, perceived mental incapacity was regarded as the predominant reason for eugenic intervention and, although reform eugenics entailed some shifts in attitudes to gender, race and class, the perspective in relation to mental incapacity remained substantially the same (Kevles 1985). The most extreme eugenic measure – sterilisation – was used against individuals labelled as mentally defective more consistently and over a longer period of time than against any other social group. Within this group there were further biases. Eugenic programmes of sterilisation were conceived and carried out primarily by men but affected mainly women (Broberg and Tydén 1996), despite being, in medical terms, procedures that carried relatively greater risks for women. In Sweden and Finland, the vast majority of those sterilised were women, with overall annual averages of 86 and 84 per cent respectively between 1935 and 1955 (Broberg and Tyden 1996; Hietala 1996). In the US, sterilisation laws applied to people in public institutions, whose residents were mainly poor and black (Kevles 1985). Similar class biases are evident in other countries (Broberg and Tydén 1996; Hietala 1996). It is therefore hard to understand how, in an otherwise critical analysis, Roll-Hansen can regard the sterilisation policies of the Nordic countries as 'a mild form of eugenics' or the Norweigan law of 1934, which made provision for the compulsory sterilisation on eugenic grounds, as 'a moderate law' (1996: 173). The implication is that sterilisation on grounds of mental incapacity continues to be regarded as reasonable.

The preoccupation with mental incapacity was the culmination of a process that ultimately located the major social ills of the second half of the nineteenth century – poverty, impairment, delinquency, crime and vice – in so-called feeble-mindedness. The key explanatory principle in the eugenic argument was the notion of inherited degeneracy and its responsibility for social pathology. The first degeneracy theorists regarded this connection as unpredictable and irregular and an extensive and shifting terminology attempted to capture the apparent variety and strength of that connection. Older terms such as idiocy, lunacy and imbecility proved inadequate to the task and prompted theorists to devise new terms such as 'moral idiocy', 'moral imbecility', 'juvenile lunacy' (Trent 1994: 20, 84, 85) and so on, to reflect the array of pathologies that were deemed to stem from degenerate genes. Theorists, however, were faced with particular problems in relation to mapping and naming the landscape of degeneracy: the invisibility of some degenerate characteristics, the problem of defining the border between the abnormal and the normal, and the difficulty of establishing distinctions between different levels of degeneracy.

The appearance of mental tests seemed to provide a way of overcoming such problems. It is no accident that individuals who pioneered mental testing in the US and Britain were also strong believers in the theory of inherited degeneracy (Kamin 1974; Radford 1991). Psychologists such as Henry Goddard who translated the Binet-Simon test into English and Lewis Terman who developed the Stanford-Binet test, promoted the idea that these tests would identify that 'class of children ... who looked in most respects like ordinary children, but who were mentally deficient' (Trent 1994: 160). According to Terman, the new tests would 'bring tens of thousands of these high grade defectives under the surveillance and protection of society ... It is hardly necessary to emphasise that the high grade cases, of the type now so frequently overlooked, are precisely the ones whose guardianship it is most important for the state to assume' (1916: 6–7, cited in Kamin 1974: 6). The tests would also enable specific categories of 'defectives' to be established on a statistical and apparently scientific basis. On the basis of his research, Goddard proposed a new classification: idiot, referring to an individual with a mental age of two years and less; imbecile, with an age of three to seven years; and moron, with an age of eight to twelve years (Trent 1994). Thus, IQ tests presumed to measure and make visible the inner stigmata of degeneracy.[5] They strengthened the idea that degeneracy was fundamentally a form of mental incapacity and that its indicators were psychological rather than physical as the early theorists had believed. In the context of the strong hereditarian ideology of the mental test pioneers, IQ tests copper-fastened the perception that degeneracy was inherited and that there was a direct causal link between mental incapacity and social pathology (Trent 1994).

During the 1910s and 1920s, largely as a result of the efforts of the mental testers and through the publication and influence of Goddard's own study of heredity and social pathology, *The Kallikak Family* (1912), references to the notion of general degeneracy decreased. The rhetoric of condemnation narrowed and coalesced around 'the menace of feeble-mindedness' because of eugenic convictions about its causes, nature and consequences (Radford 1991; Trent 1994). In eugenic discourse, feeble-mindedness was held to be inherited and immutable and the primary source of a host of social ills, from crime, through pauperism and immorality, to general social and economic inefficiency. Mental testing had shown that feeble-mindedness seemed to be more widespread in society than was generally realised. Moreover, the feeble-minded were thought to be more prolific than those of good stock. As Goddard noted: 'There are Kallikak families all about us. They are multiplying at twice the rate of the general population, and not until we recognise this fact, and work on this basis, will we begin to solve social problems' (1912: 70–1, cited in Trent 1994: 164).

Eugenic responses to feeble-mindedness were multi-faceted but, in general terms, were constructed around two objectives: to prevent the multiplication of the unfit and to encourage the better stocks to be more prolific. While there were differences of opinion on the appropriateness and likely effectiveness of birth control policies, marriage regulations, immigration controls, and financial incentives to regenerate the race, there was one issue upon which eugenicists were unanimous: the elimination of the feeble-minded. In eugenic policy, the main proposals for 'getting them off the earth' (cited in Trent 1994: 157) were sterilisation and incarceration. Each of these measures entailed a further consideration – whether the measure should be voluntary or compulsory.

The most forceful move towards sterilisation began in the US and, as early as the 1880s, officials in some American institutions were advocating a policy of this kind (Tyor and Bell 1984). Within a few years, sterilisation of the unfit commenced (Kevles 1985) and hundreds of individuals were sterilised before any enabling legislation was passed (Trent 1994).

The fact that a sterilisation bill was vetoed in the state did not prevent the enforced sterilisation of at least 270 students of the Pennsylvania Training School for the Feeble-Minded between 1889 and 1931 (Robitscher 1973). A relatively new procedure, vasectomy, was perfected by Harry C. Sharp, a physician at the Indiana State Reformatory, where residents were treated as experimental material (Kevles 1985; Miller 1996). Sharp carried out 465 vasectomies, about a third of which were said to have been requested, before sterilisation was actually legalised in the state in 1907 (Kevles 1985). From then on it became mandatory to sterilise 'criminals, idiots, imbeciles and rapists in public institutions when recommended to do so by a board of experts' and by 1914 fifteen other states had followed suit (Searle 1976: 94).

One of the main arguments used in support of a policy of sterilisation was economic. An American Eugenics Society pamphlet claimed that the costs of segregating descendants of one degenerate family ran into millions of dollars while it would have cost less than 150 dollars to have sterilised 'the original ... pair' (cited in Kelves 1985: 93). British eugenicists were also impressed by the economic argument: sterilisation in England would lead to a saving of 'about twenty million pounds per annum' (Leeper 1912a: 294). A second argument was that sterilisation was the only sure way of preventing the transmission of feeble-mindedness and mental illness. According to the eugenicists, these were inherited conditions that were not only passed on, but passed on in a prolific manner. A third argument was based on the idea that sterilisation of the unfit was required for their own good and for the good of the community. Advocates argued that sterilisation would result in greater rather than less liberty for the unfit since it would permit them to leave the institutions and marry without the danger of reproducing (McLaren 1990).

After World War I, as geneticists gained a greater understanding of heredity, they turned away from the more simplistic arguments put forward by eugenicists (Kevles 1985; McLaren 1990). But despite its declining scientific base, eugenics enjoyed its most overt public successes during the 1920s and 1930s. By 1933 twenty-eight US states had enacted eugenic sterilisation laws and, in one instance in 1927, the Supreme Court had declared the mandatory sterilisation measures enacted in Virginia to be constitutional (Kevles 1985). During the 1930s, Canadian sterilisation legislation was passed in Alberta and British Colombia. The first European sterilisation law was passed in the Swiss Canton de Vaud in

1928. Other European countries followed suit: Denmark in 1929, Danzig, Latvia and Germany in 1933, Norway and Sweden in 1934, Finland in 1935, Estonia in 1936 and Iceland in 1938.

Some eugenicists argued for voluntary rather than coercive sterilisation. In instances where the legislation specified voluntary sterilisation, however, the term was frequently misleading. Release from an institution, the offer of poor relief, or permission to marry were often conditional on an agreement to be sterilised (Searle 1976; Radford 1991; Broberg and Tydén 1996). As we have seen, eugenic measures were principally directed at individuals who were classified as mentally defective and disproportionately affected women, the poor and ethnic minorities. In many countries, eugenic measures were most thoroughly applied in public institutions whose residents came mainly from working-class and minority groups.

In countries where there was significant opposition to sterilisation policies, the main alternative policy was segregation. In Britain, most eugenicists appeared not to favour sterilisation as a means of controlling social problem groups, more because it was politically inexpedient than as a result of moral reservations or concerns about civil rights (Searle 1976; Barker 1983). While it was argued that sterilisation constituted the most economic and efficient solution to the problem of the unfit, it appeared doubtful that sufficient public support could be won in Britain for such a measure and with 'general sentiment so strong against such a radical measure ... its adoption [was] not practicable' (McLaren 1990: 42). Consequently, the argument turned to incarceration. In Ireland, too, while sterilisation was discussed, segregation was the favoured response to the problem of the unfit, not least because the Catholic Church strongly opposed sterilisation.

## DISABLING 'THE UNFIT' IN IRELAND

Eugenic debate in Ireland peaked at two particular points in time: the first during the five or six years before the outbreak of World War I and the second during the late 1920s and early 1930s. Significantly, both peaks coincided with debates concerning eugenically related issues elsewhere: first, with the Report on the Care and Control of the Feeble-minded (1908) and with proposals for legislation on mental deficiency in Britain in 1912–3; and then in 1930 with the publication of the papal encyclical,

*Casti Conubii*, which condemned sterilisation, contraception and divorce (Kevles 1985).

In international terms, the eugenics debate in Ireland was muted and sporadic. In his presidential address to the Royal Academy of Medicine in Ireland in 1912, Dr M.J. Nolan, the medical superintendent of the Down District Asylum, observed that with regard to the 'proposed sterilisation of the mentally unfit' there was 'not as much interest excited in Ireland as in England among lay and professional circles' (1912: 172). Nevertheless, international developments in eugenic thinking and policy-making were carefully tracked in Ireland, particularly by medical and theological commentators (see, for example, 48th Report of the Inspectors of Lunatics in Ireland 1898; Gerrard 1911; 1912; Davis 1929; 1931). The Irish response to the eugenics movement illustrates the significance of eugenics as a discourse of expertism and, even more importantly, it shows how people with perceived mental incapacity were subjected to eugenic evaluation.

In important respects, the Irish response to eugenics was unique and distinctive. In the broadest political and cultural senses, Ireland itself represented a seemingly dysgenic element within the context of the United Kingdom. There were several strands in this assumption: the long colonial history, the troubled political relationship with Britain, the persistent and high levels of poverty, the relatively greater proportion of the population thought to be mentally deficient, and the higher numbers confined in lunatic asylums (Finnane 1981). On the other hand, the emergence of Irish cultural nationalism during the last decades of the nineteenth century created a counter perspective that sought to highlight the distinctive identity of 'the Celtic race'. Both views were premised on notions of a distinct race and both involved some degree of eugenic thinking: on the one hand there were the degenerate Irish types portrayed in Victorian caricature (Curtis 1997); on the other hand there were calls 'to cultivate everything that is most racial, most smacking of the soil, most Gaelic, most Irish.... On racial lines then, we shall best develop' (Hyde 1894: 159).

The influence of the Catholic Church in matters of social policy was another significant factor that distinguished Ireland, particularly from countries in Northern Europe. Attempts by the state or by non-clerical experts to intervene in areas of morality, marriage and reproduction were rejected by the Catholic Church, which regarded the regulation of these matters as its sole prerogative (McEvoy 1999). Roll-Hansen (1996) notes that religious affiliation had a significant influence on the acceptance or rejection of eugenic policies in particular countries, with more extreme measures, such as sterilisation, being introduced in liberal democracies that were predominantly Lutheran. In France, the development of an active eugenics movement was possible because of the separation of public education from the Church and because of the anti-clerical character of many of the medical and scientific institutions (Moore 2004). In Ireland, the development of direct eugenic policies was curtailed by the dominance of the Catholic Church in education, including the education of doctors.

In some important respects, however, the response to eugenic ideas in Ireland was similar to that expressed in other parts of Western society. Leading medical professionals were prominent in early attempts to set up eugenics societies in Dublin and Belfast (Jones 1992). The arguments employed were the standard eugenic fare: that existing social arrangements favoured 'weaklings' and 'degenerates' over the respectable and hard-working individual (Slater 1911); that the unfit were 'multiplying at a most enormous rate' at the expense of 'the normal or the able' (D'Arcy 1914, cited in Jones 1992: 85); and that the fertility of the feeble-minded had to be controlled (Nixon 1912). With some reservations, the prevailing view among the medical experts was that feeble-mindedness was inherited (Cox 1912; Dawson 1912; Leeper 1912) and that '[i]t is by the feeble-minded that the greatest damage to posterity will be done' (*Dublin Journal of Medical Science* 1909: 133).

The expected cost of regulating feeble-mindedness was another recurring theme (Barry 1907; *DJMS* 1911; Leeper 1912; Nixon 1912). In fact, the major opposition to the extension of the Mental Deficiency Act 1913 to Ireland stemmed from cost factors rather than from rejection of the eugenic content of the legislation.[6] The apparently larger proportions of so-called defectives in Ireland were held to be responsible for an 'increasing burden of expense to the community' (Dawson 1913: 167) and if the provisions of the Mental Deficiency Act were to be extended to Ireland this would require substantial capital investment (Nixon 1912). Some experts argued that the social and economic problems connected with degeneracy were the result of 'too many marriages of an uneconomic type', specifically the unions of those whose blood was believed to be tainted – 'the submerged tenth of our cities and large towns' (Barry 1907: 458, 459). Barry proposed that the Catholic Church should deploy a little known canon law, the *ecclesiae vetitum*, to veto or obstruct such marriages since the 'enfeebled progeny' would not receive a decent upbringing and would 'become a charge on the taxpayer' (459, 462).

Contributors to religious journals by and large accepted the eugenic position with regard to the social dangers that were believed to stem from feeble-mindedness (Barry 1907; Slater 1911; Gerrard 1912; Boyd Barrett 1913; Flick 1914; O'Donnell 1920; Davis 1929; O'Neill 1931). Setting out the Catholic perspective in relation to the regulation of the feeble-minded, Gerrard observed that '[t]here is every reason why a benign Government should take charge of the dangerous units of society' (1911: 62). Because society had a right to protect itself against pauperism, crime and disease, '[s]egregation of the feebleminded and of all those who are suffering from amentia [i.e. imbecility, idiocy] of any kind is not only justifiable but is a duty' (Flick 1914: 157–8; see also Davis 1929).

The gender and class biases of eugenic arguments were a further feature that Ireland had in common with other countries. The debate in Ireland was, to all intents and purposes, a male affair. Women were thought to be more responsible for dysgenic activities. In discussing the causation of insanity, for example, Leeper attributed much of the blame to feeble-minded women who were temporary residents in the workhouses and who were permitted to consort with 'able-bodied paupers' (1912: 182–3). In a proposal to reduce the transmission of feeble-mindedness, Nixon recommended that 'defective women be kept in institutions from their sixteenth to forty-fifth year – during the entire procreative period' (1912: 200). He went on to suggest that after their forty-fifth year the women could remain in the institutions 'where they could help to earn their own living by services of various kinds' (200). Nixon felt that the feeble-minded should also be segregated on a class basis and he advocated the establishment of a separate central asylum for 'improvable imbeciles and feeble-minded from the middle class and from the class intermediate between the pauper and middle class' (201). On the other hand, several religious commentators expressed concern that eugenic policies were more likely to infringe the rights of the poor and warned that suitable precautions were necessary to avoid abuses (Gerrard 1911; O'Donnell 1920); if the state planned to regulate feeble-mindedness '*there should not be any exception for the rich*' (Gerrard 1912: 36, italics in original).

The greatest divergence of opinion concerned sterilisation and involved the Catholic Church and some sections of the medical profession. Doctors were among the most vocal advocates of sterilisation (*DJMS* 1911; Dawson 1912; Leeper 1912; 1912*a*; Nesbitt 1912), although at least two very prominent members of the medical profession in Ireland argued forcefully against it, possibly because of their religious affiliation (Nixon 1912; Nolan 1912; Jones 1992). Nolan held that the hereditarian link in mental incapacity was not well understood and therefore sterilisation was unjustified; Nixon argued that social investment in employment, housing and nutrition would remove some of the conditions that contributed to degeneracy and that the most appropriate way to deal with feeble-mindedness was institutional segregation.

Institutional segregation was also the preferred option of Catholic social theorists (Gerrard 1911; 1912; Flick 1914). They rejected sterilisation on ethical and theological grounds and because 'segregation would achieve the same end in a moral way' (O'Donnell 1920; see also Slater 1911 and Davis 1929). The question as to whether segregation should be voluntary or compulsory was an open one as far as the Church was concerned (Slater 1911; O'Donnell 1920). Some theorists noted that in the past lepers had been segregated and detained and, when more definite knowledge was available, the same measures might be employed against the feeble-minded (Slater 1911; Gerrard 1912; Davis 1929). Since the major drawback of segregation was the cost factor, theorists advocated the idea of industrial or farm colonies which would be largely self-supporting, would cater for 'every class of defective' and where each resident would 'associate only with his intellectual equals' (Gerrard 1912: 33) and be happy 'in rough but clean and sanitary shacks' (Boyd Barrett 1913: 79). Gerrard (1911) described one colony in Bavaria as a possible model. It had almost 1,500 disabled people, a staff of over 600, and several factories. The men and women were permitted to meet only on special occasions. When they did, 'the strictest vigilance is exercised when they are together ... The eugenic aim is achieved. They do not propagate their kind, nor are they themselves changed into anti-social units' (Gerrard 1911: 34–5).

Catholic social theorists warned that eugenic policies were more likely to infringe upon the rights of the poor and stressed that measures designed to control the feeble-minded should apply equally to the wealthy. However, it is also clear that the Church's opposition to sterilisation stemmed more from a concern to defend its moral hegemony over sexual and reproductive matters than from a concern for the rights of disabled people. It supported the basic eugenic argument, with the proviso that segregation rather than sterilisation be employed to prevent the propagation of feeble-mindedness. There was also a considerable degree of wishful thinking involved in believing that a colony in Ireland would provide a happy, comfortable and secure environment for disabled people (Gerrard 1912). Anyone recommending segregation in an institution had to be aware of at least some of the realities of institutional life in Ireland at that time. Boyd Barrett's description of asylums, for example, gave no grounds for optimism. Among their characteristic features were:

> the poor and monotonous diet, the repulsive prison-like surroundings, the dreary exercise yards, the hideous clothing, punishments for refractory patients ... the almost total absence of amusement and recreation ... To put it bluntly, the patients committed to asylums are condemned to a degrading and miserable imprisonment for life. (1924: 30)

## CONCLUSION

During the second half of the nineteenth century in Western Europe and North America a major shift occurred in the relationship between disability and society, one that had profound effects on the lives of people with perceived impairment. The increasing pessimism that characterised predominant attitudes and responses to impairment culminated in the eugenics movement. The merging of theories of evolution, degeneration and heredity created a template for evaluating and classifying race, class, gender, and, most importantly, mental capacity in terms of social and moral worth.

Although eugenic thinking incorporated many different political points of view and went through a number of theoretical shifts, individuals labelled as feeble-minded were the main targets of eugenic intervention. The two main kinds of intervention were sterilisation and segregation. Sterilisation was legalised across most of the US, in Alberta and British Columbia in Canada, in Germany and in all the countries of Northern Europe. Where sterilisation was made compulsory it invariably applied to those classified as mentally defective. The great majority of those sterilised were women and included disproportionate numbers of individuals who were poor, black or from ethnic minorities.

The main opposition to sterilisation came from the Catholic Church, opposition that was more a defence of Catholic moral teaching than a concern for the human and civil rights of disabled people. The Catholic Church in Ireland, the US and Britain accepted the main thrust of eugenic thinking and consequently favoured the segregation of the feeble-minded, preferably in large industrial or agricultural colonies. The creation of colonies marked a shift in perceptions of the nature and function of institutions for disabled people. At the beginning of the nineteenth century, the trend had been towards greater differentiation and the establishment of more specialised institutions. A century later, experts on anomaly were proposing the establishment of large, multi-purpose institutions for gathering together 'all ... feebleminded persons, regardless of age, sex, and degree of disability, under a single institutional roof' (Hahn Rafter 1997: 63; see also Gerrard 1911; 1912; O'Donnell 1920). This suggestion underlined the fact that colonies were seen, not as rehabilitative institutions, but as the most economic and efficient means of permanently segregating, controlling and detaining disabled people.

In the post-war period, after the murderous racial and eugenic actions that had occurred in Germany under National Socialism, eugenics rapidly disappeared from public and academic discourse (Miller 1996). However, experts who had promoted eugenics in the 1930s continued to argue for the sterilisation of disabled people (Roll-Hansen 1996) and in Canada, the US and Scandinavia, for example, this policy was maintained even into the 1960s and 1970s (Roll-Hansen 1996; Park and Radford 1998). What must be highlighted here is the long time lag between the point at which eugenics began its rapid decline in public and professional discourse and the point at which the sterilisation of disabled people began to be questioned from a human rights perspective. In spite of considerable developments in disability rights, perceived impairment continues to be seen as a ground for sterilisation (Cooney 1989).

In Ireland, eugenic thinking survived, too. For the greater part of the post-war period, the Catholic Church, with the active co-operation of the state, was involved in the management of reformatories, industrial schools, orphanages, Magdalen laundries and mother and baby homes. The segregation and detention of thousands of young women, men and children in these institutions throughout the second half of the twentieth century can be seen as a continuation of a major element in eugenic thinking and was articulated through the social policies and practices of the Catholic Church in collaboration with politicians and the general body of middle-class administrative, legal and medical professionals (Raftery and O'Sullivan 1999). Thus, Church and State authorities in Ireland continued the practice of segregation and detention as the most appropriate responses to what had been identified as social and moral pathologies by eugenicists.

Today, one of the major tasks for disability theorists and activists and their allies is the challenge presented by current developments in the field of genetics (Allen 1999; Shakespeare 1999; Ward 2001; Scally 2002). Debates on the meaning of what counts as a 'normal' or 'worthwhile' life, on 'the interests of society', and on 'responsible' human reproduction are conducted with little regard for the views of people with perceived impairments (Shakespeare 1995, 1999). Indeed, the literature of modern genetics is charged with implicit and subtle proto-eugenic values in which disability is perceived to be a personal tragedy and in which genetics offers solutions for such 'burdens', 'sufferings' and 'disasters' (Shakespeare 1999; Fletcher 2001). Moreover, the literature itself reflects a profound ignorance about disability and the lives of disabled people. As Shakespeare stresses, there is 'the need for a disabled voice in debates, and to accept that disabled people, not doctors, are the real experts on disability' (1999: 685). It is important to stress that the participation of disabled people in this debate must go beyond the stage of consultation; it must also include a place at the decision-making table (see Chapter 7, 'The Political Context and Issues of Power and Representation').

## NOTES

1.  The *Asylum Journal of Mental Science*, for example, which was circulated in Ireland throughout the 1850s, carried regular reports on activities of this kind – reviews of international publications, correspondence from abroad, notices about publications exchanged, reports about visits to institutions abroad, and so on.
2.  In Bénédict Augustin Morel's (1809–73) theory, degeneration was explained as a deviation from the normal type of humanity. It did not represent the transmission of a fixed anomaly from one body to another but rather, of something that could manifest itself in great variety of physical conditions, moral tendencies and social habits. Degeneration was a progressive pathology, with a capacity to mutate, which passed from one

generation to the next and lead to idiocy, sterility and ultimately, death (Pick 1989).

3. Drawing on Darwin's theory of evolution and on contemporary theories of degeneration, Caesare Lombroso (1835–1909) believed he had discovered a biological basis for crime. In evolutionary terms he identified his 'born criminal' as a throwback to a more primitive human type. This theory, by locating the born criminal in an evolutionary side-track, provided justification for capital punishment and control of reproduction among the so-called criminal classes (Pick 1989).

4. It is not easy to disentangle the exploitation of problem populations for careerist purposes or scientific curiosity, from interests that are more altruistic. The career of Samuel Gridley Howe serves as an example of a mixture of personal ambition and philanthropic reform (Winzer 1993; Trent 1994; Delbanco 2001). When he was director of the Perkins Institute for the Blind in Boston, Howe heard of an eight-year-old, deaf and blind girl called Laura Bridgeman. Howe saw this both as an opportunity to tackle public prejudice against disabled people and at the same time to carry out a kind of human experiment. Laura Bridgeman, he believed, 'might be made useful to science'; she was the 'unusual specimen' he was looking for (cited in Delbanco 2001: 36, 37). With Howe as her personal tutor, Laura made exceptional progress and Howe gained an international reputation as a result. As Laura moved into her teenage years, however, she 'lost the charm of childhood' (38) and Howe's attention drifted to other causes. Later, when Laura began to show some independence of mind, Howe distanced himself more and more. Howe's professional career continued to flourish; Laura Bridgeman's life, however, became one of great unhappiness, despair and unrealised potential.

5. The idea of visible, physical stigmata denoting certain internal, psychological conditions was a major element in the development of degeneration theory (Pick 1989). A similar perspective underpinned phrenology and was the central concept in Lombroso's definition of the born criminal. Photography was an important medium for disseminating these beliefs and texts in criminology, psychology, psychiatry often included photographs to illustrate the arguments being made. The development of psychometric tests indicated a shift from physical to psychological symptoms and, to use Foucault's terminology (1977), enabled a whole new set of stigmata to be brought above the horizon of visibility.

6. Although the Mental Deficiency Act of 1913 was passed while Ireland was still part of the United Kingdom, the provisions of the legislation were never extended to Ireland. The Act was sponsored by the Eugenics

Education Society and provided for the compulsory segregation and detention of certain classes of defectives (Kevles 1985). Among the perceived defectives subject to the Act were paupers, habitual drunkards, and women on poor relief at the time of giving birth or found pregnant with an illegitimate child. While Irish MPs had voted for the Mental Deficiency Act, they were not enthusiastic about its extension to Ireland, especially in view of the implications for social expenditure in Ireland if the Home Rule Bill then under consideration was successful (Jones 1992: 89–90). After the establishment of the Irish Free State in 1922, the lunatic asylums and the workhouses became the county hospitals and county homes respectively. These remained the main public institutions for the confinement of problem populations identified in the Mental Deficiency Act.

# 6

# Normalisation: Describing What Is, Prescribing What Ought to Be

One can, then, use the word 'normal' to say how things are, but also to say how they ought to be. The magic of the word is that we can use it to do both things at once. The norm may be what is usual or typical, yet our most powerful ethical constraints are also called norms.

Ian Hacking (1990), *The Taming of Chance*, 163

[Normalisation] brings five quite distinct operations into play: it refers individual actions to a whole that is at once a field of comparison, a space of differentiation and the principle of a rule to be followed. It differentiates individuals from one another, in terms of the following overall rule: that the rule be made to function as a minimum threshold, as an average to be respected or as an optimum towards which one must move. It measures in quantitative terms and hierarchizes in terms of value the abilities, the level, the 'nature' of individuals. It introduces, through this 'value-giving' measure, the constraint of a conformity that must be achieved. Lastly, it traces the limit that will define difference in relation to all other differences, the external frontier of the abnormal …

Michel Foucault (1977), *Discipline and Punish: the Birth of the Prison*, 182–3

[N]ormalization implies that contributive, positive social roles should be identified for people at risk, and corresponding positive role expectancies for them should be extended, such as those of student, worker, owner, tenant, friend, spouse, citizen, etc. In order for these role expectancies to be conveyed to devalued people, there should be normatively attractive, comfortable, and challenging service settings; age-appropriate and challenging program activities; age-appropriate and culturally-valued personal appearance of clients; as much as feasible, image-enhancing matches between the needs of clients, the nature of the program, and staff identities; status-enhancing labels and forms of address for clients, etc. Indeed, the creation of valued social roles is the highest normalization goal, and almost all other benefits will flow derivatively from it – including both competency and image enhancement in virtually all areas of people's identities …

Wolf Wolfensberger and Susan Thomas (1987), *The Principle of Normalization in the Human Services: A Brief Overview*, 14

## INTRODUCTION

In this chapter, I focus on the ideology and practice of normalisation in relation to disability. In the discussion I refer to both Irish and international contexts and suggest that the ideology of normalisation was an international feature of Western society, although there were regional differences in terms of the intensity and timing of its impact.[1] Firstly, I explore the emergence of conceptual and political challenges to long established patterns of segregation and institutionalisation. Arguing that these challenges were organised around an ideology of normalisation, I examine the development of the notion of normality in Western society. I draw on the work of Hacking (1990), Foucault (1979; 2002) and Wolfensberger (1972) and discuss the significance of normalisation as an ideological concept, a disciplinary technique and a principle for organising services for people with perceived impairments. Demands for the reform of stigmatising and oppressive institutional structures and relations were justified as a desire to normalise environments; at the same time, a normal environment was regarded as an essential prerequisite in the project of normalising people with perceived impairment. Two sections of the chapter, therefore, are devoted to explorations of these related aspects of normalising ideology and practice – environments and individuals. The final section deals with the issue of resistance, especially the resistance of disabled people to normalising discourses and practices.

In the post-World War II period, opposition to the segregation and institutionalisation of disabled people – widespread practices in the Western world for a century and a half – reached a critical juncture. This opposition materialised around two different perspectives. One was a disability activist perspective which was based on ideas of social justice and civil rights and which found expression in what eventually became known as the disability movement. The other, the particular focus of this chapter, was a professional perspective involving mainly non-disabled practitioners, academics and researchers (Deeley 2002). It was professional in the sense that opposition to established theories and practices was located among some members of professions that were directly involved in the field of disability, such as psychiatry, psychology and education, or emerged in disciplines not immediately linked to disability, such as sociology (Goffman 1961; 1963) and linguistics (Stokoe 1960).

Inevitably, because disability rights and professional perspectives challenged the same long-established institutional structures and practices, there was some overlap between them. Both appealed to ideas of human and civil rights. Both referred to the evident contradictions between political values claiming to vindicate those rights and actual social practices that led to segregation and discrimination. Both had available the same master frames of reference, such as the civil rights movement and the women's movement, for formulating concepts and mobilising support (McAdam, McCarthy and Zald 1993).

There were, however, fundamental differences between these two standpoints. As we shall see, normalisation was a fundamentally paternalistic ideology. Programmes of reform were organised for the most part by professionals, were aimed at politicians, academics, administrators and other professionals in the social services and were negotiated mainly in academic circles or in the domains of professional practice. In Ireland, for example, the debate on deinstitutionalisation was largely confined to professionals and administrators working in the field of mental health (Leane and Sapouna 1998). No strategic or participative roles were available for disabled people in this debate, nor in the arenas where policies were made and decisions taken. In this perspective, although disabled people were seen to be disempowered and discriminated against, they were also regarded as helpless and dependent. The professionals who argued for reform saw themselves as interpreters of what was in the best interests of disabled people. Nevertheless, the ideas and practices of normalisation marked a decisive shift in the relationship between disability and society. As Radford puts it, '[t]he principle of normalisation, despite its imperfections and its openness to misuse, has at least provided the mental handicap sector with a means of escape from the worst abuses conducted "in the name of eugenics"' (1991: 458).

Professional opposition to segregation and institutionalisation was articulated in different ways in different parts of the social system. In this chapter I will focus on three areas that are particularly linked to disability as a social construct – learning difficulties, mental health and special education. Professional challenges to established policies and practices in these three fields were organised around the notion of normalisation. In its most basic terms, the argument was that disabled people had a right to more normal and humane experiences, something that was being denied them if they were segregated from mainstream society. In one typical analysis, Vail (1966) summarises the case against the institutional thinking and practices that prevailed. According to this account, the critique of segregation and institutionalisation reflected 'astonishing advances in social attitudes and policy' and involved 'consciously undoing harsh traditions and replacing them with penetrating and unsentimental humanism' (vii). In the past, 'institutional relationships' had constrained individual expression and initiative, had fostered dependence and were employed as instruments of control rather than as means of promoting acceptable change; individuals were dehumanised and degraded because they were 'put away' and subjected to 'inescapable ... humiliations' (viii). Explicit comparisons were made between existing institutions and military-type establishments, forced labour camps and concentration camps. Like many critics, Vail argued for the kind of reform that would be committed to humane interventions, would reflect authentic and enlightened values, introduce self-critical and self-correcting mechanisms, foster constructive change and independence, and dispense with restrictive and punitive measures. There was, in addition, the more general expectation that new policies and practices would be based on 'day treatment and other forms of care in the community' and would promote individualised responses 'in the face of increasing mass uniformity in society' (ix).

The critique of institutionalisation was related to the larger political and social changes that were taking place in Western society during this period. Firstly, the post-war period witnessed a convergence of ideas, attitudes and movements concerned with human and civil rights. Revelations of the atrocities carried out under the Third Reich sensitised Western society to the rights of minorities and to their protection. Moreover, in the context of Cold War politics in the West, contradictions were becoming apparent between claims about social justice and freedom for all, and the actual experiences of particular social groups. Some of these concerns were expressed in a variety of UN charters and other conventions formulated during this period, including the UN Declaration' on the Rights of Mentally Retarded Persons in 1971 and the Declaration of the Rights of Disabled Persons in 1975 (Faughnan and O'Connor 1980; Whitehead 1992). Secondly, social groups with long historical experiences of oppression began to articulate a social justice agenda through civil rights and the women's movements (Whitehead 1992). These new social movements were prepared to pursue civil rights and social justice goals both on the streets and in the courts. In addition, the courts, especially in the US, seemed prepared to push out the boundaries of rights-based social policy (Bannerman Foster 1987). Thirdly, critical and well-publicised descriptions of public institutions appeared, graphically describing the abuse, filth, and over-crowding suffered by patients (Talbot 1978; Levine 1981; Morris 1993a). Sociological investigations, based on interpretive research paradigms, raised similar concerns (Goffman 1961), including the class, gender and racial biases of institutionalisation (Mercer 1974; Talbot 1978). Studies of this kind alerted public opinion to the rights of patients in psychiatric hospitals, to the treatment of people with learning difficulties in institutions, and to the experiences of students in special education. Fourthly, the emergence of the modern welfare state inaugurated an era of social citizenship in which access to education, health and social security was underwritten by the idea of social rights (Thomson 1998). The question of how social rights might be exercised, with regard to different social groups, fostered a review of professional services within the institutions themselves. In addition, conflicts between the 'old school' medical autocracy and the new professionals – nurses, psychologists, teachers, social workers – provided fertile ground for critical debate (Tyne 1992).

Official explanations of deinstitutionalisation have tended to highlight advances in medical treatment and the development of more humane and enlightened attitudes in the post-war period (Pilgrim and Rogers 1999). In relation to mental illness, for example, Talbot characterises the discovery of psychotropic drugs in the 1950s as 'perhaps the most significant development ever in the history of institutional psychiatry' (1978: 26). It is frequently suggested that the introduction of this medication enabled large numbers of people to move from the asylum into the community and thus had a decisive effect on deinstitutionalisation (Forsberg 1992). Scull (1977), however, is sceptical about this medical advance argument. He maintains that in order to reduce public expenditure, deinstitutionalisation was already under way before the introduction of psychotropic drugs, and that pharmacology, which represented a relatively cheaper technology of behavioural control, facilitated rather than initiated the process of deinstitutionalisation. Although increasing costs through the 1950s had caused some concern and raised questions about the efficiency and effectiveness of the institutions (Morris 1993*a*; Halpern *et al.* 1980), Busfield (1986) points out that the real pressure to cut costs did not emerge until the post-1970s, by which time the numbers in custodial institutions had already declined significantly.

With specific reference to mental illness, Prior (1991) argues that the main challenge to institutionalisation stemmed from a shift in psychiatric discourse rather than from a pharmacological revolution or from economic cost cutting. According to Prior, the need to accommodate Freudian concepts such as 'the psyche' and 'the unconscious' in psychiatry brought about a blurring of the traditional boundaries of normality. As a result, modern psychiatric theory and practice required more widely dispersed and more varied responses to mental health issues. New sites for the practice of psychiatry were identified and new problems were brought within the psychiatric domain (Rose 1986). The accompanying therapeutics necessitated new kinds of social contact for individuals who were diagnosed as being mentally ill, the kinds of contact that were possible in a community but not in an institutional setting (Prior 1991). A similar questioning of the boundaries of the normal, often prompted by the concerns of parents, occurred in special education and services for people with learning difficulties and led to more diverse responses (Ericsson and Mansell 1996; McGee 1990).

The shift from segregated institutions to community based provision can be seen as an essential stage in the professional project of normalisation. Numerous studies had claimed that normalising regimes were impossible in 'total institutions' (see, for example, Goffman 1961). This was the explicit premise of Wolfensberger's (1972) case against segregated institutions for people with learning difficulties: those institutions produced devalued identities for the people within them and reinforced negative attitudes among people outside. In a similar vein, arguments against segregated special education highlighted its negative impact on the emotional, social and academic development of pupils with impairment (Barton 1995). Regarding the treatment of mental illness, the aims of normalising behaviour and of building social networks were seen to be incompatible with an institutional environment (Prior 1991). Before moving on to discuss the constituents of normalising ideology and practice in these areas, however, I want to explore briefly the emergence of the concept of the normal in Western society.

## THE 'NORMAL' – WHAT IS AND WHAT OUGHT TO BE

One of the enduring legacies of scientific medicine and the science of health administration was their contribution to the modern concept of normality. In his detailed analysis of the concept, Hacking (1990) shows that, in its older sense, 'normal' was a geometric term meaning 'perpendicular' or 'at right angles'. In its modern sense, the normal first emerged in scientific medicine. The central position of pathological anatomy in medicine entailed a preoccupation with pathological structures and reactions. The normal became the inverse of the pathological in the sense that '[s]omething was normal when it was not associated with a pathological organ' (Hacking 1990: 164). At this stage in its development, the notion of the normal was contingent on the primary concept of pathology. It did not require an explicit definition; it was 'a retrospective concept, one which you can only be certain about after the last possibility for a pathological symptom has been eliminated' (Murphy-Lawless 1998: 168). In the next stage, the relationship between what was termed pathological and what was termed normal was reversed. In a definition that was first applied to the individual body (or, more correctly, organ) and then extended to the social body, the pathological was defined as a deviation from the normal. Deviation became, not something different in kind, but a departure from the normal and could be defined as something 'relative to the normal state' (Hacking 1990: 166).

In a further development, the concept of the normal was given an explicitly quantitative underpinning by the mathematician, Adolphe Quetelet. Quetelet postulated that a great many human attributes had a typical distribution pattern: the bell-shaped curve, also called normal distribution. On the basis of this belief, he introduced the idea of the *homme type*, the average man, an idea that incorporated two significant departures. Firstly, it constituted an important conceptual innovation. Although the attributes of the *homme type* were abstract, statistical creations, it was possible to think of them as actual properties of a population and to think of the *homme type* as a physical and moral reality. Secondly, the *homme type* did not refer to an average for the human species; it referred to the characteristics of a particular people or a particular racial type. The implications of this were enormous. As Hacking puts it:

> Where before one thought of a people in terms of its culture or its geography or its language or its rulers or its religion, Quetelet introduced a new objective measurable conception of a people. A race would be characterised by its measurements of physical and moral qualities, summed up in the average man of that race. This is half of the beginning of eugenics, the other half being the reflection that one can introduce social policies that will either preserve or alter the average qualities of a race. In short, the average man led to both a new kind of information about populations and a new conception of how to control them. (1990: 107–8)

The concept of normality thus became a central organising principle in both the description and evaluation of individuals and of populations. A considerable part of its potency as an instrument for interpreting conditions and behaviours derives from its capacity to represent both what 'is' and what 'ought to be'. The concept of the normal blurs the distinction between descriptive and prescriptive considerations: 'it contains not only a judgement about what is desirable, but an injunction as to a goal to be achieved' (Rose 1990: 131). And since 'normal' is also synonymous with 'average' it can draw on a mathematical underpinning to provide an apparent objectivity and impartiality. 'That is why,' says Hacking, 'the benign and sterile-sounding word "normal" has become one of the most powerful ideological tools of the twentieth century' (1990: 169).

The idea of normalisation is also a central element in Foucault's analysis (1977; 2002) of the discourse and practice of disciplinary power in modern society. Foucault maintains that normalisation is an effect of disciplinary power and operates through 'techniques of surveillance', that is, through hierarchical observation, normalising judgement and the examination (1977: 177). Surveillance is orchestrated by professional figures – schoolteachers, physicians, or psychiatrists, for example – whose authority is derived from their respective disciplines. They occupy positions in a hierarchy of observation that permits a multi-layered disciplinary gaze to be exercised 'over the entire surface to be supervised' (174). The professional gaze is normalising in that it standardises individual actions and behaviour and, through a microeconomy of evaluation, establishes distinctions between individuals in terms of 'their nature, their potentialities, their level or their value' (181). The third instrument of disciplinary power, the examination, 'combines the techniques of an observing hierarchy and those of a normalising judgement' (184) and brings individuals into a field of 'compulsory visibility' (186) and documentation. The examination makes it possible to identify and label individuals with a greater degree of certainty, 'to classify, to form categories, to determine averages' (190), and to fix 'the "marks" that characterize [each individual] and make him a "case"' (192).

Slee (1996) argues that the identification of new forms of individual pathology, such as Attention Deficit Disorder (ADD) and Attention Deficit Hyperactivity Disorder (ADHD), constitute current examples of these normalising techniques in action. Slee maintains that the crisis in education brought about by the disappearance of the unskilled youth labour market and the consequent retention of young people without post-schooling options, has produced increased levels of tension and conflict in educational systems. In this context, the new pathologies were a 'spectacular administrative convenience' that provided 'a more sophisticated and pervasive technology of control' than corporal punishment, suspension or expulsion (1996: 114). A discourse of individual pathology removes the problem from its specific political and social context and shifts the diagnostic gaze towards the student and away from the teacher, the culture and organisation of the school and from the curriculum. Moreover, the notion of an identifiable psycho-medical 'condition' makes it possible to avoid reference to such questionable and elusive categories as 'maladjustment'.

Where Foucault envisages normalisation as a pervasive technology used in the governance of individuals and populations in modern society, Wolfensberger (1972) regards normalisation as a mechanism that can be employed in the deinstitutionalisation of the social services for people with learning difficulties. For Foucault, normalisation with its disreputable origins and sinister mode of operation, constituted 'a "new microphysics" of power' (1977: 139); for Wolfensberger it was a goal worth striving for and provided a valued criterion against which abnormal structures, practices and outcomes in the social services could be measured. From the early 1960s, critics of classic nineteenth century institutions were convinced that even the best of them were not conducive to individual growth and development. They argued that custodial structures and relations needed to be replaced by 'support services to dependent people at a level that will allow them to live a life as near as possible to that which is perceived to be normal for other members of society' (O'Connor 1987: 25).

The concept of normalisation as a mechanism for deinstitutionalisation originated in Denmark (Bank-Mikkelsen 1969) and Sweden (Nirje 1969) in the late 1950s: it referred to the aim of social services to create conditions of social existence 'as close to normal living … as possible' for disabled people (Emerson 1992: 2). An essential aspect of this approach was its concern that services should reflect the basic rights of disabled people in relation to traditional quality of life indicators such as housing, education, work and leisure. During the 1960s, normalisation concepts and practices were introduced from Scandinavia into North America (Trent 1994) and were subsequently further developed and systematised by Wolfensberger (1972).

Although this particular concept of normalisation underpinned a powerful critique of established structures and practices, it tended to locate the problem more in negative mind-sets than in impoverished material circumstances. It implied that the conceptual rather than the material basis of the problem was of greater significance, and that discrimination, for example, ultimately stemmed from attitudinal rather than material sources. Normalisation, therefore, was especially preoccupied with the impact of negative imagery and labelling on disabled people (Wolfensberger 1972; Wolfensberger and Thomas 1987). Consequently, the solutions it proposed, for the most part, focused on the development of positive public and professional attitudes and dispositions towards disabled people: the primary goal was 'to create or support socially valued roles for people in their society' (Wolfensberger and Thomas 1987: 10).

In some respects, the three perspectives on normalisation discussed in this section appear very different. Nevertheless, they do share certain core properties that have a direct bearing on the lives and experiences of disabled people and their place in the social order. Firstly, each approach is concerned with making comparisons between individuals and social groups, categorising them and, overtly or by implication, ranking them.

These ideas and practices have, for disabled people, an explicit and pervasive social reality that does not usually extend to other members of
society. Secondly, the identification, evaluation and eradication of difference are implicit in each perspective. Thus, each stands in opposition
to egalitarian measures such as recognition and solidarity which, as
Kwiotek (1999) points out, are essential to the notion of disability rights.
Thirdly, each perspective endorses the deployment of rehabilitative or
therapeutic programmes designed to correct perceived individual and
social anomalies; each, therefore, underpins the idea of adjustment
which forms such a central element in the medical model of disability
(Oliver 1990).

   In summary then, normalisation represented one element in a much
broader critique of dominant and subordinating ideologies present in
Western society during the post-war period. While both the normalisation
and disability rights movements emerged from the same socio-political
matrix and had some shared objectives, there were important differences
between them. Although both challenged the thinking behind the large-
scale, segregated institutions that were then typical of the social services
sector, the normalisation movement was largely the product of professional concerns and perspectives and did not include disabled people at a
strategic level in policy making or decision taking.

## NORMALISING ENVIRONMENTS

The ambiguity in the above heading captures the dual nature of normalising ideology and practice – on the one hand, the idea that environments
may need to be normalised and, on the other, that normal environments
are expected to have normalising effects on individuals who are located in
them. Thus, normalisation has implications for the conceptual and material infrastructures of institutions and services as well as for individual
actions and dispositions. Although normalising ideology and practice has
been articulated in different ways in different environments in the social
services sector, a number of recurring themes can be identified. Among
the most significant of these are: firstly, a particular set of assumptions
that have shaped the concepts of 'community' and 'care'; secondly, an
emphasis on dispersal and assimilation as the most appropriate policy
responses to the difficulties experienced by disabled people; thirdly, an
approach suggesting that the construction of disability has a conceptual

rather than a material basis; and finally, an understanding of the social world as a consensual and undifferentiated entity.

Normalising ideology and practice attaches particular importance to the idea of the community. The perception of what is normal is associated with the community as opposed to the institution and, within the community, with family or family-like care as opposed to residential care. In a report on services 'for mentally and physically handicapped persons', for example, the National Economic and Social Council (NESC) stated:

> The handicapped child should be able to enjoy a normal life in the community using facilities available to the public at large. If for some reason a handicapped person cannot live with his/her own family, the residential care provided should approximate as far as possible to an ordinary home. (1980: 12)

The council went on to argue that a crucial aspect in the achievement of integration was a willingness on the part of the community at large to accept and 'welcome the handicapped into schools, community and workplaces' (12).

Community based provision for people with impairments has existed for centuries and, even at the high point of institutional foundation between 1850 and 1950, substantial numbers of people with impairment continued to live in the community (Bartlett and Wright 1999). Care work in this form was usually unpaid and was undertaken mainly by women (Symonds 1998). Under normalisation, however, the idea of community provision took on a new meaning. It came to be seen as a morally superior and therapeutically more effective location than the institution for providing treatment and care, as well as being more attractive to public authorities in terms of expenditure (NESC 1987: 3). In relation to learning difficulties and mental illness, the concepts of community and community care had positive social meaning and were linked to the notion that ordinary people could participate in care (4–5). Community care implied locally based services, more humane and personal responses to vulnerable people, and a recognition of 'the need for the integration and participation of the handicapped to the greatest extent possible at various levels of society' (Dept. of Health 1980: 12). Care in this context was equated with normalisation and was regarded as the most 'appropriate and preferred [form] for children, the elderly, disabled and handicapped persons' (NESC 1987: 3).

The question of who would do the actual caring was largely taken for granted. When it was addressed, it was generally assumed to be women's work (Symonds 1998). Thus, in the organisation of home help services in Ireland, 'the typical recruit would be a middle-aged woman with time to spare from her other household duties who was attracted to the idea of helping to normalise the living conditions of a person or family in need of care' (Dept. of Health 1972). O'Donovan (1997) observes that this model of care continues to be endorsed by the health boards in Ireland where ideal home helps are defined as 'caring and capable mature women who have some experience of caring and whose interest in the work is not determined primarily by the level of pay' (Lundstrom and McKeown 1994: 156). On this basis the dominant perception is of home-based care as philanthropic, gendered, 'non-work', and quasi-waged (O'Donovan 1997: 149).

In her analysis of care, Dalley (1996) argues that an ideology of familism underlies all contemporary forms of social organisation of daily living, including those aspects that involve caring. The ideology of familism not only generates particular sets of relations with regard to caring in the domestic sphere but also reproduces the same patterns in the public sphere. Among the more significant aspects of these processes are the gendered division of care labour, the regulation of women to the domestic sphere, the confirmation of the 'natural' role of women as care-givers and the articulation of these relations in both private and public domains. In the ideology of familism, social care is expected to closely replicate the family form and policies are premised on a 'family is best' model. There is a consensus among policy makers, academic experts and practitioners that care is best provided at home and that, where family care is not available, 'home like conditions' or 'nearest approximations' should be introduced. During the 1980s, there was considerable emphasis in the critical literature that community care, in fact, amounted to family care and that family care meant care provided by women. Care work, therefore, was regarded as a gender issue, with implications for the exploitation of women (Finch and Groves 1983). Although more recent research suggests a more complex picture in terms of gender, Dalley concludes that care work is something 'women tended to do more, more often and more intimately' (1996: 13).

Writing from a disability rights perspective, Morris (1993) maintains that the feminist critique of care only as an exploitation issue for carers has colluded with the creation of dependency, has excluded the voices of disabled people, and has failed to challenge the fact that poverty is a fundamental factor in the debate. Morris argues that community care has never been simply about providing services to people in their own homes as an alternative to residential care; it has also implied the development of policies and practices to enable people to control their own lives and live independently. She maintains that the preoccupation of feminist research with the burden of care on women and with the interests of carers has constructed disabled and older people as dependent, has diverted attention away from their interests and preferred options and, in some instances, has involved proposals for a return to residential provision. Morris points out that the economic independence of carers is not the only point at issue; a more fundamental problem is the poverty and economic dependence of disabled people. This, Morris believes, is the problem that must be addressed.

Care in the community implies a normalising environment because it involves a more widespread distribution of people with perceived impairment in the social world. An important element in the ideology of normalisation is the conviction that 'when deviancies and stigmata increase in number, severity, or variety, they tend to have a multiplicative ... impact upon observers' (Wolfensberger and Thomas 1987: 15). Accordingly, the greater the level of deviancy or degree of stigmatisation, the greater will be the normalising impact of reducing the number of deviant people in the group. One Irish report stressed that 'large numbers of highly dependent intellectually disabled people should not be placed in one location' and that new provision should be organised in small clusters of three or four houses at a number of locations (Dept. of Health 1990: 39). Consequently, normalising of the environment was organised around two strategies – dispersal and assimilation. The dispersal of disabled people through the social world operates in the interests of 'reduced visibility' and on the assumption that it provides greater access to 'appropriate role models' (Szivros 1992: 115); assimilation will then be relatively more successful.

Integration in education is based on similar practices. It is, as Corbett and Slee argue, 'inherently assimilationist. It holds firm to a traditional notion of ideal types, both of people and of institutions. According to this model, the emphasis is upon deficit, diagnosis, categorisation and individual treatment ...' (2000: 134). Although integration involves promoting opportunity, it does so at the expense of eradicating difference. In integration discourse, the expectation is that pupils from the special school sector will 'be ready for' and 'able to cope' in normal, mainstream schools. There is no reciprocal expectation that the mainstream school must negotiate a new ethic because it is presumed that what happens there is already normal and, therefore, unproblematic (McDonnell 2000). The business of adjusting and accommodating to the new situation is left to the pupil being integrated and thus there is little impetus to fashion new curricula, teaching methodologies, or learning environments for a more diverse pupil population.

In many instances in Ireland and other countries, pupils being integrated were simply shifted to separate facilities on the mainstream campus (McDonnell 2003). Like family care in the context of the community, functional integration (The Warnock Report 1978) was regarded as the most normal option; however, if this was not possible, family-like alternatives were available. Thus, integration could be locational, where pupils 'with special needs' simply shared a campus with 'ordinary' pupils, or it could be social, where the pupils spent occasional periods in the mainstream environment. An important corollary, therefore, in normalising the environment was the practice of establishing 'a continuum of provision' or 'the least restrictive environment' (Dept. of Health 1984: 45, 49; NESC 1987: 4). This practice was grounded in the conviction that if 'full integration' was not possible (NESC 1980: 12) then there was 'the prospect of at least a reasonably normal and integrated social life' (Dept. of Health 1984: 17). In these circumstances the aim was to make provision as normal as possible and thus achieve an equivalent reduction in the manifestation of difference.

Indeed, the ideology and practices of normalisation involves a fundamental rejection of difference. In relation to learning difficulties, Szivros (1992) identifies two distinct normalising responses to difference. In his analysis of the means of normalisation, Wolfensberger (1972) refers to the need for the environment to highlight the presentation and promotion of social images and attitudes emphasising an individual's similarity to, rather than difference from, others. The objective is to create conditions that enhance public perceptions of people with learning difficulties and thus facilitate their integration in mainstream society. In contrast, Nirje's (1969) formulation regards difference as more acceptable in itself and places less emphasis on the idea of inculcating behaviour that corresponds to some culturally accepted norm. Szivros (1992) goes on to argue that the formulation proposed by Wolfensberger became the predominant model to be taken up by social services in many countries because it was presented as a systematic programme and couched in empiricist language.

Normalisation was influenced by notions of individual rights and ran counter to a custodial model of care. It proposed instead a training model whereby disabled people would, as far as possible, be socially educated to adopt patterns of behaviour that would allow them to be accepted in the wider community. It also presupposed public awareness training to enable the wider community to develop more positive attitudes towards disabled people. In this framework, disability was interpreted as a product of prejudices, negative attitudes and labelling. Accordingly, the sources of problems were to be found in the minds and hearts of people rather than in the material world, problems that could be overcome by rational argument, by disability awareness training and by ensuring that accurate information was disseminated (Riddell 1996). If aspects of the material world were thought to be in need of change this was done more in order to create positive impressions than because they presented disabling barriers.

Normalisation has been and continues to be a powerful force in policy-making and practice in the social services in Western society. Its practices are easily incorporated into the structures of social and liberal democracy and it reinforces rather than presents a radical challenge to the status and power of professionals. Normalisation is functionalist in its assumptions about the relationship between professionals and disabled people. It presupposes homogeneity in environments where community care, mainstreaming and the creation of valued social roles are in fact problematic practices. That mainstream schools, for example, are significantly differentiated in terms of class, gender and ability relations has never constituted an appreciable factor in the integration debate (McDonnell 2000). Normalisation reflects a consensual view of the social order and, as we shall see, assumes that professional experts are best placed to determine the true interests of disabled people. Its most abiding concerns are grounded in a constructionist interpretation of disability since it highlights issues such as values, attitudes and perceptions (Oliver 1990; Barnes 1996).

If normalising programmes were considered necessary to counter prejudices in the environment, they were regarded as being equally necessary to enhance the personal competencies of disabled individuals. Thus, in addition to a means criterion, Wolfensberger identifies behaviour as another important dimension of normalisation. This dimension applies to the individual and involves promoting the development of individual competence 'beyond the point of being merely physically adaptive, to the point of being socially normative' (Szivos 1992: 113). The primary purpose of these normalising programmes was to enable devalued individuals to pass as normal.

## NORMALISING INDIVIDUALS

The normalisation of individuals involves a set of legitimising ideologies and practices that have been a recurring presence in the relationship between disability and society. Firstly, normalisation interacts with a discourse of expertise. It relies on experts in the human sciences to set and regulate the boundaries of the normal. Secondly, the primary focus of normalisation is the individual. Although, as we have seen, normalisation has implications for environments, that is a secondary concern. Consideration of the environment derives in the first place from the desire to normalise anomalous individuals. Thirdly, normalisation implies pathology and is premised on the existence of some condition or disposition within the individual that is seen to be in need of rehabilitation and therapy. Finally, normalisation lays claim to humanitarian motives because it represents a challenge to the oppression of the total institution. The next four sections are devoted to explorations of the connections between these explanatory ideologies and the organising ideology of normalisation.

### Expertism

Normalisation has been a movement involving, for the most part, professional workers in or associated with the various social services. Its theoretical assumptions and practices have been underpinned by discourses of professional expertise. An important factor in the genesis of new social movements is the presence of glaring contradictions between highly salient political and social values and conventional institutional practices (McAdam, McCarthy and Zald 1996). In this context, therefore, it is not surprising that, initially, the most active normalisation movements developed in Scandinavia and the US, countries that had formalised in legislation and practice the more extreme eugenic responses to perceived impairment (Kirkebaek 2002; 2002a). The pronounced shift away from established practices was in large measure due to the concern of some professional workers to distance themselves from the negative effects of such practices – the absence of humanitarian attitudes, the lack of individual treatment, the degrading physical surroundings and conditions, and the gross violation of human and civil rights.

Psy-complex knowledge and practices (Ingleby 1983) have portrayed users of social services mainly as objects of the clinical gaze of professionals. In the area of mental health, for example, Pilgrim and Rogers (1999) argue that this understanding of the relationship between professionals and service users is evident in the academic literature and training upon which professional formation is based. The views of patients tend to be excluded from clinical research and patients themselves regarded as passive objects of study. Individual characteristics and feelings are seen as data likely to invalidate rather than illuminate research. In particular, patient views that contradict the views of professionals are treated with suspicion and professional narratives carry greater claims to validity and truth. Moreover, since patients are believed to be irrational or in denial about their perceived condition, they are thereby assumed to be incapable of holding valid viewpoints. To question an expert diagnosis or treatment or to refuse to comply with medication instructions are themselves taken as symptomatic indicators of a mental health problem. The views of patients are often conflated with the views of relatives and important differences between them may be glossed over; diverging patient views are explained away in terms of patient pathology. Finally, research often frames patient views in terms that suit professionals; studies may adopt victim-blaming attitudes and focus on the patients' problems rather than the problems thrown up by professional or institutional practices (Pilgrim and Rogers 1999).

If the views of users of mental health services are regarded with suspicion, people with learning difficulties are assumed to be incapable of expressing reliable views at all. Goodley and Rapley (2002) demonstrate how psychological practices are deployed in the production of intellectually impaired identities. For example, a socially constructed and reified attribute – a so-called acquiescence bias, that is, 'the tendency to say yes regardless of the question content' among 'mentally retarded persons' (Sigelman *et al.* 1981, cited in Goodley and Rapley 2002: 129) – is deemed to render invalid and untrustworthy their own accounts of their actions, beliefs or feelings. This perspective literally leaves space only for expert discourse. Similarly, the recommendations of a recent working group 'on the implementation of the health strategy in relation to persons with a mental handicap' in Ireland left no space for any input from or participation by service users themselves in policy making (Dept. of Equality and Law Reform 1996). Ironically, the report was entitled 'Enhancing the Partnership', a partnership of the Department of Health, the Health Boards and the 'voluntary bodies providing services to people with mental handicap' (3). Clearly, the professionals who produced the report regarded service users themselves as having little of value to contribute.

Equally, in the educational sector, Corbett and Slee (2000) maintain that the voices of professionals have dominated the ideology of integration. Professionals speak for students with special needs, whom they know as objects of their expert discourses (McDonnell 2000) and the starting point for intervention is the identification and evaluation of individual defect. In this framework, the job of special education experts is to minimise and manage difference, 'to resolve issues of fit' (Slee 1997: 411). As Tomlinson argues, 'dealing with special education *is* now the province of professionals, almost immune from alternative discourses and views of other groups such as parents and civil rights activists' (1996: 177, italics in original). In Ireland, professional expertise in relation to special needs education has been reinforced, and the whole debate surrounding integration dominated by an exceptional privileging of psychological discourse (see, for example, Dept. of Education 1993: 30–2). As Billington (2000) and Slee (1995) demonstrate, psychology provides the expert underpinning for a new technology of individualisation in education. In this context, disability is rarely perceived to be a form of discrimination but is frequently seen as an individual condition that must be identified and assessed in order for an appropriate placement to be made. Thus, the exclusionary strategies and the barriers operating in the mainstream system are less likely to be scrutinised.

The discourses that define, measure and categorise mental illnesses, learning difficulties and special needs in education are uniformly discourses of expertise. Perhaps the situation is best illustrated by one particular investigation relating to the education of deaf children. In an analysis of thirteen US textbooks on special education, Hoffmeister (1996) compared content derived from a psycho-medical interpretation of deafness (an expert perspective) with content informed by a socio-cultural (Deaf community) perspective. His findings clearly showed that, in relation to the education of deaf pupils, the most significant issues and ideas conveyed to readers were those that were products of discourses of professional expertise.

A similar analysis can be conducted on the most recent major report on special education in Ireland, the Report of the Special Education Review Committee (Dept. of Education 1993), the details of which are summarised in Table 6.1. In the table, topics 1–5 refer to matters essential to a socio-cultural understanding of deafness, while topics 6–10 refer to topics central to a psycho-medical approach (Hoffmeister 1996). In terms of content, topics are discussed, sometimes at length, mentioned in one or two sentences, noted in a word or two, or are not discussed at all. Although a report published today on the education of deaf children would undoubtedly give much greater consideration to the concerns of the Irish Deaf community (and, therefore, to topics 1–5), Table 6.1 demonstrates that a discourse of expertise is likely to continue to exert considerable influence on such a report.[2]

Their theoretical frameworks, their models of practice and their tools of the trade have oriented the human science professions towards a technical understanding of problems and an engineering approach to solutions (Skrtic 1995; Oliver 1992). These orientations create and are creations of an essentialist interpretation of disability, that is, a definition of disability as an inherent characteristic of the individual. Understanding disability in essentialist terms involves a search for solutions on two general fronts: through adjustment and rehabilitation of the disabled person and, more importantly, through the deployment of greater degrees of professional expertise. Consequently, in the field of disability, research and expenditure are mainly directed at training more professionals, increasing the level of professional specialisation, developing new or more accurate measuring instruments, and intensifying processes of identification, assessment and categorisation (see, for example, Dept. of Education 1993). These efforts are premised on an essentialist definition of disability.

**Table 6.1: Content Analysis of Topics Considered
Relevant to the Education of Deaf Pupils**

|  | **Topics** |
| --- | --- |
| 1. Deaf Community | Not discussed |
| 2. Sign Language | Noted |
| 3. Deaf Culture | Not discussed |
| 4. Bilingualism | Not discussed |
| 5. Interpreting | Noted |

Pages devoted to a Socio-cultural Model of Deafness   0

|  |  |
| --- | --- |
| 6. Categories of Deafness | Discussed at length |
| 7. Prevalence of Deafness | Discussed at length |
| 8. Causes of Deafness | Mentioned |
| 9. Measuring Deafness | Discussed at length |
| 10. Hearing aids | Not discussed |

Pages devoted to a Psycho-medical Model of Deafness   6

*Source*: Dept. of Education (1993), *Report of the Special Education Review Committee*, Dublin: The Stationery Office.

## Essentialism

Essentialism is a perspective that defines disability as a condition or deficit inherent in the individual. It interprets disability as having a biological or physiological rather than a social origin. As we have suggested, it is a perspective that is particularly associated with professional expertise that tends to generate positivist, quantitative research and underpin engineering solutions and care models in social policy (Oliver 1992; 2002). At a fundamental level, essentialism protects the interests of the experts. Professionals tend to resist explanations that situate the problem in the environment (Riddell 1996; Pilgrim and Rogers 1999). In terms of economic interests and professional affiliation, it is difficult for experts to turn their diagnostic gaze onto structures and relations because it involves criticism of their employers or the institutions in which they are employed. Moreover, professionals in one field

fear that if they do not provide a legitimating framework for state policies, then professionals from a related field may be found to do so
(Stone 1985).

It is also difficult to avoid essentialist perspectives in the highly
individualist and competitive context of Western capitalist society. The
individualising gaze creates the context in which cases are produced,
leading in turn to the 'Foucault paradox' (Meadmore 1993: 30). The
increasing individualisation of special educational needs, for example,
purports to create better conditions to enable pupils with special educational needs to make progress in school. This, however, is accomplished
at a cost. The more intensely and thoroughly the individual is brought
under the professional gaze, the more the essentialist perspective is
strengthened. In addition, if programmes of intervention fail, explanations will be all the more sought in the deficiencies of the pupil (Drudy
and Lynch 1993).

However, in the face of increasing criticism of professional authority, of essentialist understanding of problems, and of positivist
approaches to research, professionals have been obliged to direct their
gaze towards the environment. One result has been the emergence of
interpretative approaches to research and enlightened policy making
(Oliver 1992; 2002). Since interpretative approaches are frequently
concerned with issues such as attitudes, values, expectations, and perceptions, a discursive space has become available for the articulation of
insider views and experiences. If interpretative approaches have not
entirely displaced essentialist interpretations of disability, they have
moderated them. From an interpretative position, the problem of disability can be located in the negative perceptions and conceptualisa-
tions of others rather than in the bodies and minds of disabled people
(Oliver 1990).

By taking account of insider perspectives, normalisation represented
a departure from a purely essentialist understanding of disability (Nirje
1969; Wolfensberger 1972). Instead of withering away, however, essentialism continues to surface as a powerful explanatory device to explain
policy failures in areas such as integration and community care. Riddell
(1996) argues that in Britain, for example, while there was some initial
shift away from essentialist thinking in education policy, especially in
the late 1970s, more recent developments suggest a resurgence of such

thinking. Thus, while it may have been moderated, essentialism remains a powerful ideological device that permits professionals and policy makers to explain their failures in terms of the individual deficits of service users rather than in terms of deep-rooted structural and relational inequalities.

A recent example from the field of education in Ireland illustrates some of the tensions and contradictions that emerge when attempts are made to link an essentialist understanding of disability with measures related to social justice (McDonnell 2003a). In May 1999, an expert advisory group on certificate examinations published a discussion paper on proposals for changes in arrangements for candidates with special needs. This paper was followed by a report in January 2000. The expert group acknowledged that for certain students the Leaving Certificate Examination

> does not adequately represent the achievements that it purports to measure. This arises partly from the fact that the scope of the present examination is fairly limited. Although there is provision for other kinds of assessment (e.g. oral and practical competencies), the examination relies heavily on performance on written papers which are administered under controlled conditions in a limited time frame at the end of students' secondary school careers. Furthermore, unlike the experience in other countries, the Examination does not involve any element of continuous assessment by a student's own teachers. Assessment either in written, oral or aural format is by external examiners ... Some candidates experience difficulty, or may even find it impossible, to communicate what they know in this situation. (Dept. of Education and Science 1999: 1)

It is clear, then, that the format of the examination presents barriers to some students and the disability stems, not from individual impairment, but from a particular administrative or structural format that excludes certain students. In spite of this, it is the essentialist model of disability contained in the Education Act 1988 that informs the discussions and subsequent recommendations of the expert group. Disability is seen as an 'individual human condition' (Dept. of Education and Science 1999: 1) and thus the problems that disabled people face are reduced 'to their own personal inadequacies or functional limitations' (Oliver 1990: 7). At no point in its deliberations did the expert group display any awareness of disability as a contested phenomenon; it merely assumed that there is consensus about how it should be understood. The real problem is perceived to be located in the student rather than in the structure and format of the examination. This conceptual position then shapes the discussion that follows, defining the key principles and issues and determining how these are to be addressed. The weakness of this perspective is most striking with reference to deaf candidates. While the expert group suggests that pupils 'with impaired hearing' may seek exemption from the aural components of examinations (Dept. of Education and Science 2000), the central and more critical cultural and linguistic barriers faced by deaf pupils (Lane 1993; McDonnell 1996) are completely overlooked and the question of access for deaf pupils is not answered.

While essentialist theories and practices are widespread among the human science professions, they have particularly marked applications in the field of disability. When essentialist concepts are employed more generally, notions of deficit and deficiency may be inferred rather than declared. In the field of disability, however, essentialism operates in a much more explicit way; here, differences are interpreted not as simple deviations from a norm but as individual pathologies.

## Individualised Pathology

Our conceptions of the normal are not simply generalisations derived from our accumulated experience of normal people; instead, criteria of normality are developed by experts on the basis of their claims to scientific knowledge about the human condition (Rose 1990; Slee 1995). The concept of the normal has not been gleaned from studies of the normal; rather, it has taken shape around the study of those who were perceived to deviate from the normal – the troubled, the delinquent, the impaired (Rose 1990). In the field of disability, the construction of individual pathology performs several functions in relation to how problems are defined: it masks their political and economic roots; it turns attention away from their institutional contexts; it provides a locus for the exercise of professional expertise; and it facilitates the employment of a rhetoric of care and cure.

Two threads run through the ideology and practices of normalisation as they are expressed in different parts of the social system. Firstly, as we have seen, they represent a distinct move away from the segregated residential approaches of the nineteenth and twentieth centuries and the care and treatment practices with which those institutions were associated. Secondly, this shift invoked points of reference that were based on taken-for-granted assumptions about normal structures and relations. There is no doubt that normalisation represented a challenge to the prejudice and discrimination that sought to exclude disabled people from mainstream society (Booth 1988). At the same time, however, ideologies and practices of normalisation continued to be driven by an understanding that defined disability as individual pathology and that granted privileged roles to professional experts (Slee 1995). Normalisation, as Meekosha and Jakobowicz put it, is 'a form of paternalistic reform ... albeit clothed in the language of a liberation movement' (1996: 80).

The reference to the use of language is revealing since language is the key medium for transforming difference into pathology. Because of its power to generate and fix meaning in the social world, disability activists, theorists and researchers have become sensitised to ways in which language is used. Particular criticism has been levelled at the use of explicitly pathologising terminology in relation to disability (Barnes *et al.* 1999). Despite this, however, pathologising language continues to appear, even in contexts where particular care and attention are given to its use. Examples of this may found in the definitions of disability employed in recent legislation in Ireland (Education Act 1998; Equal Status Act 2000; see also Chapter 7 below).

As I have already suggested, language and terminology were crucial factors in the principle of normalisation. Wolfensberger and Thomas propose that one of the major goals of normalisation would be achieved by '[p]resenting, managing, addressing, labelling, and interpreting' individuals and the social systems in which they were located in a manner that enhanced their social images, and by '[s]haping cultural values, attitudes, and stereotypes, so as to elicit maximal feasible acceptance of individual differences' in society (1987: 11). While this position represented a challenge to marginalisation and oppression, it failed to address more deep-rooted inequalities. As some disability theorists have argued, while attitudes and values are relevant, material structures are of crucial importance in the creation of disability (Oliver 1990; Barnes 1996). Moreover, disabled people are not convinced that 'enhanced social images' are suffi-cient to achieve more equitable life chances; hence the case for anti-discrimination legislation 'with an appropriate mechanism to enforce it' (Barnes 1992: 20).

Paradoxically, normalising practices can lead to an increase as well as a reduction in the extent to which individuals are pathologised. This can be seen in processes of integration in education. Students likely to be mainstreamed are those who are expected 'to fit in' and 'be able to cope' and whose prospects depend largely upon their capacity to negotiate the existing mainstream system. This is a form of sponsored mobility (Turner 1961) that provides selected students with opportunities to acquire the for-mal educational credentials offered in mainstream schooling and reduces the possibility of those students being labelled. However, students who are deemed 'not ready', or for whom integration is thought to be 'impractical' or 'unrealistic', are consequently even more excluded, more stigmatised and more distanced from the mainstream school.

Nevertheless, normalisation has proved to be very durable in terms of ideology and practice in the social services. It attracted professionals because it was congruent with the notion of professional expertise as an authoritative, diagnostic and humane activity and was easily incorporated into expert practices. It appealed to policy makers because its programmes suggested reform without constituting a radical challenge to existing structures and relations. It was acceptable to politicians because it seemed to underwrite cheaper and more effective responses than were available through the existing services. Above all, normalisation was presented as a progressive and humanitarian alternative to the inequalities of segregation and residential institutionalisation.

## Humanitarianism

A major claim of professional expertise is that its practices are framed in humane ethical values (Rose 1996). Professionals are assumed to be ser-vice oriented with a commitment to use their knowledge and skills on behalf of the needs of their clients. Moreover, they claim that the extended training and education they receive and the specialised knowledge and skills they possess puts them in a position to interpret the needs of their clients objectively and 'to know better what is good for the client than the client himself' (Skrtic 1995: 7).

This humane perspective, however, is contingent on disabled people accepting the interpretation of disability, the definition of the problem and the framing of the solution proposed by the professional. Refusal or resistance is likely to give rise to a further pathologising of the individual and to be interpreted as proof of their difficulties – a failure to come to terms with the disability, an incomplete negotiation of the process of adjustment, or a manifestation of anger at being the victim of a tragedy (Oliver 1996a). The issue of humanitarianism is a thorny one since it is bound up with notions of solidarity and affect, values that traditionally have been excluded from the rationalist and positivist discourses that have dominated social theory (Nussbaum 1995). It is further complicated by the fact that coercive and oppressive social measures are frequently cloaked in humanitarian rhetoric (Foucault 1977) and that expressions of concern and promises of improvement and reform are often not transformed into substantive action (McDonnell 2000).

The normalisation project in relation to disability illustrates some of the difficulties associated with the operation of expertise and service within a framework of humanitarian values. Wolfensberger's principle of normalisation identified negative societal attitudes and prejudices as the source of the devaluation and exclusion of disabled people. Although this challenged essentialist understandings of disability, it failed to address, with the same degree of vigour, the reality of discriminatory social structures. It assumed that a change of professional hearts and minds would be sufficient to effect a transformation in the lives of disabled people in a materially unequal society. However, it is possible for positive and humanitarian attitudes to co-exist alongside profoundly unequal economic relations and, as Oliver contends, better attitudes do not in themselves guarantee better life chances for disabled people (1990).

The integration movement in education reflects similar difficulties and contradictions. It fits into the broad debate about equality of opportunity that has been central to research and analysis in education over the past forty years and, in particular, can be seen as a reaction against the inequalities of segregated special schooling. Studies such as those carried out by Coard (1971) and Mercer (1974) have shown that working-class and black children and children from other ethnic groups were over-represented in the special school sector. Integration emerged in opposition to segregated schooling and ensured that at least some disabled pupils would have access to a comprehensive curriculum, have opportunities to participate in the everyday activities of mainstream school life, and circumvent the labelling associated with special schooling. However, as I have indicated, integration is a selective practice that has disabling side effects and is based on assimilation rather than on the recognition of difference.

Although the normalisation project was informed by humanitarian principles in that it 'contributed a framework designed to reverse the negative effects of institutional malpractice' (Brown and Smith 1992: 151), it was also driven by a conviction that professionals knew what was best for disabled people. There were no channels for the articulation of disabled people's perspectives; neither was it easy for service users to challenge the definitions, assessments or treatments decided on by professionals. Normalisation was a paternalistic rather than a reciprocal project. Service users were expected 'to behave in an accommodating way ... to "obey" rather than challenge their care givers' (Walmsley 1989: 5).

## NORMALISATION AND RESISTANCE

Two aspects of resistance are evident in the context of normalisation. On the one hand, normalisation challenged the institutional and segregative social service model that had been developed and consolidated in Western society over the century from 1850 to 1950. The challenges came from three quarters: firstly, from elements within the professions that had overseen, supported and gained from institutionalisation; secondly, from disciplines outside medicine, the field of knowledge that had provided the main conceptual underpinning for institutionalisation; and thirdly from organisations of services users, their advocates and their supporters. In turn, the ideology and practice of normalisation itself began to be questioned as a result of a growing awareness among disabled people of its limits and inequities.

Of the areas that provide the focus of analysis in this chapter – mental illness, learning difficulties and special education – the most sustained and widely researched critique of residential segregation has been in relation to mental illness. In the asylum phase, mental illness was believed to be biological in origin and treatment and therefore necessitated some form of physical intervention. During the 1960s a number of critics from within psychiatry, such as Szasz (1961), Laing (1967) and Cooper (1968), rejected this biologically informed approach and its coercive responses and proposed instead services that were based on voluntary psychological approaches in community settings (Pilgrim and Rogers 1999). Residential institutions and the asylum tradition also came under attack from studies conducted from sociological (Goffman 1961) and historical (Foucault 1971; Rothman 1983; Scull 1979) perspectives. These studies challenged the humanitarian, progressive claims of the medical model of mental illness and argued that dominant practices were primarily about the segregation and social control of a problem population.

In challenging established practices, the anti-psychiatry movement, however, did not so much empower service users as create alternative sets of expert practices. Because expert theory and practice are so deeply implicated in both the creation and the criticism of processes of definition, identification and treatment, resistance among service users to professional perspectives in the field of mental health has been particularly hard to develop and sustain. Professional expertise resists the acceptance of lay knowledge. And since its legitimacy is premised on the idea of prolonged education and training, grounded in science, and codified in a curriculum of formal study, professional expertise cannot admit points of view that fall outside its jurisdiction. To do so would undercut the very basis of its authority.

In spite of these difficulties, associations of 'survivors of psychiatric systems' are a growing phenomenon and have managed to exert some practical influence on research, participation and funding in mental health services (Pilgrim and Rogers 1999: 202–4). The main stimulus to service users' movements has come from civil libertarian objections to the coercive role of psychiatry in society. These movements are heterogeneous and reflect a variety of ideological positions on how mental health should be conceptualised, on relations with professionals, and on forms of treatment. Despite these differences, survivor movements have given rise to user-led services, self-help groups as well as user-defined forms of intervention, service provision and treatment (Wilson and Beresford 2002).

With regard to services for people with learning difficulties, the professional challenge to segregated institutions (Nirje 1969; Wolfensberger 1972) received crucial support from organisations of parents. Indeed, parent and advocate groups such as the International League of Societies for the Mentally Handicapped played a leading role in disseminating normalisation concepts and practices (Trent 1994). In Ireland, voluntary organisations of parents and their supporters were particularly influential in the normalisation movement, not only in providing information but also in being directly involved in funding, establishing and running new facilities (Robins 1992; Dept. of Education 1993). Services for people with learning difficulties were overwhelmingly residential until the late 1950s when the first 'day educational and care facilities' began to be established by voluntary groups (Robins 1986: 195).

The shift towards integration in education in Ireland was also strongly influenced by a preference among parents for community based rather than residential facilities. The first stage of normalisation during the 1960s and 1970s was represented by the establishment of separate day facilities for pupils perceived to have special needs. From the 1970s, however, a further pattern of provision began to emerge when pupils were placed either in special classes attached to mainstream schools or within mainstream classes (McGee 1990). Up to the late 1990s, the number of pupils in special schools remained relatively stable, while those in special classes attached to mainstream schools more than doubled (McDonnell 2003). During the same period, there was only a small increase in the number of pupils with special needs enrolled in ordinary classes in mainstream schools (Dept. of Education and Science 2001).

Normalisation represented a shift towards community based facilities, that is, a form of provision constituted on a relatively smaller scale and situated in the locality rather than at a distance. But community based provision does not necessarily mean a relatively greater degree of inclusion for disabled people. As we have seen, although the pattern of development in integration, for example, did indicate normalising tendencies, it also generated considerable degrees of resistance on the part of mainstream schools. Thus, normalising practices in special education often resulted in *re-* rather than *de*institutionalisation – the creation of segregated, community based provision to replace centralised residential facilities.

Provision for pupils with learning difficulties remains largely segregated, albeit in special classes rather than special schools (McDonnell 2003) and there is very strong resistance to dispensing altogether with segregated facilities. As the members of Special Education Review Committee put it, 'we favour as much integration as is appropriate and feasible with as little segregation as is necessary' (Dept. of Education 1993: 22). What is 'appropriate', 'feasible' or 'necessary' is determined by relations of power and the politics of presence in arenas where policies are made and decisions taken. These arenas are likely to be occupied by non-disabled professionals and educational mediators whose interests do not necessarily coincide with the interests of disabled people. Similarly, in mental health services, professionals have been reluctant to dispense with hospital based treatment (Pilgrim and Rogers 1999).

## CONCLUSION

Although the principle of normalisation has been most specifically applied to policy development and implementation in the field of disability, it has also been used more broadly in the social services sector. In this more general sense, normalisation represented a challenge to centralised, custodial institutions and was expressed in different ways in different services. In the field of mental health, normalisation was related to deinstitutionalisation and the idea of community care, and in special education with the integration movement. But normalisation involved more than a change in institutional structures. It was underwritten by a discourse of professional expertise and had an important function in the regulation of disabled people.

Normalising ideology and practices were directed at both environments and individuals. The community represented the normal environment as opposed to the centralised institution, while normal care was family or family-like care. Disability was perceived to be the product of the interaction between an individual condition and a set of negative social and professional attitudes in relation to that condition. It was assumed that the major barrier to the social integration of disabled people was to be found in prejudicial attitudes and perceptions. Normalising solutions, therefore, were concentrated, firstly, on fostering positive professional and public attitudes towards devalued people and, secondly, on normalising the individual conditions that had given rise to negative perceptions.

The ideology and practices of normalisation were grounded in professional expertise. Professionals defined, identified and evaluated the problem and determined the shape of solutions. Despite the fact that normalisation incorporated a social dimension in its perspectives, disability was still perceived to refer to a difference that was pathological in nature. The object of normalising expertise was to remove or diminish that difference. Normalisation opposed the abuses and degradation of the total institution and drew upon the image of the modern, enlightened professional battling against the forces of ignorance and intolerance (Robins 1986). The rhetoric of humanitarianism and social progress proved to be a powerful device for masking professional interests. The transfer of mental health services from the asylum to the general hospital was justified in terms of deinstitutionalisation and community care; in reality, this meant the integration of the psychiatric profession rather than the integration of people with mental illness (Pilgrim and Rogers 1999).

Normalisation bridged the gap between modern and postmodern institutional responses to disability. In doing so, it encompassed both continuity and change. Continuity is reflected in the enduring dominance of centralised, segregated, psycho-medical responses to disability. In relation to mental illness, the continuing and substantial presence of hospital based in-patient responses which retain their coercive orientation is more about mental pathology than mental health (Pilgrim and Rogers 1999: 162–3). Change is evident in the parallel, though smaller presence of a looser set of structures and systems that were more dispersed and flexible, and were situated in normal settings. In special needs education similar kinds of continuity and change are evident. Segregated special schooling remains a significant presence in the educational landscape. At the same time more diverse, individualistic programmes may be found in normal classrooms, supported by specially designed pupil programmes and special needs assistant personnel. Normalisation has indeed underwritten a continuum of services that maintains the traditional segregated institution in the background.

The ideology of normalisation failed to recognise and acknowledge the importance of difference. In fact, the main objective of normalising practices was the eradication or attenuation of difference; normalisation was perceived to have worked when disabled people had 'passed as normal' in the community. A disability rights perspective, emerging in the same political and social contexts, contested the ideology and practices of normalisation. Disabled activists and theorists highlighted the fact that the key issues were the recognition of difference rather than its assimilation, the representation of disabled people's perspectives rather than the exercise of expertise, and the belief that the material as much as the conceptual world was at the root of discrimination and inequality.

NOTES

1. Due to the relatively slow pace of social policy development in Ireland for much of the post-war period, there were evident time lapses between the introduction of normalising policy measures (deinstitutionalisation in relation to mental illness and integration in education, for example) in the field of disability in the US and Britain, for example, and their appearance in Ireland. Nevertheless, when these did emerge in Ireland, the conceptual frameworks, the theoretical perspectives, and the practices recommended tended to mirror their international counterparts quite closely. While such an international exchange of ideas had been a notable feature of the nineteenth century, they became particularly marked during the post-war period. For similar influences in education, see Drudy and Lynch (1993: 64).

2. An advisory committee on the education of deaf and hard-of-hearing children in Ireland was established by the Minister for Education and Science Noel Dempsey in December 2001. Some of the historical tensions and differing perspectives in relation to this topic were reflected in the decision, in 2004, of the then Minister Mary Hannafin to disband the committee. In 2006 the newly appointed National Council for Special Education was invited to complete the work of the advisory committee. Subsequently, the Centre for Deaf Studies at Trinity College Dublin was awarded the tender to review the existing documentation and compile a report (Leeson 2007).

# 7

# Disability and Equality

There is little doubt that during the latter half of the twentieth century our understanding of disability and the complex process of disablement has been transformed. Since the emergence of the international disabled people's movement in the late 1960s, traditional individualistic medical explanations for the various economic and social deprivations encountered by disabled people and their families have gradually given way to a more socio/political account widely referred to as the 'social model of disability'.... Mike Oliver first coined the phrase in 1983 to reflect the growing demand by disabled people for:

> ... nothing more fundamental than a switch away from focusing on the physical limitations of particular individuals to the way the physical and social environments impose limitations on certain groups or categories of people (Oliver 1983: 23).

Since then much has been written about the social model by both activists and writers from within and without the disabled people's movement. The result has been that the social model has been a, if not the, major catalyst for the increasing politicisation of large numbers of disabled people and their allies throughout the world ... It has also provided a firm foundation for the development of a fully formed 'materialist' account of the social creation of disability in the modern world ... as well as a workable analytical framework with which to understand and explain the particular type of institutional discrimination encountered by people labelled 'disabled' because of perceived impairment ...

Colin Barnes (2000), 'A Working Social Model?
Disability, Work and Disability Politics in the 21st Century',
*Critical Social Policy*, 20(4): 441, 443.

INTRODUCTION

In the preceding chapters I have discussed a series of organising
ideologies that have shaped the relationship between disability and
society – exclusion, medicalisation, institutionalisation, eugenic theory
and normalisation. I have explored how these ideologies have interacted with another set of legitimating ideologies in which, for example,
disability is perceived to be an individualised and pathological deficit
or condition, a matter for expert evaluation and intervention, and the
assumed object of humanitarian progress. In this chapter, I discuss a
conceptual framework that adopts a very different perspective on disability – a social model of disability – that is, the idea of disability as
a form of oppression that invokes responses premised on rights, social
justice and equality. In addition, this framework represents an insider
perspective; it derives from the experiences and theorising of disabled
people themselves and their allies (Campbell and Oliver 1996; Oliver
1996).

That disability can be seen as an equality issue has given rise to new
ways of understanding the relationship between disability and society. A
great deal of recent work, especially in the field of disability studies,
describes disability as a form of social, political and cultural oppression
(Barton 1996; Davis 1997; Shakespeare 1998; Barnes *et al.* 1999; Thomas
1999; Tregaskis 2002; Barnes and Mercer 2003). Accordingly, theorists
and activists refer to disablism in the same way that they would refer to
oppressions such as sexism or racism. This social model of disability has
involved a very significant shift in focus from individual conditions to
environmental barriers, and has already had some impact on public policy
and perceptions of disability (European Commission 1999;
Eurobarometer 2001; National Disability Authority 2002). It constitutes a
challenge to a long established medical model of disability which, nevertheless, continues to exert considerable influence on policy and practice
(McDonnell 2000; 2003).

According to the medical model, disability is a personal and limiting
characteristic of the individual – some abnormality, disorder or deficiency
is perceived to cause the disability (Oliver 1990; Barnes and Mercer 2003).
Thus, disability is understood to be a personal problem of and for the individual concerned, and solutions are offered primarily in terms of individual (re)adjustment. The key practices in this approach are identification

(finding out what the condition is), assessment (measuring its extent), categorisation (allocating the individual to a group with a similar or related condition), and rehabilitation (professional intervention aimed at overcoming or minimising the condition). The purpose and expectation of these measures is that individuals will eventually accommodate, to a greater or lesser extent, to their environments.

Practices informed by the medical model are usually conducted in a clinical/medical setting and, while the applied expertise may involve professionals of various kinds, it generally reflects a hierarchy of knowledge dominated by medical personnel and by medical discourse. If individuals oppose this perspective, the rejection is construed as a denial of the reality of their 'condition' and is interpreted as an unsatisfactory form of adjustment (Oliver 1990). Within the medical model, of course, some problems are regarded as having their source in society rather than in the individual. Problems of this kind, however, tend to be characterised as stemming from the prejudices and attitudes of others, rather than from the material structures of society. As a result, interventions are frequently couched in terms of programmes and projects designed to raise awareness and to change mind-sets rather than material conditions.

From the 1960s the beginnings of an alternative perspective on disability began to appear (Barnes 1996; 1998; Tregaskis 2002). Although this perspective or model took somewhat different forms in different places and at different times, the forms all shared several important features. Firstly, they made a distinction between impairment and disability and challenged the idea of disability as personal deficit or tragic condition. Secondly, they defined disability as the product of a relationship between individuals and society and proposed that disability was the end result of exclusionary social structures and relations, in terms of architecture, occupational procedures, value systems, economic practices, educational services, social policies, legal processes, and so on. As Harlan Hahn put it, 'disability stems from the failure of a structured social environment to adjust to the needs and aspirations of citizens with disabilities *rather* than from the inability of a disabled individual to adapt to the demands of society' (1986: 128). A social model submits that it is not the fact that a person must use a wheelchair that signifies a disability; rather, it is an environment of steps and narrow doors that creates a disability. Thus, the emergence of a social model shifted the focus of analysis from individuals and perceived impairments to environments, inclusion and rights.

Disability theorists have identified three distinct challenges to the medical model of disability (Oliver 1990; Barnes 1996; 1998). One, drawing on structural functionalist and social deviance theories in sociology, defined disability as a social construct. Barnes (1996; 1998) identifies this approach as primarily American, emerging during the late 1960s and early 1970s and owing much to the Independent Living Movement and the ideology of normalisation. Its advocates argued that disability is a product of modern industrial society: in which hostile physical and social environments restrict the rights and freedoms of disabled people (De Jong 1979); in which the modern state uses an administrative notion of disability to control access to the welfare system (Stone 1984); in which human service industries must create disability dependency in order to remain in existence (Wolfensberger 1972; 1989); and in which the multi-million-dollar 'disability business' produces clients and consumers (Albrecht 1992).

The main criticism of this approach has been that it is premised on 'free' market assumptions of self-sufficiency and consumer choice while ignoring the inequalities of that market and the crucial role that Western capitalism has played in the creation of disability (Oliver 1990; Barnes 1996; 1998). This second approach is based on materialist grounds and defines disability as a social creation, the product of modern capitalist society. Where a social constructionist perspective tends to locate the problem in the mind-set of able-bodied society – in attitudes, beliefs and values – a social creationist perspective emphasises material structures and institutions (Oliver 1990). Barnes (1996) regards this latter approach as typical of a number of British authors, many of whom are disabled people themselves, such as Hunt (1966), Finkelstein (1980) and Oliver (1990). Oliver, who first coined the term 'social model of disability' (Barnes 2003: 4), argues that a core ideology of individualism and peripheral ideologies of medicalisation and rehabilitation underpinned the social creation of disability and were closely associated with capitalist development. Moreover, in capitalist societies, because of the way work shapes social relations and identity, and because disabled people are regarded as being unable to work at 'normal' rates and levels of productivity, they are defined as being dependent and in need.

The social model of disability has been instrumental in politicising disabled people and their allies throughout the world (Barnes 1998; 2000; Tregaskis 2002). It has provided a conceptual foundation for an analysis of the social creation/construction of disability in the modern world and has supplied a framework for understanding and explaining structures and processes of discrimination experienced by disabled people. However, social model theory is not without its critics, primarily from feminist and postmodernist standpoints. One line of criticism is that it constitutes a form of grand theorising and consequently has overlooked individual narratives and experiences in terms of gender (Morris 1993*a*; 1996; Thomas 1999), ethnicity (Stuart 1993; Begum *et al.* 1994), and impairment (French 1993; Hughes and Paterson 1997; Hughes 1999; Thomas and Corker 2002).

Thus, a third approach emphasises the cultural production and reproduction of disability through the representation and stigmatisation of disabled people as 'other', through negative imagery in literature and the general media, and through disabling attitudes and values (Hevey 1992; Shakespeare 1994; Barnes 1996; 1998; Peters 1996; Wendell 1996; Corker and Shakespeare 2002). Several critics acknowledge the contribution of the social model to changing public policies and perspectives on disability and point out that their intention is to develop and expand rather than undermine social model explanations (French 1993; Shakespeare and Watson 1997; Thomas 1999; Tregaskis 2002). Others emphasise the need to undertake a social analysis of impairment in the context of discourses on the body and initiate a dialogue between disability and impairment (Hughes and Paterson 1997; Corker and French 1999; Hughes 1999; Corker and Shakespeare 2002). Barnes, however, warns that 'a potentially endless variety of competing and ever-changing discourses' will cloud the meaning of disability and its impact on economic, political and social lives of disabled people (2000: 444).

At a fundamental level, disability is about some form of inequality, whatever the differing emphases in social model theory. One way, therefore, of overcoming the problem identified by Barnes is to explore disability through an egalitarian framework. As we have noted, a very substantial body of evidence indicates that disabling oppressions and injustices are multidimensional. Not only do a disproportionate number of disabled people live in poverty, their lack of material resources is intimately connected with cultural marginalisation and exclusion from networks of power. For disabled people, the oppressions of misrecognition, powerlessness and poverty do not operate in any fixed order of precedence or importance. Rather, different inequalities are foregrounded in differing contexts and circumstances. Similarly, the affective dimension establishes a link between 'private troubles' and 'public issues' (Borsay 1986) and facilitates an analysis of the psychological and emotional fallout from disabling political, social, and cultural structures and practices. The affective dimension also opens a channel for the analysis of impairment as a social phenomenon. In brief, then, a multidimensional egalitarian analysis facilitates the holistic approach advocated by Thomas (1999).

In applying an egalitarian framework, I will draw on a conceptual model proposed by Lynch, Cantillon and Baker (2001) that identifies four core contexts in which inequalities can be generated and which operate through corresponding sets of social relations. These are: the economic context and relations of distribution and redistribution; the socio-cultural context and relations of respect and recognition; the political context and relations of power and representation and the affective context and relations of dependence and interdependence. In the following sections I will explore these four primary dimensions of equality in relation to disability with particular reference to recent discussion and policy development in Ireland.

## THE ECONOMIC CONTEXT AND ISSUES OF DISTRIBUTION AND REDISTRIBUTION

Issues of distribution and redistribution are important dimensions of equality. They raise particular questions about economic relations in society and the ways in which different kinds of resources, especially economic resources, are shared out. Although obviously interconnected with other dimensions of equality such as recognition and representation, for the purposes of the analysis here, I focus specifically on issues of distribution and redistribution. The economic resources that people can call upon play a crucial role in determining their life chances. Life chances in turn are closely connected to education and employment: education creates the primary route to paid employment and employment not only determines the level of one's income but also influences access to a whole range of other social, cultural and political opportunities and resources. In a medical model of disability, low levels of employment are accounted for in terms of individual deficits, limitations and inadequacies (Oliver 1990). In contrast, socio-political accounts explain unemployment and welfare dependency in terms of systematic exclusion (Barnes 1991; Dept. of Equality and Law Reform 1996).

The direct links involving disability, employment and poverty are well established (Dept. of Equality and Law Reform 1996; European Commission 1999; Conroy 2003; Harbison 2003; McManus 2003). On every major economic criterion, disabled people are worse off than their non-disabled peers. In an international context, disabled people as a social group are poorer than the general population; likewise, people living in poverty are significantly more likely to be disabled. With regard to Ireland, McManus observes that '[t]he risk of poverty in these households [where the reference person is 'ill/disabled'] is twice the average for all households' (2003: 62).

Harbison (2003) identifies three determining factors in the link between disability and poverty. Firstly, relatively lower education and employment levels lead to a loss of income. Even when educational levels are similar between disabled people and other groups, the former are still more likely to be unemployed (Neufeldt and Albright 1998). The relatively lower incomes received by disabled people reduce access to other resources such as housing, health and education. Secondly, impairment frequently involves additional costs for individuals and households with regard to medicines, equipment, and adaptations to buildings. There is also the further loss of earnings foregone by members of households who fulfil caring roles. Thirdly, factors such as the lack of appropriate transportation, problems of access to buildings, negative attitudes, and educational exclusion all create barriers to the world of work.

Current evidence suggests that rates of unemployment among disabled people in Ireland are significantly higher than in the population as a whole and that, where disabled people are in employment, it is often poorly paid and of low status. Only 40 per cent of those 'with a disability/health problem' between the ages of fifteen and sixty-four were in employment in 2002, compared with a rate of 65 per cent for the population as a whole in the same age category (CSO 2002: 1). In terms of disability only, surveys by disability organisations point to levels of over 70 per cent (Dept. of Equality and Law Reform 1996; National Rehabilitation Board 1994).

Exclusion of disabled people from the workforce results in a high level of dependency on social welfare payments and benefits in kind. Good (2003) estimates that 80 per cent of disabled people in Ireland depend to varying degrees on welfare provisions from a combination of state, non-government and private services. Welfare payments based on disability create both practical and ideological difficulties. Practical difficulties arise from the fragmented and unco-ordinated ways in which welfare is provided. This complex system is complicated further by a serious information deficit – a lack of information and of access to information – and the patchy and scattered nature of the information itself (Dept. of Equality and Law Reform 1996). In addition, the personal lives of people receiving welfare are subject to a degree of public scrutiny and judgement that does not apply to people whose incomes are derived from investments, salaries or wages.

Individuals and social groups whose main sources of income come through welfare payments are likely to be perceived and treated in negative ways. On the one hand, neo-liberal approaches to social policy have placed greater emphasis on paid work as the principal mechanism for the distribution of goods and services. On the other, the orientation to competition and individualism is particularly problematic for those who are excluded from the labour market by structural inequalities, discriminatory attitudes and stigmatisation (Cantillon *et al.* 2001). Within the ideology of the market, welfare provision is perceived to create dependency as well as a perception that those who receive welfare payments are exploiting a complacent system. With specific reference to disability, it is important to remember that such beliefs led to the eugenic oppression of disabled people in Western society for the greater part of the twentieth century (see Chapter 5).

The serious inequalities experienced by disabled people in the labour market have led to the development of policies based on three general principles (Conroy 2003; European Commission 1998; 1999): through legislation to prevent discrimination on the grounds of disability; through programmes of affirmative action in favour of disabled people; and through target or quota systems in which a certain percentage of positions are filled by workers categorised as disabled. Several EU countries, including Ireland, have introduced policies based on combinations of some or all of these principles (European Commission 1998). In Ireland, the Employment Equality Act (1998) constitutes an example of the legislative principle. In basic terms, the Act forbids discrimination against employ-ees, trainees or job seekers with a disability and obliges employers to do all that is reasonable to accommodate workers with a disability, subject to a nominal cost. As Conroy points out, the Act 'sets some economic rights in law. It shifts attention away from individual impairments to disabling environments. It conveys a message that discrimination is not tolerated' (2003: 52). On the other hand, there is no definition of what constitutes a nominal cost and no guidance is offered as to how such a cost might be estimated. While the Act effectively signals a shift towards a social model of disability, its understanding of disability is firmly based on medicalised notions of individual conditions, malfunctions and disfigurements.

Positive action that focuses on the supply side of labour covers a very wide range of practices, including advice and information services, voca-tional training schemes, disability awareness training programmes, sup-ported employment, and sheltered workshops (Barnes 2000; Conroy 2003). Among the major disappointments in this area, in terms of raising employment levels, has been the failure to capitalise on the very consid-erable investment in vocational training for disabled people under the European Social Fund between 1973 and 1993–94, especially since it pre-ceded a period of exceptional shortages in the Irish labour market (European Social Fund Evaluation Unit 1996; Kwiotek 1996; Conroy 2003). The total budget for training disabled people between 1973 and 1993–94 amounted to €615 million of which almost €360 million came directly from the European Social Fund. Evaluation of the programme showed that the majority of participants left training for reasons other than employment or further training, that the measures undertaken lacked clear aims and objectives and that there were serious mismatches between the expectations of the trainees, the nature of the training provided and the eventual outcomes (European Social Fund Evaluation Unit 1996). Furthermore, disabled people were excluded from well-paid and high sta-tus positions in the initiatives themselves (Murray 1998). The overall con-clusions of the evaluation seem to bear out Oliver's charge that there is a professional basis for the creation of dependency and that 'in a fundamen-tal sense it is professionals who are dependent upon disabled people ... for their jobs, their salaries, their subsidised transport, their quality of life and so on' (1990: 90–1).

More recently, however, under a supported work initiative, the unequal and unprotected status of disabled people in sheltered workshops has begun to be addressed. Heretofore, disabled people in sheltered work-shops were not regarded as employees in terms of employee legislation. However, measures to integrate sheltered workshops into the labour market and to regulate wage rates, conditions of employment, and contracts are expected to be part of the new programme (Conroy 2003). While initiatives such as these represent an improvement on the past, because they tend to highlight the functional limitations of individuals, some critics regard their contribution as minimal and likely to do little to bring about substantive change (Hyde 1995; Barnes 2000).

The idea of a percentage target or quota refers to a form of affirmative action or positive discrimination that focuses on the demand side of the labour market and has a significant presence in several member states of the EU (European Commission 1999). Advocates of intervention of this kind point to the success of government intervention in including disabled people in the UK workforce in the period 1939–45 and afterwards (Barnes 2000). In Ireland, a 3 per cent voluntary quota system in the civil and public services has been in operation since 1977 (Dept. of Equality and Law Reform). Although widely endorsed by successive governments, employer bodies and trade unions, the 3 per cent target has not been achieved by all public service employers (Conroy and Fanagan 2001). Reporting on the success or otherwise of this system is difficult since it depends on the consent of employees to be categorised as disabled. One of the major drawbacks of quota systems operating in many European countries (European Commission 1999) is the tendency for employers to favour applicants with what are perceived to be 'less severe disabilities' (Samorodov 1996, cited in Conroy 2003: 50).

In terms of a general pattern of change, the EU has been slow to implement legally binding measures to prevent or reduce discrimination against disabled people in the world of work. However, article 13 of the Treaty of Amsterdam, ratified in 1997 together with a directive under this article adopted in 2000, represent a step forward (Conroy 2003). The latter measure has particular significance for Ireland in that it is based on reasonable accommodation for disabled persons without reference to nominal costs. It does, however, stipulate that employers are not obliged to accommodate to the extent that it entails a disproportionate burden. In terms of an equality framework, these developments can be seen as moving economic opportunities for disabled people somewhat beyond the boundary of formal equality (Baker 1998). However, the fact that a doubling of

participation rates of disabled people in the Irish workforce will be necessary in order to achieve a level of parity with non-disabled workers
(Conroy 2003), indicates that economic equality has not yet reached even
a modest level of liberal equality.

A more radical approach to the issue of economic equality questions
the centrality given to the meaning and organisation of work in Western
society, whereby the ability to labour in some socially recognised way is
seen as a requirement for full membership of society (Abberley 1996;
Barnes 2000). Work is regarded as central in establishing an identity: the
work you do tells who you are. Participation in the workforce is a condition of social inclusion and consequently the demand for access to work
is seen as crucial in the struggle for equality. Abberley points out that
making the capacity to perform work a condition of citizenship is fraught
with difficulties. He argues that even if societies make sincere and profound attempts to integrate disabled people into the workforce, some will
still be excluded and 'in any possible work-based Utopia, will not be capable of producing goods or services of social value' (1996: 71).

Barnes (2000) argues that social inclusion must involve a redefinition
of work. The manner in which work is organised in Western society –
around the pursuit and maximisation of profits, waged labour and competition between individual workers – effectively disables people with any
perceived form of functional limitation or impairment. But it is possible
to organise work around more inclusive principles such as social necessity, obligation and interdependence. Barnes (2000) goes on to identify
practical ways in which this might be done. Grants, currently given to the
voluntary sector, for example, could be reserved for organisations controlled and run by disabled people who have an admirable record in
employing disabled people (Oliver and Barnes 1998). Interestingly, in its
report on training for disabled people in the European Union, the European
Social Fund Evaluation Unit (1996: 112) recommended the promotion of
policies to encourage disabled people to become providers of goods and
services in the field of training. The expansion of user-led services in the
UK, such as the employment of personal assistants and sign language
interpreters, has meant that more and more disabled people are involved in
service provision of one kind or another (Barnes 2000; Barnes and Mercer
2006). User-led services also help to promote civil rights for disabled people and to ensure that 'you get what you want, not what other people want
for you' (Morris 1994: 1). Barnes (2000) argues that reconceptualising

the meaning of work is not unknown in modern societies. The women's movement, for example, has successfully redefined work to include housework and childcare. In this context, the emergence of the disability arts movement has generated a range of cultural activities involving disabled and non-disabled participants and has established the possibility of creating identities and lifestyles not determined by the 'ability to participate in a labour market constructed around conventional able bodied/minded ideals' (Barnes 2000: 453).

Another significant aspect of the economic dimension of disability involves the distribution of services. The class based two-tier health service operating in Ireland demonstrates that the affluent members of society get first call on the health services (O'Shea and Gillespie 2006; Tussing and Wren 2006). What is true of the health services in general, is also true for the mental health sector in particular. Recent studies of service provision in mental health report large-scale inequalities in terms of access to services and resources (Amnesty International 2003; Tussing and Wren 2006). People experiencing the greatest levels of deprivation and disadvantage receive the most poorly developed services; most resources are directed at the most affluent. An earlier study found that unskilled manual workers were four times more likely than higher professionals to be admitted to hospital for the first time for schizophrenia (Barry *et al.* 2001: 7).

In addition to concerns about economic marginalisation, during the 1990s increasing attention has been given to the social and cultural dimensions of discrimination experienced by disabled people (Hevey 1992; Barnes 1996; Shakespeare 1994; 1996). These studies, which are closely related to the focus on 'the politics of recognition' in the work of theorists such as Fraser (1995; 2000) and Baker *et al.* (2004), demonstrate how processes such as cultural domination, misrepresentation and stereotyping cause distinct kinds of disability inequality.

## THE SOCIO-CULTURAL CONTEXT AND ISSUES OF RESPECT AND RECOGNITION

The respect and recognition dimensions of equality are principally concerned with social and cultural relations in society. Injustices experienced by some groups in society, though frequently related to economic inequalities, can have distinctive socio-cultural roots (Young 1990; Fraser 1995;

Lynch *et al.* 2001; Baker, *et al.* 2004; Thompson 2006). Indeed, as Fraser (1995; 2000) has argued, claims for the recognition of difference have, to a great extent, displaced claims for redistribution as the primary egalitarian struggle. Nevertheless, it is clear from the discussion in the preceding section that the dynamics of respect and recognition are intimately connected with the material and financial circumstances of the lives of disabled people. As Sayer (2003) points out, since recognition implies an effort to live and act in ways that deserve recognition, it is connected to the need to be able to access material conditions that support such ways of living and acting.

The overlapping of economic and socio-cultural inequalities is especially evident in Young's analysis of marginalisation (1990). For Young, marginalisation constitutes one of the most dangerous forms of oppression. Members of marginalised social groups not only experience poverty, they also risk a loss of self-respect because they are excluded from useful participation in ordinary social life. Through welfare payments they are made into dependants and their lives are subject to detailed scrutiny by the social services. There is no arena where they can legitimately contest and counter such actions and practices; their expected role is to accept and obey what they are ordered to do.

Cultural imperialism, another 'face of oppression' identified by Young, has a more direct significance for disabled people in the context of respect and recognition. In cultural imperialism, the dominant meanings and values in society render other meanings and values invisible or, where they are visible, they are stigmatised and devalued as 'other'. The experiences and values of the dominant group are universalised and instituted as normal because this group has access to, and control of, the means of communication and interpretation. Through cultural stereotyping, the differences manifested by minority groups are characterised as inferior or deviant and members of these groups find themselves defined from the outside. Their images of themselves are influenced by the judgements of the dominant group and, as a result, they experience a double consciousness. From an insider perspective, minority group members may see themselves as having great potential, being full of hope and capable of achievement. But the message they receive from the dominant culture is that they are inferior, dependent 'children of a lesser god' (Medoff 1982).

For three decades or more, disabled theorists and researchers and their allies have been arguing, firstly, that conceptual frameworks derived from

medical and individualised models of disability have created a basis for
the marginalisation and oppression of disabled people and, secondly, that
alternative theoretical models must be developed if inclusive and more
egalitarian policies and services are to be established (Hahn 1985; Borsay
1986; Abberley 1987; Oliver 1990; Barnes 1991; Morris 1991). Despite
these critiques, psycho-medical definitions of disability continue to exert
the most powerful influence on social and cultural practices in Ireland,
and misrecognition, invisibility and a lack of respect towards disabled
people have characterised institutional and administrative structures and
practices.

Several recent instances in legislation, planning and policy-making
demonstrate these socio-cultural inequalities. One blunt example is the
manner in which disability is defined in recent Irish legislation such as the
Education Act 1998, the Employment Equality Act 1998 and the Equal
Status Act 2000. Further examples of misrecognition and trivialisation are
evident in the Green Paper on Education (Dept. of Education 1992), in a
discussion paper (Dept. of Education and Science 1999), and in the Report
on Arrangements for the Assessment of Candidates with Special Needs in
Certificate Examinations (Dept. of Education and Science 2000).
According to section 2 of the Equal Status Act, disability means:

a)  the total or partial absence of a person's bodily or mental func-
    tions, including the absence of a part of the person's body;
b)  the presence in the body of organisms causing, or likely to cause,
    chronic disease or illness;
c)  the malfunction, malformation or disfigurement of a part of a per-
    son's body;
d)  a condition or malfunction which results in a person learning dif-
    ferently from a person without the condition or malfunction; or
e)  a condition, illness or disease which affects a person's thought
    processes, perception of reality, emotions or judgement, or which
    results in disturbed behaviour.

Psycho-medical definitions of this kind locate the problem within the
individual and construct disability as a form of pathology. As a result, the
socio-political relationship between people and their environments is
obscured, and circumstances that, from a socio-political point of view,
constitute experiences of discrimination and inequality are transformed

into individual deficits (Swain *et al.* 1993; Phtiaka 1997; Vlachou 1997; Persson, 1998). By defining people in terms of given problems, service providers, for example, are then predisposed to interpret any difficulties that arise as being due to the perceived limitations or deficiencies of the people for whom the service is intended.

Legislators responsible for the Education, Employment Equality and Equal Status Acts ignored the theorising and the conclusions of disabled people themselves. The option to employ definitions based on the perspectives of psycho-medical experts marginalised disabled people and rendered invisible at least twenty-five years of critical research and commentary – often by disabled people themselves. The incorporation of a medical model of disability in the legislation is an example of cultural imperialism that dismisses the perspectives of disabled people, misrepresents their concerns and breaches a fundamental principle of equality.

The Green Paper on Education (Dept. of Education 1992) provides a second example of socio-cultural inequality. It contains an extensive discussion on gender and equity in education and acknowledges the existence of gender bias in the educational system. It stresses the need for schools to be alert to the influence of the hidden curriculum in reinforcing stereotypes and to ensure that the achievements and contributions of women are emphasised in the curriculum. The report notes the absence of women from positions of authority and power in the education system and stresses the need for appropriate role models if girls and young women 'are to develop themselves to their full potential' (Dept. of Education 1992: 70). The report then goes on to outline a detailed programme to promote gender equity in education.

The Green Paper also demonstrated an awareness that equity in relation to disability was an issue for the educational system and emphasised the need for greater equality, 'especially for those who are disadvantaged ... physically or mentally' (Dept. of Education 1992: 5). There was, however, a requirement to explore the view that 'disability is the result of disabling political and social processes which treat a functional impairment as a reason to disadvantage or marginalise individuals' (Cooney 1995: 249). The report, however, failed to consider any discussion or analysis along those lines. Moreover, although the Green Paper proposed a programme of affirmative action to address the problem of gender inequality, no similar programme was suggested for dealing with the inequalities that existed in relation to disability.[1] An obvious question is, if a programme of affirmative action was thought to be necessary to work towards gender equality, why wasn't a similar programme proposed in relation to disability? It appears that the concerns of disabled people were trivialised and the case for disability equality was not taken seriously.

Instances of misrecognition and cultural imperialism are also evident in the stigmatising language and terminology used in psycho-medical discourses on disability (Christensen 1996; Peters 1996; Swain and Cameron 1999). Language both reflects and shapes how we perceive and understand our world and its role in political and social processes has been recognised by many of the new social movements seeking human and civil rights. Just as it is in relation to gender (Spender 1980), race (Labov 1973), and ethnicity (Cummins 1984), language is also a site of cultural struggle with regard to disability. Just as the term 'black' has been redefined in a way that valorises and recognises its reference group, terms such 'Deaf' (Wrigley 1996) and 'disabled' (Oliver 1990; Brennan *et al.* 1991) have been redefined to convey political and cultural values.

There are a number of ways of looking at the relationship between language and disability. Firstly, as we have stressed, disability rights theorists and activists attach considerable importance to definitions and terminology. They have drawn attention to negative connotations associated with deficit laden terms and to the ways in which language usage can reinforce notions of helplessness and dependency (Barnes 1992; 1992*a*). In this analysis, language and terminology are seen as more than surface features of disability relations. Acts of naming and explaining are central to identity; the capacity to define oneself, to name one's own world and experiences and to have these definitions and accounts accepted are regarded as crucial elements in the politics of recognition and representation (Young 1990; Lynch *et al.* 2001). Oliver (cited in Brennan *et al.* 1991: 44) argues that 'disabled people know only too well that taking control of what they are going to be called is not a triviality. It is much more important than that; it's part of a wider process of empowering ourselves to take control of all aspects of our lives.'

A second way of looking at the issue is to suggest that what something is called is not the key issue. Instead, what matters is the underlying set of deep structures and relations – such as who is named and who does the naming – to which particular uses of language and terminology refer. Thus, a simple change of terminology without a corresponding change in deep structures will make no substantial difference to the lives of disabled people. In tracing the changing terminology used to refer to some disabled people – from idiocy, feeble-mindedness, mental subnormality and mental handicap, to learning impairments and intellectual disabilities – Jenkins (1998) notes that, while the most recent term is assumed to be superior, it does not necessarily carry a lesser stigma. The proper targets for struggle, therefore, are underlying structures and relations and when these are changed the appropriate language will follow.

A third argument draws attention to the ways in which the language of rights, introduced by disability activists and academics, can be co-opted or colonised for cosmetic purposes. In this way, important conceptual distinctions, such as that between 'disability' and 'impairment', may be glossed over. For example, the phrase 'people with disabilities' may be seen in a positive light. However, it also continues to convey the message that disability is an individual condition and thus masks or denies the socio-political causes of disability (Barnes 1992a). In the field of education, Slee discusses how the language of rights and equity can be deployed to provide token adjustments to traditional practices, to disempower disabled students, and to privilege 'those professionals who work "in their best interests"' (1996: 107). An acceptable surface is produced while disabling deep structures remain unchallenged and unexposed. Similarly, many current terms in special education deprive disability of its meaning as a socio-political indicator of inequality and discrimination and, for the most part, are employed only as more acceptable substitutes for 'handicap' (McDonnell 2000; 2003). Language, therefore, is significant not only in terms of its place in the politics of recognition and representation but also in terms of its potential as a rhetorical, masking or diversionary instrument. Of course it is important to use language that shows respect and consideration. The point here, however, is a different one and concerns the contested reality to which the term 'disability' refers. The fact that disability is still equated with psycho-medical conditions continues to direct the problematising gaze towards the individual rather than towards disabling professional practices or organisational structures.

Resistance to the erasure of the social and political dimensions of disability has come, firstly, from the demand by disabled people that their experience be recognised and, secondly, from the development of disability studies as an academic discipline in its own right. As Barnes *et al.* observe, the connections between the everyday struggles of disabled people and the scholarly work produced by disabled and non-disabled academics has allowed disability studies to 'challenge the traditional disciplines of medicine, sociology and psychology with regard to the legitimacy of the knowledge they have produced about disability' (2002: 252). However, the relationship between the disability movement and the academy is not straightforward (Oliver 1996). While direct experience of a social reality is important for developing a political response, to recognise as authentic only those voices that reflect direct experience runs the risk of marginalisation (Barnes *et al.* 2002: 253). Arguing that, by itself, direct experience is not enough, Finklestein (1996) maintains that the experience of disabling barriers must be linked to a political analysis that seeks to explain them and propose ways of eradicating them. Consequently, a reciprocal relationship is essential: the disability movement 'can provide the direct experience, the academy can provide a coherent … analysis' (Barnes *et al.* 2002: 253).

The prospect of establishing and sustaining a relationship of mutual recognition and respect between the disability movement and the academy is made all the more difficult by the traditional conservatism of the latter and by its claim to be the ultimate arbiter of what counts as meaningful knowledge. Moreover, the increasing marketisation of academic life, the emphasis on economic viability, and the intensification of links between academic activities and business interests not only calls into question the 'the very nature of what constitutes critical thought in university life' but increases the possibility that the work, ideas and experiences of disabled people will be colonised (Barnes *et al.* 2002: 256–7). The task of maintaining a constructive dialogue between the disability movement and the academy prompts two important questions: how can disability related academic activity be made both accessible and accountable to the wider community and how can grassroots activists acquire 'a presence' in the academy? These questions bring us to issues of power and representation and the third important dimension of an equality framework.

## THE POLITICAL CONTEXT AND ISSUES OF POWER AND REPRESENTATION

Representation is closely linked to issues of redistribution and recognition but is distinct from them. Representation is typically concerned with relations of power, dominance and subordination. It is particularly implicated in socio-political contexts where problems are defined and researched, where policy is made, where solutions to problems are devised and promoted, and where action may be undertaken to remedy lapses in the actual implementation of policy. With regard to disability, representation can be understood in a number of senses. A considerable amount of research has been carried out on the cultural aspects of representation, that is, how disability is defined and portrayed in different public media (Darke 1998; Barnes *et al.* 1999). Less attention has been given to the political dimensions of representation – the idea of 'voice' or 'presence', for example, in the making and implementation of policy. In this section, I concentrate on exploring the idea of representation as 'a politics of presence' (Phillips 1995), with particular reference to the domains of administrative and professional authority. I focus especially on ideas of empowerment and expertise in modern society, the tensions that may lie between them, and the implications of these for relations between disabled people and professionals.

Representation raises obvious questions about who can speak for or make decisions on behalf of others. However, as Phillips (1995) points out, the crucial issue may not be who should speak or decide, but rather whether those who might challenge certain voices or contest certain decisions are actually present to undertake that contention. In the field of disability, it is now commonplace for service providers, for example, to observe that accountability and quality entails the empowerment of service users (see, for example, Dept. of Health 1996; 1997). This leads to the further question of what exactly might be involved in practices of empowerment. The initiation, development and implementation of policy all involve several kinds of activity with implications for representation and empowerment. At a discursive level, consultation represents a minimal degree of representation but, beyond consultation, selections have to be made among proposals, priorities established and decisions taken about the ordering of such priorities. Then, at the level of action, policies have to be implemented and perhaps sanctions initiated or a veto introduced.

Phillips (1995) argues that when policies are worked out *for* rather than *with* a politically excluded constituency – and disabled people are one such constituency – they are unlikely to engage with all the relevant concerns. Representation and empowerment require a contesting presence at all stages of the process, from consultation through to implementation, since none of these matters can be taken as settled in advance. New problems, constraints and interpretations are likely to emerge at every stage and '[w]hen there is significant under-representation of disadvantaged groups at the point of final decision, this can and does have serious consequences' (44). Moreover, a disability presence must be more than token: relative to other interests it must have an equal chance to promote, moderate or rebuff proposals.

In the field of disability it is not unusual to have a complete lack of representation, not only at the stages of prioritisation and decision taking, but even at a basic consultative level. Expert working groups are particularly problematic in this respect. A recent exercise in the development of a health strategy,[2] for example, stresses the importance of '"people-centredness" ... as a key principle' and observes how submissions received by the experts raised the matter of 'participation in decision-making' (Dept. of Health and Children 2001: 48). Yet, members of the steering group, the project team and the inter-departmental group that prepared the strategy were all 'insiders' – civil servants or representatives of the health boards. Moreover, one of the main problems identified at the consultation stage was that 'patients and clients often have to adapt to the way the system works, rather than the system responding to their needs' (48). At the same time, the work of the strategy groups proceeded on the assumption that insiders were immune from those same forces and pressures that shape the way the system works.

A politics of presence rejects the assumption that experts, or guardians, uniquely know what is in the best interests of others and emphasises that policies devised under such conditions contradict the basic principles of empowerment and people-centredness. Neither is a politics of presence content to leave decisions to the altruistic assertions of professional work or to its presumed objectivity (Skrtic 1995). As one activist in the field of mental heath put it, 'many of the mistakes in mental health care come from a helping attitude. But they want to help you without asking you, without understanding you, without involving you, in your best interests' (Gombos, cited in Love 2003).

Numerous instances can be cited of an absence of representation at crucial stages in policy making in relation to disability. From the 'working party' of the 1970s and 1980s (see, for example, Dept. of Health 1975; 1980) to the 'review' or 'expert group' of the 1990s (Dept. of Education and Science 2000; Dept. of Health 1996; 1997), disabled people are seen as passive recipients of services determined by others. The more recent policy-making efforts are perhaps more indefensible in that they combine a rhetoric of empowerment with an absence of representation. The report, 'Towards an Independent Future', for example, was the 'first detailed review of services for persons with physical and sensory disabilities since ... 1984' (Dept. of Health 1996: 5). The review group held that service provision must be guided by principles of equity, quality and accountability and stated that '[p]eople with disabilities are increasingly asserting their right to control their own lives and to be involved in decision making in relation to their care. Their views must be sought and taken into account in planning services' (27). Yet, there was no representation for disabled people themselves in the review group. No recommendations were made or measures suggested as to how disabled people might exercise control or be involved in decision making. Two aspects of the report are especially telling. In its introductory discussion the report refers to the 'confusion' surrounding definitions of disability when, from the perspective of social model theory, the key issue is that definitions are not so much confusing as contested. A more serious problem arises in a recommendation for research in which the report unquestioningly accepts and promotes a medical model: 'The Department of Health in consultation with the Health Research Board should develop a strategy for promoting medical/scientific research into conditions causing physical and sensory disabilities' (110).

Arguments are rightly made that disabled people should have recourse to appropriate sanctions to deal with delaying tactics and non-compliance in the implementation of new policies. Given their lack of representation in actual policy and decision making, it is essential that disabled people have recourse to measures that can be used to resist policies that are inimical to their interests and well-being or that fail to meet the concerns that they have identified and prioritised. Young argues that social justice requires a form of participatory democracy that includes 'group veto power' to ensure 'the effective recognition and representation of the distinct voices and perspectives of those ... constituent groups that are oppressed or disadvantaged' (1990: 84). If the power of a veto of this kind is thought to be essential for the protection of minority interests on an international stage such as the EU,[3] it must be regarded as being equally essential for the protection of minority group interests within national boundaries. Furthermore, the possibility of exercising a veto would ensure that minority voices are seriously engaged, listened to and negotiated with as policy is being developed.

A politics of presence must be based on principles of popular control and political equality (Phillips 1995). Control is only a pious aspiration unless people are actually present and equality is not achieved if some groups have more leverage than others. A striking feature about responses to disability in modern Irish society is the degree of leverage exercised by discourses of expertise. That an individualistic, medical model of disability constitutes the dominant theoretical perspective is, as we have seen, well illustrated in recent legislation and in practices in fields such as education (McDonnell 2000; 2003), employment (Conroy 2003), social welfare (McManus 2003) and research (Woods 1996).

At issue here is a dominant-subordinate relationship between expert and 'disabled' perspectives and the question of how empowerment can occur in a field so dominated by expertise. Rose defines professional expertise as 'a particular kind of social *authority*, characteristically deployed around *problems*, exercising a certain *diagnostic* gaze, grounded in a claim to *truth*, asserting technical *efficiency*, and avowing *humane* ethical virtues' (1996: 86, italics in original). To these we add a further characteristic: professional expertise is *exclusionary*. Lay people are usually excluded from processes of definition and interpretation since a fundamental claim of professional expertise is that only it can objectively and therefore legitimately decode the true nature of a problem, that only experts can speak with authority about what is in the individual's best interests, and that they carry out these responsibilities in a context of care. It is this presumption of authority and care that creates the institutionalised paternalism so frequently found in disablist policy-making (McDonnell 2000).

In modern societies, expert discourses carry considerable weight and exert a profound influence on both public and private responses to disability. The presence of experts in the field creates vested interests that constitute powerful sites of resistance to the perspectives of disabled people (Oliver 1990). Bannerman Foster (1987) points to the symbiotic relationship that exists between experts and the state: while experts rely on the state to legitimate their authority and, in most cases, to pay their salaries, the state depends upon experts to legitimate its activities and implement its policies. The particular interests of experts in fields such medicine, psychology, or education often bear little or no relation to the interests of disabled people (Potts 1983; Lane 1993). In addition, since expert discourses generate asymmetrical power – relationships between those who evaluate and those who are evaluated – disabled people are in the weakest position to ensure that their interests get priority (McDonnell 1992).

Because of its orientation to technical efficiency, expertism (see Troyna and Vincent 1996), in its search for solutions, simply demands more expert practices, namely, more detailed identification measures, more extensive or intrusive clinical procedures, greater numbers of experts, and further training and professional development for those experts already working in the field (see, for example, Dept. of Education 1993). Expertism asserts that disability-related problems can be conquered or diminished by the application of technology or by more scientific management (Skrtic 1995). It promotes the deployment of new technologies which may be exercised on those whose difficulties are not at all amenable to technical interventions. Expertism is sustained by a rhetoric of on-going progress and improvement. However, when unsuccessful expert interventions are criticised, a frequent defence is that such criticisms are out of date and not applicable to the most recent developments. In the ideology of expertism, the most significant breakthrough is always just around the corner.

Expert practices of identification, assessment and classification, which sustain and inform the medical model of disability, profess to be neutral. However, such interventions have transformative effects because they involve more than claims to evaluate disability objectively (Dant and Gregory 1991). By interpreting human differences as pathologies and deficits, medical discourse creates people with problems. Subjective experiences of exclusion or oppression are neutralised by being translated into charts, profiles and scales. Moreover, such individualised evaluation masks the inequalities produced by disabling relationships between individuals and their environments (Oliver 1990).

Another important aspect of representation relates to the training and professional formation of experts. Radford's comments about the role of the university in the social creation of 'mental deficiency', through 'the authority of "science" and the rise of professionalism' (1994: 10), are equally applicable to its role in the social creation of disability. On the one hand, according to Radford, the efforts of the university to develop a critique of expertism have been 'indifferent at best ... [and] ... sometimes obstructionist', while on the other, it supported policies that culminated in 'custodial incarceration, sterilization and even extermination' (1994: 15–6). Therefore a pertinent question is: to what extent have current university research and training programmes incorporated and accommodated rights-based perspectives on disability?

The establishment of new and dedicated centres for disability, Deaf and equality studies, and the explicit articulation of disability rights perspectives in some university programmes, can be seen as positive developments (McDonnell 2003). There is, however, cause for concern regarding the composition and orientation of longer established programmes in education, psychology and medicine, and in nursing and rehabilitation studies. Firstly, the exploitation of disabled individuals and groups for education and training purposes is an issue that remains to be addressed. While it is clearly necessary to have informed and skilled personnel working in the various services, there is a danger that the experience, knowledge and skills of disabled people will be used mainly for the professional advancement of others (Oliver 1990; 1996). Secondly, social model theory appears to have had limited general impact on the academy (Oliver 1996a). With some exceptions (see, for example, Department of Adult and Community Education, NUI Maynooth 2006–7; Equality Studies Centre, UCD 2000; and Centre for Deaf Studies, TCD 2005–6), there is little evidence of any robust programmes of affirmative action being undertaken to promote academic and professional formation for disabled people in Ireland. Thirdly, it is difficult to establish whether the emergence of social model theory has resulted in significant structural or conceptual shifts in the overall content of courses. Thus, although courses in special needs education have incorporated elements of social model theory, a strong orientation to clinical and individualised understandings of disability persists.

It would of course be wrong to deny expertise or the training of professionals any part in the repertoire of responses to impairment. What is being questioned here is the fact that professionals have monopolised the arenas where recognition is affirmed and representation manifested. Shakespeare (1996), for example, notes the degree to which discourses concerning sexuality and intimate relationships are controlled by professionals and the extent to which the perspectives of disabled people themselves have been excluded. The next section addresses these and related concerns which constitute a further dimension in an equality framework – the affective domain.

## THE AFFECTIVE CONTEXT: ISSUES OF DEPENDENCE AND INTERDEPENDENCE

The affective domain refers to the emotional lives of individuals, and to intimate personal and social relations. Again, the affective is closely connected with other dimensions of equality, such as economic status and recognition. For example, inadequate income, inaccessible places of recreation and ineffective public transport will limit opportunities for social interaction. The affective dimensions of human life and experience are also significant in their own right. They are particularly important in establishing self-esteem and a secure identity, and in developing the confidence, the capacities and the opportunities to engage in rewarding emotional relationships with others. The affective dimension of equality implies relations of dependence and interdependence, integral aspects of the human condition (Nussbaum 1995; Kittay 1999). As human beings, we all experience both dependency and interdependency at different times in our lives; indeed from the intimate to the impersonal, being human involves living within networks of interdependency (Kittay 2001; Lynch et al. 2001; Baker et al. 2004).

Social theorists have tended to consider the affective domain as private and personal rather than an issue for public policy and to regard the emotions as being peripheral if not irrelevant to the development of a more egalitarian society. Several recent studies, however, have drawn attention not only to ways in which the state regulates the affective aspects of our lives, but more significantly to the importance of love, care and solidarity relations in human development (Lynch and McLaughlin 1995; Nussbaum 1995; Kittay 1999; Lynch et al. 2001; Baker et al. 2004). Nussbaum, for example, rejects the traditional opposition between emotion and reason in Western thought, in which it has been customary to denigrate the emotions, to attribute an excessively emotional nature to women and to non-Western peoples, and to assume that the emotions inhibit or extinguish the capacity to reason. She argues instead that emotions are in fact 'intelligent and discriminating elements of personality, closely related to belief and judgement' (1995: 365).

In a similar vein and in the context of disability, Kittay (1999; 2001) argues that, far from being peripheral, the reality of human dependency and interdependency is a defining characteristic of what it means to be a person. In the tradition of liberal equality, the struggle of marginalised groups for resources, recognition and representation has been premised on notions of independence, rationality and self-sufficiency. In this frame-work, there seems to be little room for individuals whose rationality and capacity to reason may be impaired. Kittay goes on to argue that, in real-ity, personhood with all its attendant rights 'has little to do with rational-ity and everything to do with *relationships* – to our world and to those in it' (2001: 568). Independence in modern society, according to Kittay, is largely a fiction, regardless of our abilities or disabilities. She proposes that having a capacity to be in affective and interdependent relationships with others should be brought to the centre of what it means to be a person.

Kittay's argument addresses important aspects of the social model, especially where 'profound problems experienced by people with certain impairments are difficult, if not impossible, to solve by social manipula-tion' (French 1993: 17). Moreover, by presenting alternative concepts of care and dependency, in which neither givers nor receivers may be exploited, she offers a resolution to some of the difficulties identified by Morris (1993*a*). In shifting the basis for equality and social justice from the human capacity to reason to the capacity to be interdependent, Kittay underlines the significance of the affective domain with particular regard to disability.

The affective sphere is of great concern to disabled people, not only because it is associated with complex and sensitive issues, but also because it is a relatively neglected area of research and discussion (Shakespeare 1996; Evans *et al.* 2003). The Department of Equality and Law Reform's Report of the Commission on the Status of People with Disabilities (1996) emphasises that any list of equal rights must include the right of disabled people 'to the same degree of fulfilment through rela-tionships and sexuality as anyone else' (231). Among the barriers to ful-filment identified in the report are the stereotypes that surround the 'body beautiful' and the stigma associated with perceived impairment. Shakespeare *et al.* (1996) essentially make the same points in their analy-sis of the sexual politics of disability. Narrow concepts of physical beauty exert a powerful influence on the attitudes of the general public as well as on the attitudes of disabled people themselves. In addition, the cultural representation of impairment in the media is a major factor in creating and disseminating negative images and perceptions of disabled people (Barnes *et al.* 1999). Thus, disabling social and emotional relations are more likely

to stem from prejudice, ignorance and discrimination than from individual conditions.

Underpinning these barriers to fulfilment in intimate relationships are
discourses that regard disabled people as asexual. Disabled people report
experiences of being managed without the same levels of respect given to
non-disabled people, of being left unclothed in hospitals for long periods
as members of staff went about their work, and of being treated as if their
appearance was of no consequence (Dept. of Equality and Law Reform
1996). The invisibility of disabled people as autonomous sexual actors
and the assumption that impairment displaces sexual worth are reflected
in the failure of professional services to take sexuality seriously.
Consequently, disabled people's self-images and their perceptions of
themselves as attractive individuals and potential sexual partners are
undermined (Shakespeare 1996).

These inequalities are also associated with eugenic ideology, particularly where it relates to the issue of reproduction. While the idea that disabled people might have a sexual life is considered strange, that they might
desire to have children is 'seen as irresponsible' (Evans, cited Morris 1991:
20–1). The explicit purpose of the large scale institutionalisation and sterilisation of disabled people that occurred in Europe and North America
over the greater part of the twentieth century was aimed at preventing the
reproduction of the so-called unfit. While Ireland never introduced sterilisation legislation, there was considerable support for other eugenically
inspired measures (Jones 1992). The Report of the Commission on the
Status of People with Disabilities expressed concern that sterilisation of
disabled people, particularly women, takes place in Ireland without any
information being available as to whether an informed and voluntary decision is being made by the disabled person. The report went on to recom-
mend 'that sterilisation of people with disabilities on the grounds of their
disability alone should be legally prohibited' and that 'where sterilisation
is being considered, every effort must be made to ensure that informed and
free consent exists'(Dept. of Equality and Law Reform 1996: 236).

Several recent studies highlight the need to replace the assumptions of
non-disabled professionals with a discourse that foregrounds the views of
disabled people themselves (Shakespeare *et al.* 1996; Hypatia 2001–2002;
Walmsley and Johnson 2003). While most attention has been given to het-
erosexual relations, Shakespeare (1996) argues that research, social policies and support services must be sensitive to differences in sexual

orientation among disabled people. He further emphasises that opportunities to form consensual emotional or sexual relationships should not be denied to disabled people who attend day centres or live in residential homes. Intimate relationships are highly significant for most adults and to ignore their importance constitutes a failure to consider disabled people as fully human.

A recent Irish study (Evans *et al.* 2003) sought the views and opinions of people with learning difficulties on personal relationships. The study also reported on the views and opinions of parents and siblings and of staff in facilities providing services for people with learning difficulties. There were considerable differences among the three groups in their perceptions of, and attitudes towards, relationships. Most of the people with learning difficulties whose views were reported in the study had developed personal relationships and did not see any reason why emotions and feelings should not be expressed. Some stated that personal relationships were not allowed in facilities providing services and there was considerable discontent about the lack of privacy as well as intrusive forms of supervision. Several participants 'reported that they had relationships "behind the staffs' backs"' (Evans *et al.* 2003: 133). In terms of the future, most hoped to get married and have children.

In contrast, very few parents/carers believed that intimate relationships or marriage were acceptable or possible. Parental opposition to such relationships was apparent to the individuals concerned and this was believed to have a negative impact on their right to be happy. In contrast, staffs in the centres were more supportive of personal relationships, believing that a different 'type of relationship … should be allowed for different ability levels'. The study reported that '[i]n terms of having a boyfriend/girlfriend (intimate) or marriage, only a small proportion (5–25 per cent) of staff believed those of moderate/severe ability levels should be allowed such a relationship with about half (48–55 per cent) believing those with a mild ability level should be allowed such relationships' (Evans *et al.* 2003: 135). Among its conclusions, the study recommended that the views of service users should be represented in drawing up guidelines for personal relationships and the fact that people with learning difficulties have sexual feelings and want to express these feelings should be recognised. In addition, the development of personal relationships should be facilitated in such a way that an individual's privacy is respected, 'yet at the same time ensuring relationships and behaviour are appropriate and that the individual is protected against abuse' (Evans *et al.* 2003: 138).

Shakespeare (1996) also warns of the risks of exploitative or abusive relationships where disabled people are concerned and maintains that disabled people experience disproportionately high levels of physical and sexual abuse. Clearly, institutionalisation, dependency and the frequent invasion of private and physical space, create social contexts and social opportunities where abuse and exploitation can occur. Furthermore, in the delivery of care and support services, disabled people are vulnerable to possible discriminatory attitudes ranging from insensitivity to homophobia on the part of care-workers, counsellors and other professionals. To date, these particular features of the affective dimension of disability remain largely unresearched in Ireland.

It is important, however, to mention positive developments. The Report of the Commission on the Status of People with Disabilities has addressed some key issues regarding sexuality and relationships and made several important recommendations. In particular, recommendations that incorporate a direct role for disabled people themselves in policy making and decision taking should be endorsed (Dept. of Equality and Law Reform 1996). The growth of the disability movement itself has created opportunities for cultivating personal and social relationships and for developing a positive disability identity (Shakespeare 1996). There is also a new willingness among disabled people to see the affective domain in terms of rights and entitlements, to take legal action in pursuit of these rights (Saxton 1993), and to challenge social structures and relations which deny disabled people opportunities to lead emotionally fulfilling lives (Morris 1991; Kallianes and Rubenfeld 1997).

## CONCLUSION

The discussion in this chapter has focused on an ideological position that defines disability as a form of oppression, a standpoint articulated through what has been called the social model of disability. The chapter has located disability within a framework that provides an explicit egalitarian dimension to the analysis of disability relations in society. The application of egalitarian theory makes it clear that disability is a multidimensional form of oppression. Disabled people experience injustice and inequality in several interrelated ways: through poverty and

unemployment, through non-recognition and invisibility, through powerlessness and absence from key policy and decision making arenas,
through oppressive forms of dependency, and through the lack of control and autonomy in the development and maintenance of intimate
interpersonal relationships.

Postmodernist critics have rejected what they regard as the grand theorising of the social model of disability (Barnes 2000). They may also
argue that the application of egalitarian theory has the same universalising
purpose. However, given the long history of ideologies, structures and
practices of disablement, as Lynch and Lodge (2002) argue, there is a
place for universalising, provided that it has regard for difference and
diversity and for the politics of theory making. Barnes and Mercer (2003)
also emphasise the need to maintain a collective and integrated challenge
to the asymmetrical nature of relations of power operating in the field of
disability.

In addressing the problem of desirable, alternative social systems,
egalitarian theory distinguishes between deep and surface structures and
looks to transformative rather than affirmative remedies (Fraser 1995;
2000). A standpoint incorporating these perspectives is essential at a time
when disability relations are entering a new and critical phase in Irish
society, when a new socio-political paradigm is being established, when
new policies are being developed, and guidelines for new practices are
being introduced (Kwiotek and McDonnell 2003; McDonnell 2000; 2003;
Nolan 2003). As these responses take shape, from the point of view of disabled people, what is put in place must go beyond the reproduction of old
structures and the reformulation of old relations. A real danger in the current period of transition is that change will not go beyond the cosmetic
and that older organising ideologies will remain entrenched, invisible but
influential. Furthermore, if the deep structures that govern the distribution
of resources, the quality of recognition, the exercise of power and the
nature of dependency are not confronted and transformed, the exclusion
and oppression of disabled people will be reproduced even under the best
intentioned and well-supported programmes of change.

The purpose of this study has been to identify the primary ideologies
around which interpretations of and responses to disability have been
organised in Western society and to explore how these ideologies have
been explained and justified. These conceptual frameworks and the practices associated with them not only have a long history, but have become

so deeply entrenched in the machinery of the social system that they are often regarded as natural phenomena rather than as social creations. While the interpretative challenge to these perspectives came from the development of a social model of disability, the political challenge came from the development of modern disability movements and their struggles for equality and social justice. The legitimacy of this struggle has gained a considerable degree of national and international recognition and acknowledgement (Quinn and Bruce 2003).

Among the more positive recent developments in Ireland are an increasingly activist disability movement and a growing perception that disability is an equality issue (Dept. of Equality and Law Reform 1996; Toolin 2003). The 'Get Your Act Together' conference, for example, was organised in 2001 by the Disability Federation of Ireland, the Forum of People with Disabilities, People with Disabilities Ireland, and the National Association for the Mentally Handicapped of Ireland, in opposition to the proposed Disability Bill. The focus of the conference was the failure to sufficiently address the equality and rights concerns of disabled people in the Bill. The disability movement and disability studies have demonstrated that disability is part of a broad and fundamental concern for social justice in economic, social, political and affective domains. They offer an alternative to individualised and deficit models of people. There is also a growing awareness that, in relation to disability, oppression and discrimination are the products of long established and deep-rooted ideologies that underpin current organisational structures and institutional practices. The degree to which these are tackled and overcome is an important barometer of equality in society.

In Ireland, progress on this front remains an open question. Disability activist, Donal Toolin, puts it:

> How far Irish society will go in the development of law and policy responses that demonstrate more than a rhetorical commitment to the equality of disabled people remains to be seen. Much will depend on fundamental and radical shifts taking place from where power currently lies in frequently unaccountable entities to one that locates the desires and needs of disabled people at the centre. The direct involvement of disabled people and the extent of their involvement in that power shift will fundamentally inform the nature of which rights are articulated and given effect. (2003: 181)

NOTES

1.  A disability equality programme based on the guidelines and proposals
    suggested for tackling gender inequality (Dept. of Education 1992: 9–10)
    might have included the following:

    (a) All education institutions, at first, second and third levels, to develop
        and publish an active policy to promote disability equality. Annual
        reports to record progress in implementing this policy.
    (b) All administrative bodies in education to promote disability representa-
        tion in their membership. Disability awareness to be embodied in staff
        development programmes and to be promoted in the student body.
    (c) A systematic examination of teaching materials to take place regu-
        larly, and action taken to withdraw or adapt unsuitable material.
        Courses to be proofed to determine how disability issues should be
        addressed.
    (d) People with disabilities to be regarded as the primary source of infor-
        mation on their needs and on the restrictions they currently experience
        in the education system. Disability activist organisations to be con-
        sulted in designing equality codes and in promoting equal citizenship.
    (e) Inclusive education to be actively encouraged, but not imposed, as the
        norm in first and second level schools. Regard for the particular needs
        of different groups – for example, the need for deaf pupils to learn in
        an environment where the primary language is sign language.
    (f) Institutions of higher education to operate a reserved places policy to
        bring participation rates into line with other students. Special atten-
        tion to be given to women with disabilities in the operation of a
        reserved places policy.
    (g) The Department of Education to promote greater participation by
        people with disabilities in management at all levels in the
        Department. Participation by people with disabilities in the inspec-
        torate to be implemented.

2.  The health strategy included important proposals for the development of
    services in relation to disability (Dept. of Health and Children 2001).
3.  Unanimous decisions by the Council of the EU are required in several
    important areas, 'such as common foreign and security policy, police and
    judicial cooperation in criminal matters, asylum and immigration policy,
    economic and social cohesion policy and taxation. In other words each
    Member State has a veto on European measures in these sectors'
    (European Commission 2001: 9).

# Bibliography

Abberley, P. (1987), 'The Concept of Oppression and the Development of a Social Theory of Disability', *Disability, Handicap and Society*, 2(1): 5–19.

Abberley, P. (1996), 'Work, Utopia and Impairment', in L. Barton (ed.), *Disability and Society: Emerging Issues and Insights*, Harlow, Essex: Addison Wesley Longman, 61–79.

Adams, Thomas McStay (1990), *Bureaucrats and Beggars: French Social Policy in the Age of the Enlightenment*, Oxford: Oxford University Press.

AHEAD (1994), Committee on Access and Participation of Students with Disabilities in Higher Education, Report to the Higher Education Authority, Dublin: AHEAD.

Akenson, D. (1970), *The Irish Education Experiment*, London: Routledge and Kegan Paul.

Albrecht, G. (1992), *The Disability Business*, London: Sage.

Albrecht, G. (2002), 'American Pragmatism, Sociology and the Development of Disability Studies', in C. Barnes, M. Oliver and L. Barton (eds.), *Disability Studies Today*, Cambridge: Polity Press, 18–37.

Allan, J. (1999), *Actively Seeking Inclusion: Pupils with Special Needs in Mainstream Schools*, London: Falmer Press.

Allen, G. (1999), 'Genetics, Eugenics and the Medicalisation of Social Behaviour: Lessons from the Past', *Endeavour*, 23(1), 10–19.

Althusser, L. (1971), 'Ideology and Ideological State Apparatuses', in L. Althusser (ed.), *Lenin and Philosophy and Other Essays*, London: NLB, 121–73.

Amnesty International (Irish Section) (2003), *Mental Illness: The Neglected Quarter*, Dublin: Author.

Andrews, J. (1975), *A Paper Landscape: The Ordnance Survey in Nineteenth Century Ireland*, Oxford: Clarendon Press.

Armstrong, D., Armstrong, F. and Barton, L. (eds.) (2000), *Inclusive Education: Policies Contexts and Contemporary Perspectives*, London: David Fulton.

Armstrong, F., Belmont, B. and Verillon, A. (2000), 'Vive la différence? Exploring Context, Policy and Change in Special Education in France: Developing Cross-Cultural Collaboration', in F. Armstrong, D. Armstrong

213

and L. Barton (eds.) *Inclusive Education: Policies, Contexts and Contemporary Perspectives*, London: David Fulton, 60–77.

Ashley, W. (1906), *An Introduction to English Economic History and Theory. Part* II: *The End of the Middle Ages*, 4th edition, London: Longmans, Green and Co.

*Asylum Journal of Mental Science* (1854), July; (1854*a*), November; (1856), January, London: Longman, Brown, Green, Longman and Roberts.

Baker, J. (1998), 'Equality', in S. Healy and B. Reynolds (eds.), *Social Policy in Ireland: Principles, Practices and Problems*, Dublin: Oak Tree Press, 21–42.

Baker, J., Lynch, K., Cantillon, S. and Walsh, J. (2004), *Equality: From Theory to Action*, Basingstoke: Palgrave-Macmillan.

Bank-Mikklesen, N. (1969), 'A Metropolitan Area in Denmark: Copenhagen', in R. Kugel and W. Wolfensberger (eds.), *Changing Patterns in Residential Services for the Mentally Retarded,* Washington: President's Committee on Mental Retardation, 227–54.

Banks, B. (1872), *Compendium of the Irish Poor Law*, Dublin: Alexander Thom.

Bannerman Foster, S. (1987), *The Politics of Caring*, Lewes: The Falmer Press.

Barker, D. (1983), 'How to Curb the Fertility of the Unfit: the Feeble-Minded in Edwardian Britain', *Oxford Review of Education*, 9(3), 197–211.

Barnes, C. (1991), *Disabled People in Britain and Discrimination: A Case for Anti-Discrimination Legislation*, London: Hurst, in association with the British Council of Organisations of Disabled People.

Barnes, C. (1992), 'Institutional Discrimination against Disabled People and the Campaign for Anti-Discrimination Legislation', *Critical Social Policy*, 12(1), 5–22.

Barnes, C. (1992*a*), *Disabling Imagery and the Media: An Exploration of the Principles for Media Representations of Disabled People*, Halifax: British Council of Disabled People and Ryburn Publishing.

Barnes, C. (1995), *Exploring the Divide: Illness and Disability*, Leeds: The Disability Press.

Barnes, C. (1996), 'Theories of Disability and the Origins of the oppression of Disabled People in Western Society', in L. Barton (ed.), *Disability and Society: Emerging Issues and Insights*, Harlow, Essex: Addison Wesley Longman, 43–60.

Barnes, C. (1998), 'The Social Model of Disability: A Sociological Phenomenon Ignored by Sociologists?' in T. Shakespeare (ed.), *The Disability Reader: Social Science Perspectives*, London: Cassell, 65–78.

Barnes, C. (2000), 'A Working Social Model? Disability, Work and Disability Politics in the 21st Century', *Critical Social Policy*, 20(4), 441–57.

Barnes, C. (2003), 'What a Difference a Decade Makes: Reflections on doing "Emancipatory" Disability Research', *Disability and Society*, 18(1), 3–17.

Barnes, C. and Mercer, G. (eds.) (1996), *Exploring the Divide: Illness and Disability*, Leeds: The Disability Press.

Barnes, C. and Mercer, G. (eds.) (1997), *Doing Disability Research*, Leeds: Disability Press.

Barnes, C. and Mercer, G. (2003), *Disability*, Cambridge: Polity Press.

Barnes, C. and Mercer, G. (2006), *Independent Futures: Creating User-Led Disability Services in a Disabling Society*, Bristol: Polity Press.

Barnes, C., Mercer, G. and Shakespeare, T. (eds.) (1999), *Exploring Disability: A Sociological Introduction*, Cambridge: Polity Press.

Barnes, C., Oliver, M. and Barton, L. (eds.) (2002), *Disability Studies Today*, Cambridge: Polity Press.

Barnes, J. (1989), *Irish Industrial School 1868–1908*, Dublin: Irish Academic Press.

Barry, D. (1907), 'Our National Degeneracy and a Forgotten Matrimonial Impediment', *The Irish Theological Quarterly*, vol. 2, October, 458–64.

Barry, J., Sinclair, H., Kelly, A., O'Loughlin, R., Hardy, D. and O'Dowd, T. (2001), *Inequalities in Health in Ireland: Hard Facts*, Department of Community Health and General Practice, Trinity College Dublin.

Bartlett, P. and Wright, D. (eds.) (1999), *Outside the Walls of the Asylum: The History of Care in the Community, 1750–2000*, London: The Athlone Press.

Barton, L. (1995), 'Segregated Special Education: Some Critical Observations', in G. Zarb (ed.), *Removing Disabling Barriers*, London: The Policy Studies Institute, 27–37.

Barton, L. (1996), 'Sociology and Disability: Some Emerging Issues', in L. Barton (ed.), *Disability and Society: Emerging Issues and Insights*, Harlow, Essex: Addison Wesley Longman, 3–17.

Baynton, D. (1993), '"Savages and Deaf-Mutes": Evolutionary Theory and the Campaign against Sign Language in the Nineteenth Century', in J. Van Cleeve, (ed.), *Deaf History Unveiled: Interpretations from the New Scholarship*, Washington, DC: Gallaudet University Press, 92–112.

Begum, N., Hill, M. and Stevens, A. (eds.) (1994), *Reflections: The Views of Black Disabled People on their Lives and Community Care*, London: CCETSW.

Beier, A.L. (1985), *Masterless Men: The Vagrancy Problem in England 1560–1640*, London: Methuen.

Belfast Charitable Society (1832), 61st Annual Report, Belfast: Thomas Mairs.

Billington, T. (2000), *Separating, Losing and Excluding Children*: *Narratives of Difference*, London: Routledge/Falmer.

Binet, A. and Simon, T. (1914), *Mentally Defective Children*, London: Edward Arnold.

Blume, S. (2000), 'Reflections on Bio-Ethics from a Deaf Viewpoint', in L. Leeson (ed.), *Looking Forward*: *EUD in the 21st Century – The Deaf Citizen in the Third Millennium*, Coleford, Glos.: Forest Books, 116–26.

Bogucka, M. (1997), 'Health Care and Poor Relief in Danzig (Gdansk): The Sixteenth and first half of the Seventeenth Century', in O. Grell and A. Cunningham (eds.), *Health Care and Poor Relief in Protestant Europe 1500–1700*, London: Routledge, 204–19.

Booth, T. (1988), 'Challenging Conceptions of Integration', in L. Barton (ed.), *The Politics of Special Educational Needs*, London: The Falmer Press, 99–121.

Borsay, A. (1986), 'Personal Trouble or Public Issue: Towards a Model of Policy for People with Physical and Mental Disabilities', *Disability, Handicap and Society*, 1(2): 179–96.

Borsay, A. (2002), 'History, Power and Identity', in C. Barnes, M. Oliver and L. Barton (eds.), *Disability Studies Today*, Cambridge: Polity Press, 98–119.

Bourdieu, P. (1997), 'The Forms of Capital', in A.H. Halsey, H. Lauder, P. Brown and A. Stuart Wells (eds.), *Education, Culture, Economy and Society*, Oxford: Oxford University Press, 46–58.

Boyd Barrett, E. (1924), 'Modern Psycho-Therapy and Our Asylums', *Studies*, vol. 13, March, 29–43.

Boyd Barrett, J. (1913), 'The Medical Examination of School Children', *Studies*, vol. 2, June, 73–80.

Brennan, M., Turner, G. and Thoutenhoofd, E. (eds.) (1991), *Language, Community and Culture*, Course Book, Deaf Studies Research Unit, University of Durham.

Broberg, G. and Roll-Hansen, N. (eds.) (1996), *Eugenics and the Welfare State*: *Sterilization Policy in Denmark, Sweden, Norway and Finland*, East Lansing: Michigan State University Press.

Broberg, G. and Tydén, M. (1996), 'Eugenics in Sweden: Efficient Care', in G. Broberg and N. Roll-Hansen (eds.), *Eugenics and the Welfare State*: *Sterilization Policy in Denmark, Sweden, Norway and Finland*, East Lansing: Michigan State University Press, 77–150.

Brock Committee (1934), Report of the Departmental Committee on Sterilisation, cmd. 4485, London: HMSO.

Brown, H. and Smith, H. (eds.) (1992), *Normalisation: A Reader for the Nineties*, London: Routledge.

Browne, A. (1995), 'Bartholomew Mosse, 1712–59: Founder and First Master', in A. Browne (ed.), *Masters, Midwives and Ladies-in-Waiting: The Rotunda Hospital 1745–1995*, Dublin: A. & A. Farmar, 1–20.

Burke, H. (1987), *The People and the Poor Law in 19th Century Ireland*, Dublin: Women's Education Bureau.

Burke, H. (1993), *The Royal Hospital Donnybrook*, Dublin: The Royal Hospital Donnybrook and The Social Science Research Centre, University College Dublin.

Busfield, J. (1986), *Managing Madness*, London: Hutchinson.

Byrne, M. (1980), 'Educational Provision for the Mentally Handicapped in Ireland', in J. Coolahan (ed.), *Proccedings of the 5th Annual Conference of the Educational Studies Association of Ireland*, Dublin: The Educational Studies Association, 10–25.

Campbell Ross, I. (ed.) (1986), *Public Virtue, Private Love: The Early Years of the Dublin Lying-in Hospital*, Dublin: The O'Brien Press.

Campbell, J. and Oliver, M. (1996), *Disability Politics: Understanding Our Past, Changing Our Future*, London: Routledge.

Campling, J. (ed.) (1981), *Images of Ourselves: Women with Disabilities Talking*, London: Routledge and Kegan Paul.

Cantillon, S., Corrigan, C., Kirby, P. and O'Flynn, J. (eds.) (2001), *Rich and Poor: Perspectives on Tackling Inequality in Ireland*, Dublin: Oak Tree Press.

Carlson, E. (2001), *The Unfit: A History of a Bad Idea*, Cold Spring Harbour, NY: Cold Spring Harbour Laboratory Press.

Carroll-Burke, P. (2000), *Colonial Discipline: The Making of the Irish Convict System*, Dublin: Four Courts Press.

Cassell, R. (1997), *Medical Charities, Medical Politics: The Irish Dispensary System and the Poor Law 1836–1872*, Dublin: The Royal Historical Society/The Boydell Press.

Catholic Institution for the Deaf and Dumb, Annual Reports 1846–, Dublin: Author.

Census of Ireland 1841 (1843), Report of the Census Commissioners appointed to take the Census of Ireland, Dublin: Alexander Thom.

Census of Ireland 1851 (1854), General Report, Part III: Report on the Status of Disease, Dublin: Alexander Thom.

Census of Ireland 1861 (1863), Part III: Vital Statistics, Dublin: Alexander Thom.

Census of Ireland 1881 (1882), Part II: General Report, Dublin: Alexander Thom.

Central Statistics Office (2002), Quarterly National Household Survey: Disability in the Labour Force, Second Quarter, Dublin: CSO.

Centre for Deaf Studies, University of Dublin, Trinity College (2005–06), Student Handbook.

Christensen, C. (1996), 'Disabled, Handicapped or Disordered: "What's in a Name?"' in C. Christensen and F. Rizvi (eds.), *Disability and the Dilemmas of Education and Justice*, Buckingham: Open University Press, 63–78.

Coakley, D. (1988), *The Irish School of Medicine: Outstanding Practitioners of the 19th Century*, Dublin: Tara House.

Coakley, D. (1995), *A Short History of the Royal City of Dublin Hospital, Baggot Street*, Dublin: The Board of Governors, Royal City of Dublin Hospital, Baggot Street.

Coard, B. (1971), *How the West Indian Child is Made Educationally Subnormal in the British Educational System*, London: New Beacon.

Cohen, S. and Scull, A. (1983), *Social Control and the State: Historical and Comparative Essays*, Oxford: Martin Robertson.

Connolly, S. (1989), 'Aftermath and Adjustment', in W.E. Vaughan (ed.), *A New History of Ireland, Vol. V: Ireland under the Union 1801–1870*, Oxford: Clarendon Press, 1–23.

Connolly, S. (1989*a*), 'Union Government 1812–23', in W. Vaughan (ed.), *A New History of Ireland, Vol. V: Ireland under the Union 1801–1870*, Oxford: Clarendon Press, 48–73.

Conrad, L., Neve, M., Nutton, V., Porter, R. and Wear, A. (1995), *The Western Medical Tradition: 800 BC to AD 1800*, Cambridge: Cambridge University Press.

Conroy, P. (2003), 'Employment Policy', in S. Quin and B. Redmond (eds.), *Disability and Social Policy in Ireland*, Dublin: University College Dublin Press, 45–56.

Conroy, P. and Fanagan, S. (2001), Research Project on the Effective Recruitment of People with Disabilities into the Public Service, 2000, Dublin: The Equality Authority and the Department of Justice, Equality and Law Reform.

Cook, H. (1997), 'From Scientific Revolution to Germ Theory', in I. Loudon (ed.), *Western Medicine*, Oxford: Oxford University Press, 80–101.

Coolahan, J. (1981), *Irish Education: Its History and Structure*, Dublin: Institute of Public Administration.

Coolahan, J. (1988), 'Imperialism and the Irish National School System', in J.A. Mangan, *Benefits Bestowed*, Manchester: Manchester University Press, 76–93.

Cooney, T. (1989), *Sterilisation and the Mentally Handicapped*, Dublin University Law Journal, 11(1), 56–73.

Cooney, T. (1995), 'Recommendations', in P. Callaghan (ed.), *Legislation, Disability and Higher Education, A Comparative Study: Europe and the USA*, Dublin: AHEAD Education Press, 249–57.

Cooper, D. (1968), *Psychiatry and Anti-Psychiatry*, London: Tavistock.

Corbett, J. and Slee, R. (2000), 'An International Conversation on Inclusive Education', in D. Armstrong, F. Armstrong and L. Barton (eds.), *Inclusive Education: Policy, Contexts and Comparative Perspectives*, London: David Fulton, 133–46.

Corker, M. and French, S. (eds.) (1999), *Disability Discourse*, Buckingham: Open University Press.

Corker, M. and French, S. (1999a), 'Reclaiming Discourse in Disability Studies', in M. Corker and S. French (eds.), *Disability Discourse*, Buckingham: Open University Press, 1–11.

Corker, M. and Shakespeare, T. (eds.) (2002), *Disability/Postmodernity: Embodying Disability Theory*, London: Continuum.

Cox, Dr (1912), Report of the Transactions of the Royal Academy of Medicine in Ireland, *Dublin Journal of Medical Science*, vol. 133, April, 292.

Crawford, E. (1999), 'Typhus in 19th Century Ireland', in E. Malcolm and G. Jones (eds.), *Medicine, Disease and the State in Ireland, 1650–1940*, Cork: Cork University Press, 121–37.

Crossman, V. (1996), *Politics, Law and Order in 19th Century Ireland*, Dublin: Gill and Macmillan.

Cullen, Cardinal P. (1870), Royal Commission of Inquiry into Primary Education (Ireland), vol. iv, Minutes of Evidence ..., H.C. 1870, xxviii, pt. iii.

Cummins, J. (1984), *Bilingualism and Special Education: Issues in Assessment and Pedagogy*, Cleveland, Avon: Multilingual Matters.

Curtis, L. Perry (1997), *Apes and Angels: The Irishman in Victorian Caricature*, rev. edition, Washington: Smithsonian Institution Press.

Dalley, G. (1996), *Ideologies of Caring: Rethinking Community and Collectivism*, 2nd edition, London: Macmillan.

Dant, T. and Gregory, S. (1991), 'The Social Construction of Deafness', Block 3, Unit 8 of D251, *Issues in Deafness*, A Social Sciences Second Level Course, Milton Keynes: The Open University.

D'Arcy, C. (1914), *Northern Whig*, 12 February.

Darke, P. (1998), 'Understanding Cinematic Representations of Disability', in T. Shakespeare (ed.), *The Disability Reader: Social Science Perspectives*, London: Cassell, 181–97.

Davis, H. (1929), 'Sterilization of the Mentally Deficient', *The Catholic Medical Guardian*, 7(2), 47–56.

Davis, H. (1931), 'State Sterilization of the Mental Defective', *The Clergy Review*, February, 165–76.

Davis, K. (1993), 'On the Movement', in J. Swain, V. Finkelstein, S. French and M. Oliver (eds.), *Disabling Barriers – Enabling Environments*, London: Sage, in association with the Open University, 285–92.

Davis, L. (ed.) (1997), *The Disability Studies Reader*, New York: Routledge.

Davis, L. (1997), 'Constructing Normalcy: The Bell Curve, the Novel, and the Invention of the Disabled Body in the 19th Century', in L. Davis (ed.), *The Disability Studies Reader*, New York: Routledge, 9–28.

Dawson, W.R. (1912), 'Report of the Transactions of the Royal Academy of Medicine in Ireland', *Dublin Journal of Medical Science*, vol. 133, April, 292.

Dawson, W.R. (1913), 'The Mental Deficiency Bill and its Proposed Extension to Ireland', *Dublin Journal of Medical Science*, vol. 135, March, 161–67.

Dear, M. and Woolch, J. (1987), *Landscapes of Despair: From Deinstitutionalisation to Homelessness*, Cambridge: Polity Press.

Deeley, S. (2002), 'Professional Ideology and Learning Disability: An Analysis of Internal Conflict', *Disability and Society*, 17(1), 19–33.

De Jong, G. (1979), *The Movement for Independent Living: Origins, Ideology and Implications for Disability Research*, Michigan: University Centre for International Rehabilitation.

Delbanco, A. (2001), 'An Experiment in Darkness', *The New York Review*, 20 September, 36–39.

Department of Adult and Community Education, National University of Ireland Maynooth (2006–7), Certificate in Disabilities Studies Course Handbook.

Department of Education (1965), Report of the Commission of Inquiry on Mental Handicap, Dublin: The Stationery Office.

Department of Education (1972), 'The Education of Children who are Handicapped by Impaired Hearing', Dublin: The Stationery Office.

Department of Education (1992), 'Education for a Changing World', Green Paper on Education, Dublin: The Stationery Office.

Department of Education (1993), Report of the Special Education Review Committee, Dublin: The Stationery Office.

Department of Education (1995), 'Charting our Education Future', White Paper on Education, Dublin: The Stationery Office.

Department of Education and Science (1999), 'Arrangements for the Assessment of Candidates with Special Educational Needs', Discussion Paper, Dublin: Department of Education and Science.

Department of Education and Science (2000), 'Arrangements for the Assessment of Candidates with Special Educational Needs in Certificate Examinations', Report to the Minister for Education and Science, Dublin: Department of Education and Science.

Department of Education and Science (2001), Statistical Report 1999–2000, Dublin: The Stationery Office.

Department of Equality and Law Reform (1996), 'A Strategy for Equality', Report of the Commission on the Status of People with Disabilities, Dublin: The Stationery Office.

Department of Health (1972), Home Help Services, Circular 11/72.

Department of Health (1975), 'Training and Employing the Handicapped', Report of a Working Party, Dublin: The Stationery Office.

Department of Health (1980), 'Services for the Mentally Handicapped', Report of a Working Party, Dublin: The Stationery Office.

Department of Health (1984), 'Towards a Full Life', Green Paper on Services for Disabled People, Dublin: The Stationery Office.

Department of Health, Needs and Abilities (1990), 'A Policy for the Intellectually Disabled', Report of the Review Group on Mental Handicap Services, Dublin: The Stationery Office.

Department of Health (1996), 'Towards an Independent Future', Report of the Review Group on Health and Personal Social Services for People with Physical and Sensory Disabilities, Dublin: The Stationery Office.

Department of Health (1997), 'Enhancing the Partnership', Report of the Working Group on the Implementation of the Health Strategy in Relation to Persons with a Mental Handicap, Dublin: The Stationery Office.

Department of Health and Children (2001), 'Quality and Fairness: A Health System for You', Health Strategy, Dublin: The Stationery Office.

Department of Justice, Equality and Law Reform (1999), 'Towards Equal Citizenship', Progress Report on the Implementation of the Recommendations of the Commission on the Status of People with Disabilities, Dublin: Stationery Office.

Dickson, D. (1988), 'In Search of the Old Irish Poor Law', in R. Mitchison and P. Roebuck (eds.), *Economy and Society in Scotland and Ireland 1500–1939*, Edinburgh: John Donald, 149–59.

Digby, A. (1996), 'Contexts and Perspectives', in D. Wright and A. Digby (eds.), *From Idiocy to Mental Deficiency: Historical Perspectives on People with Learning Difficulties*, London: Routledge, 1–21.

Digby, A. (1997), 'The Patient's View', in I. Loudon (ed.), *Western Medicine*, Oxford: Oxford University Press, 291–306.

Dobbs, A. (1729), *An Essay on the Trade and Improvement of Ireland*, Dublin: A. Rhames for J. Smith and W. Bruce.

Donajgrodski, A. (1977), '"Social Police" and the Bureaucratic Elite: A Vision of Social Order in the Age of Reform', in A. Donajgrodski (ed.), *Social Control in Nineteenth Century Britain*, London: Croom Helm, 51–76.

Drake, R. (1996), 'A Critique of the Role of Traditional Charities', in L. Barton (ed.), *Disability and Society: Emerging Issues and Insights*, Harlow, Essex: Addison Wesley Longman, 147–66.

Drake, R. (1999), *Understanding Disability Policy*, London: Macmillan.

Dreyfus, H. and Rabinow, P. (1982), *Michel Foucault: Beyond Structuralism and Hermeneutics*, Brighton: The Harvester Press.

Driver, F. (1993), *Power and Pauperism: The Workhouse System, 1834–1884*, Cambridge: Cambridge University Press.

Drudy, S. and Lynch, K. (1993), *Schools and Society in Ireland*, Dublin: Gill and Macmillan.

Dublin Directory (1825), *The Gentleman's and Citizen's Almanac*, Dublin: Stewart and Hopes.

*Dublin Journal of Medical Science* (1909), vol. 127, February.

*Dublin Journal of Medical Science* (1911), vol. 131, June.

*Dublin Penny Journal* (1836), vol. iv, no. 196, April 2.

Education Act 1988, Dublin: The Stationery Office.

Edwards, D. (ed.) (2004), *Regions and Rulers in Ireland 1100–1650*, Dublin: Four Courts Press.

Elias, N. (1994), *The Civilising Process: The History of Manners and State Formation and Civilization*, Oxford: Blackwell.

Emerson, E. (1992), 'What is Normalisation?', in H. Brown and H. Smith (eds.) *Normalisation: A Reader for the Nineties*, London: Routledge, 1–18.

Employment Equality Act 1998, Dublin: The Stationery Office.

Equal Status Act 2000, Dublin: The Stationery Office.

Equality Studies Centre, University College Dublin (2000), 'Education for Transformation', 10th Anniversary Report.

Ericsson, K. and Mansell, J. (1996), 'Introduction: Towards Institutionalisation', in J. Mansell and K. Ericsson (eds.), *Deinstitutionalisation and Community Living: Intellectual Disability Services in Britain, Scandanavia and the USA*, London: Chapman and Hall, 1–16.

Eurobarometer (2001), *Europeans and Disability*, Brussels: European Commission.

European Commission (1998), Compendium on Member States' Policies on Equality of Opportunity for People with Disabilities, Directorate-General for Employment, Industrial Relations and Social affairs, Unit V/E.4.

European Commission (1999), 'Raising Employment Levels of People with Disabilities: The Common Challenge', Luxembourg: Office for the Official Publications of the European Communities.

European Commission (2001), 'The Institutions and Bodies of the European Union: Who's Who in the European Union', Luxembourg: Office for Official Publications of the European Communities.

European Social Fund Evaluation Unit (1996), 'Training for People with Disabilities', Summary Report, Dublin: Author.

European Union (2000), Council of Ministers, Council Directive 2000/43/EC, Establishing a General Framework for Equal Treatment in Employment and Occupation, *Official Journal of the European Communities*, L 303/16 of 2000.

Evans, D., Healy, E. and McGuire, B. (2003), 'The Development of Personal Relationships and Sexuality Guidelines for People with Learning Disabilities', in *Using Emancipatory Methodologies in Disability Research*, Conference Proceedings, Inaugural NDA Disability Research Conference, 3 December 2002, Dublin: National Disability Authority, 129–39.

Fahey, T. (1987), 'Nuns in the Catholic Church in Ireland in the Nineteenth Century', in M. Cullen (ed.), *Girls Don't Do Honours*, Dublin: Women's Education Bureau, 7–30.

Faughnan, P. and O'Connor, S. (1980), *Major Issues in Planning Services for Mentally and Physically Handicapped Persons, Part II*, Dublin: National Economic and Social Council.

Finch, J. and Groves, D. (eds.) (1983), *Labour of Love: Women, Work and Caring*, London: Routledge and Kegan Paul.

Fine, M. and Asch, A. (eds.) (1988), *Women with Disabilities: Essays in Psychology, Culture and Politics*, Philadelphia: Temple University Press.

Finkelstein, V. (1980), *Attitudes and Disabled People*, Geneva: World Health Organisation.

Finklestein, V. (1991), 'Disability: An Administrative Challenge', in M. Oliver (ed.), *Social Work: Disabled People and Disabling Environments*, London: Jessica Kingsley, 19–39.

Finklestein, V. (1996), 'Outside "Inside Out"', *Coalition*, April, 30–6.

Finnane, M. (1981), *Insanity and the Insane in Post-Famine Ireland*, London: Croom Helm.

Finzsch, N. and Jütte, R. (1996), *Institutions of Confinement: Hospitals, Asylums and Prisons in Western Europe and North America, 1500–1950*, Cambridge: Cambridge University Press.

Fischer, R. and Lane, H. (eds.), *Looking Back: A Reader on the History of Deaf Communities and their Sign Languages*, Hamburg: Signum Press.

Fissell, M. (1991), 'The Disappearance of the Patient's Narrative and the Invention of Hospital Medicine', in R. French and A. Wear (eds.), *British Medicine in an Age of Reform*, London: Routledge, 92–109.

Fitzgerald, P. (1994), *Poverty and Vagrancy in Early Modern Ireland*, unpublished Ph.D. thesis, Queen's University Belfast.

Fleetwood, J. (1983), *The History of Medicine in Ireland*, 2nd edition, Dublin: Skellig Press.

Fletcher, A. (2001), '"Three Generations of Imbeciles are Enough": Eugenics, the New Genetics and People with Learning Difficulties', in L. Ward (ed.), *Considered Choices: The New Genetics, Prenatal Testing and People with Learning Disabilities*, Kidderminster: British Institute of Learning Disabilities, 72–107.

Flick, L. (1914), 'Eugenics and Mental Diseases', *The Ecclesiastical Review*, vol. 51, August, 151–8.

Forsberg, E. (1992), 'The "long term mentally ill"', in P.G. Svensson and B. Starrin (eds.), *Health Policy Development for Disadvantaged Groups*, Oslo: Scandinavian University Press, 13–57.

Foucault, M. (1971), *Madness and Civilization: A History of Insanity in the Age of Reason*, London: Tavistock.

Foucault, M. (1976), *The Birth of the Clinic: An Archaeology of Medical Perception*, London: Tavistock.

Foucault, M. (1977), *Discipline and Punish: The Birth of the Prison*, London: Allen Lane.

Foucault, M. (1979), *A History of Sexuality, Vol. 1*, London: Allen Lane.

Foucault, M. (1980), *Power/Knowledge: Selected Interviews and Other Writings 1972–1977*, New York: Harvester Wheatsheaf.

Foucault, M. (1982), 'The Subject and Power', in H. Dreyfus and P. Rabinow, (eds.), *Michel Foucault: Beyond Structuralism and Hermeneutics*, New York: Harvester Wheatsheaf, 208–26.

Foucault, M. (2002), *Essential Works of Foucault 1954–1984, Vol. 3*, London: Penguin, edited by James D. Faubion.

Fownes, W. (1725), *Methods Proposed for Regulating the Poor, Supporting of Some and Employing Others, According to their Several Capacities*, Dublin: J. Hyde.

Fraser, N. (1995), 'From Redistribution to Recognition? Dilemmas of Justice in a 'Post-Socialist' Age', *New Left Review*, 212, 68–91.

Fraser, N. (2000), 'Rethinking Recognition', *New Left Review*, 2(3), 107–120.

Freeman, T. (1989), 'Land and People c. 1841', in W. Vaughan (ed.), *A New History of Ireland, Vol. V: Ireland Under the Union 1801–1870*, Oxford: Clarendon Press, 242–71.

Freidson, E. (1963), *The Hospital in Modern Society*, New York: The Free Press.

French, S. (1993), Disability, Impairment or Something in Between? in J. Swain *et al.* (eds.), *Disabling Barriers – Enabling Environments*, London: Sage, in association with The Open University, 17–25.

French, S. (ed.) (1994), *On Equal Terms: Working with Disabled People*, Oxford: Butterworth-Heinemann.

Geary, L. (2004), *Medicine and Charity in Ireland 1718–1851*, Dublin: University College Dublin Press.

Gemerek, B. (1994), *Poverty: A History*, Oxford: Blackwell.

Gerrard, T. (1911), 'The Catholic Church and Race Culture', *The Dublin Review*, vol. 149, July, 49–68.

Gerrard, T. (1912), *The Church and Eugenics*, London: P.S. King and Son.

Gerrard, T. (1913), 'The Mental Deficiency Bill', *The Dublin Review*, vol. 152, January, 21–40.

Gilbert, J. (1891), *Calendar of Ancient Records of Dublin, Vol. II*; (1892) *Vol. III*, Dublin: Joseph Dollard.

Gilman, S. and Chamberlain, J. (eds.) (1985), *Degeneration: The Dark Side of Progress*, New York: Columbia University Press.

Goddard, H. (1912), *The Kallikak Family: A Study in the Heredity of Feeble-Mindedness*, New York: Macmillan.

Goffman, E. (1961), *Asylums: Essays on the Social Situation of Mental Patients and Other Inmates*, New York: Doubleday.

Goffman, E. (1963), *Stigma: Notes on the Management of a Spoiled Identity*, Harmondsworth: Penguin.

Good, A. (2003), 'The Mixed Economy of Welfare: State, NGOs and the Private Sector', in S. Quin and B. Redmond (eds.), *Disability and Social Policy in Ireland*, Dublin: University College Dublin Press, 139–54.

Goodley, D. and Rapley, M. (2002), 'Changing the Subject: Postmodernity and People with "Learning Difficulties"', in M. Corker and T. Shakespeare (eds.), *Disability/Postmodernity: Embodying Disability Theory*, London: Continuum, 127–42.

Gould, S. (1987), *The Mismeasure of Man*, rev. edition, London: Penguin Books.

Gramsci, A. (1971), *Selections from the Prison Notebooks*, London: Lawrence and Wishart, edited and translated by Q. Hoare and G. Nowell Smith.

Gregory, S. and Hartley, G. (1991), *Constructing Deafness*, London: Pinter Publishers in association with The Open University.

Grell, O. (1997), 'The Protestant Imperative of Christian Care and Neighbourly Love', in O. Grell, and A. Cunningham (eds.), *Health Care and Poor Relief in Protestant Europe 1500–1700*, London: Routledge, 43–65.

Grell, O. and Cunningham, A. (eds.) (1997), *Health Care and Poor Relief in Protestant Europe 1500–1700*, London: Routledge.

Griffiths, P. (1996), 'Masterless Young People in Norwich, 1560–1645', in P. Griffiths, A. Fox and S. Hindle (eds.), *The Experience of Authority in Early Modern England*, Basingstoke: Macmillan Press, 146–86.

Hacking, I. (1990), *The Taming of Chance*, Cambridge: Cambridge University Press.

Hahn, H. (1985), 'Disability Policy and the Problem of Discrimination', *American Behavioural Scientist*, 28(3), 293–318.

Hahn, H. (1986), 'Public Support for Rehabilitation Programs: The Analysis of US Disability Policy', *Disability, Handicap and Society*, 1, 121–138.

Hahn Rafter, N. (1997), *Creating Born Criminals*, Chicago: University of Illinois Press.

Halpern, J., Sackett, K., Binner, P. and Mohr, C. (1980), *The Myths of Deinstitutionalisation: Policies for the Mentally Disabled*, Boulder, Co.: Westview Press.

Hansen, B. (1996), 'Something Rotten in the State of Denmark: Eugenics and the Ascent of the Welfare State', in G. Broberg and N. Roll-Hansen (eds.), *Eugenics and the Welfare State: Sterilization Policy in Denmark, Sweden, Norway and Finland*, East Lansing: Michigan State University Press, 10–76.

Harbison, J. (2003), 'Poverty and Disability: A Northern Ireland Perspective', in S. Quin and B. Redmond (eds.), *Disability and Social Policy in Ireland*, Dublin: University College Dublin Press, 155–70.

Harrison, R. (1995), 'Medical Education at the Rotunda Hospital 1745–1995', in A. Browne (ed.), *Masters, Midwives and Ladies-in-Waiting: The Rotunda Hospital 1745–1995*, Dublin: A. & A. Farmar, 66–76.

Hevey, D. (1992), *The Creatures Time Forgot: Photography and Disability Imagery*, London: Routledge.

Hickey, D. (1997), *Local Hospitals in Ancien Régime France: Rationalisation, Resistance, Renewal, 1530–1789*, Quebec: McGill-Queen's University Press.

Hietala, M. (1996), 'From Race Hygiene to Sterilization: The Eugenics Movement in Finland', in G. Broberg and N. Roll-Hansen (eds.), *Eugenics and the Welfare State: Sterilization Policy in Denmark, Sweden, Norway and Finland*, East Lansing: Michigan State University Press, 195–258.

Hill, C. (1974), *Change and Continuity in Seventeenth Century England*, London: Weidenfeld and Nicolson.

Himmelfarb, G. (1984), *The Idea of Poverty: England in the Early Industrial Age*, London: Faber.

Hobbes, T. (1996), *Leviathan*, Oxford: Oxford University Press, edited by J. Gaskin.

Hoffmeister, R. (1996), 'Cross-Cultural Misinformation: What does Special Education say about Deaf People?', *Disability and Society*, 11(2), 171–89.

Hoppen, K.T. (1989), *Ireland Since 1800: Conflict and Conformity*, Harlow, Essex: Longman.

Howard, J. (1789), *An Account of the Principal Lazarettos in Europe*, Warrington: William Eyres.

Hufton, O. (1974), *The Poor of 18th Century France 1750–1789*, Oxford: Clarendon Press.

Hughes, B. (1999), 'The Constitution of Impairment: Modernity and the Aesthetic of Oppression', *Disability and Society*, 14(2), 155–72.

Hughes, B. (2000), 'Medicine and the Aesthetic Invalidation of Disabled People', *Disability and Society*, 15(4), 555–68.

Hughes, B. (2002), 'Disability and the Body', in C. Barnes, M. Oliver and L. Barton (eds.), *Disability Studies Today*, Cambridge: Polity Press, 58–76.

Hughes, B. and Paterson, K. (1997), 'The Social Model of Disability and the Disappearing Body: Towards a Sociology of Impairment', *Disability and Society*, 12(3), 325–40.

Hunt, P. (1966), *Stigma: The Experience of Disability*, London: Geoffrey Chapman.

Hyde, D. (1894), 'The Necessity for De-Anglecising Ireland', in C.G. Duffy, G. Sigerson and D. Hyde (eds.), *The Revival of Irish Literature*, London: T. Fisher Unwin, 117–61.

Hyde, M. (1995), 'Fifty Years of Failure: Employment Services for Disabled People in the UK', *Work, Employment and Society*, 10(4), 683–700.

Hyland, A. and Milne, K. (eds.) (1987), *Irish Educational Documents, Vol. 1*, Dublin: Church of Ireland College of Education.

*Hypatia* (2001), Special Issue: *Feminism and Disability*, Part I, 16(4); (2002), Part II, 17(3).

Ignatieff, M. (1983), 'State, Civil Society and Total Institutions: A Critique of Recent Social Histories of Punishment', in S. Cohen and A. Scull (eds.), *Social Control and the State: Historical and Comparative Essays*, Oxford: Martin Robinson, 75–105.

Ingleby, D. (1983), 'Mental Health and Social Order', in S. Cohen and A. Scull (eds.), *Social Control and the State: Historical and Comparative Essays*, Oxford: Martin Robinson, 141–88.

Ingram, M. (1996), 'Reformation of Manners in Early Modern England', in P. Griffiths, A. Fox and S. Hindle (eds.), *The Experience of Authority in Early Modern England*, Basingstoke: Macmillan, 47–88.

Inspectors of Lunatics in Ireland (1855), Seventh Report; (1898), Forty-eighth Report, Dublin: Alexander Thom.

Ireland (1786), Journal of the House of Commons of the Kingdom of Ireland.

Ireland, W. (1900), *The Mental Affections of Children: Idiocy, Imbecility and Insanity*, 2nd edition, London: Churchill.

Jenkins, R. (1998), 'Culture, Classification and (In)competence', *Questions of Competence: Culture, Classification and Intellectual Disability*, Cambridge: Cambridge University Press, 1–24.

Jewson, N. (1976), 'The Disappearance of the Sick-Man from Medical Cosmology, 1770–1870', *Sociology XII*, 369–85.

Johnson, T. (1972), *Professions and Power*, London: Macmillan.

Jones, C. (1989), *The Charitable Imperative: Hospitals and Nursing in Ancien Régime and Revolutionary France*, London: Routledge.

Jones, C. (1996), 'The Construction of the Hospital Patient in Early Modern France', in N. Finzsch and R. Jütte (eds.), *Institutions of Confinement: Hospitals, Asylums and Prisons in Western Europe and North America, 1500–1950*, Cambridge: Cambridge University Press, 55–74.

Jones, G. (1992), 'Eugenics in Ireland: the Belfast Eugenics Society, 1911–15', *Irish Historical Studies*, 28, 81–95.

Jones, K. and Tillotson, A. (1965), *The Adult Population of Epileptic Colonies*, London: British Epilepsy Association and International Bureau for Epilepsy.

Jütte, R. (1997), 'Health Care Provision and Poor Relief in Early Modern Hanseatic Towns: Hamburg, Bremen and Lübeck', in O. Grell, and A. Cunningham (eds.), *Health Care and Poor Relief in Protestant Europe 1500–1700*, London: Routledge, 105–28.

Kallianes, V. and Rubenfeld, P. (1997), 'Disabled Women and Reproductive Rights', *Disability and Society*, 12(2), 203–21.

Kamen, H. (1984), *European Society 1500–1700*, London: Hutchinson.

Kamen, H. (2000), *Early Modern European Society*, Routledge: London.

Kamin, L. (1974), *The Science and Politics of I.Q.*, New York: Wiley.

Kelly, F. (1988), *A Guide to Early Irish Law*, Dublin: Dublin Institute for Advanced Studies.

Kelly, J. (1986), 'The Context and Course of Thomas Orde's Plan of Education of 1787', *The Irish Journal of Education*, 20(1), 3–26.

Kelly, J. (1999), 'The Emergence of Scientific and Institutional Medical Practice in Ireland, 1650–1800', in E. Malcolm and G. Jones (eds.),

*Medicine, Disease and the State in Ireland, 1650–1940*, Cork: Cork University Press, 21–39.

Kelly, M. (1978), *Selection and Transmission Processes within the Irish National System of Education 1831–1900*, unpublished Ph.D. Thesis, University of Cambridge.

Kevles, D. (1985), *In the Name of Eugenics: Genetics and the Uses of Human Heredity*, New York: Alfred Knopf.

Kidd, A. (1999), *State, Society and the Poor in Nineteenth Century England*, Basingstoke: Macmillan.

Kinealy, C. (1994), *The Great Calamity: The Irish Famine 1845–52*, Dublin: Gill and Macmillan.

Kirkebaek, B. (2002), Normalisation Seen as an Anti-dogma Project: The Danish Foundation and Formulation of the Normalisation Concept, Personal Communication.

Kirkebaek, B. (2002*a*), The Mentally Deficient and the Period of Normalisation, Personal Communication.

Kittay, E. (1999), *Love's Labour: Essays on Equality, Women and Dependency*, New York: Routledge.

Kittay, E. (2001), 'When Caring is Just and Justice Caring: Justice and Mental Retardation', *Public Culture*, 13(3), 557–79.

Kühl, S. (1994), *The Nazi Connection: Eugenics, American Racism and German National Socialism*, Oxford: Oxford University Press.

Kuhn, T. (1962), *The Structure of Scientific Revolutions*, Chicago: Chicago University Press.

Kwiotek, R. (1999), *The Need for a Disability Equality Model*, unpublished Master of Equality Studies thesis, Equality Studies Centre, University College Dublin.

Kwiotek, R. and McDonnell, P. (2003), 'Disability in an Equality Framework', *Studies*, 92(366), Summer, 151–160.

Kyle, J. and Woll, B. (1985), *Sign Language: The Study of Deaf People and Their Language*, Cambridge: Cambridge University Press.

Labov, W. (1973), 'The Logic of Non-Standard English', in N. Keddie (ed.), *Tinker, Tailor ... The Myth of Cultural Deprivation*, Harmondsworth: Penguin, 21–66.

Ladd, P. (2003), *Understanding Deaf Culture: In Search of Deafhood*, Clevedon: Multilingual Matters.

Laing, R. (1967), *The Politics of Experience and the Bird of Paradise*, Harmondsworth: Penguin.

Lane, H. (1984), *When the Mind Hears*, London: Penguin Books.

Lane, H. (1993), *The Mask of Benevolence*, New York: Vintage Books.

Lane, H. (2002), 'Do Deaf People have a Disability?', *Sign Language Studies*, 2(4), 356–79.

Larkin, E. (1967), 'Economic Growth, Capital Investment, and the Roman Catholic Church in Nineteenth-Century Ireland', *American Historical Review*, 72(3), 852–884.

Leane, M. and Sapouna, L. (1998), 'Deinstitutionalisation in the Republic of Ireland', in J. Campbell and R. Manktelow (eds.), *Mental Health Social Work in Ireland: Comparative Issues in Policy and Practice*, Aldershot: Ashgate, 101–121.

Lee, G. (1996), *Leper Hospitals in Medieval Ireland*, Dublin: Four Courts Press.

Leeper, R. (1912), 'A Note on the Cause of Insanity in Ireland', *Dublin Journal of Medical Science*, vol. 133, March, 180–87.

Leeper, R. (1912a) 'Report of the Transactions of the Royal Academy of Medicine in Ireland', *Dublin Journal of Medical Science*, vol. 133, April, 294.

Leeson, L. (2007), NCSE /Advisory Committee Report, Personal communication.

Lennon, C. (1999), 'Dives and Lazarus in Sixteenth Ireland', in J. Hill and C. Lennon (eds.), *Luxury and Austerity: Historical Studies XXI*, Dublin: University College Dublin Press, 46–65.

Levine, M. (1981), *The History and Politics of Community Mental Health*, Oxford: Oxford University Press.

Lewis, J. (1997), 'Medicine, Politics, and the State', in I. Loudon (ed.), *Western Medicine*, Oxford: Oxford University Press, 277–90.

Lindsay, D. (1987), 'The Sick and Indigent Roomkeepers' Society', in D. Dickson (ed.), *The Gorgeous Mask: Dublin 1700–1850*, Dublin: Trinity History Workshop, 132–56.

Lis, C. and Soly, H. (1979), *Poverty and Capitalism in Pre-Industrial Europe*, Hassocks, Sussex: The Harvester Press.

Lonsdale, S. (1990), *Women and Disability*, London: Macmillan.

Loudon, I. (ed.) (1997), *Western Medicine*, Oxford: Oxford University Press.

Love, S. (2003), Preface in *Mental Illness: The Neglected Quarter*, Dublin: Amnesty International (Irish Section), 4.

Luddy, M. (1988), Women and Charitable Institutions in Nineteenth Century Ireland, *Women's Studies International Forum*, 11(4), 301–5.

Luddy, M. (1995), *Women and Philanthropy in Nineteenth-Century Ireland*, Cambridge: Cambridge University Press.

Lundstrom, F. and McKeown, K. (1994), *Home Help Services for Elderly People in Ireland*, Dublin: National Council for the Elderly.

Lynch, K., Cantillon, S. and Baker, J. (2001), *Equality: Frameworks for Change*, Revised Draft of Paper presented to the National Economic and

Social Forum, Dublin: Equality Studies Centre, University College Dublin.

Lynch, K. and Lodge, A. (2002), *Equality and Power in Schools*: *Redistribution, Recognition and Representation*, London: Routledge Falmer.

Lynch, K. and McLaughlin, E. (1995), 'Caring Labour and Love Labour', in P. Clancy, S. Drudy, K. Lynch and L. O'Dowd (eds.), *Irish Society*: *Sociological Perspectives*, Dublin: Institute of Public Administration, 250–92.

Lyons, F.S.L. (1973), *Ireland Since the Famine*, London: Fontana.

Lyons, J.B. (1991), *The Quality of Mercer's*: *The Story of Mercer's Hospital, 1743–1991*, Dublin: Glendale.

McAdam, D., McCarthy, J. and Zald, M. (eds.) (1996), *Comparative Perspectives on Social Movements*: *Political Opportunities, Mobilizing Structures and Cultural Framings*, Cambridge: Cambridge University Press.

McAvoy, S. (1999), 'The Regulation of Sexuality in the Irish Free State 1929–1935', in E. Malcolm and G. Jones (eds.), *Medicine, Disease and the State in Ireland, 1650–1940*, Cork: Cork University Press, 253–66.

McCartney, D. (1987), *The Dawning of Democracy*: *Ireland 1800–1870*, Dublin: Helicon.

MacDermott, W. (1910), 'Science and Evolution', *New Ireland Review*, 33, 339–49.

MacDonagh, O. (1977), *Ireland*: *The Union and Its Aftermath*, London: George Allen and Unwin.

MacDonagh, O. (1989), 'Ideas and Institutions 1830–1845', in W.E. Vaughan (ed.), *New History of Ireland, Vol. 5*, Oxford: Oxford University Press, 193–217.

McDonnell, P. (1979), *The Establishment and Operation of Institutions for the Education of the Deaf in Ireland, 1816–1889*, unpublished essay, Education Department, University College Dublin.

McDonnell, P. (1992), 'Vested Interests in the Development of Special Education in Ireland', *Reach*, 5(2), 97–106.

McDonnell, P. (1992a), 'Giving it up for Lent: Colonising Language', paper given at the Fourth Annual Conference of the Irish Association of Teachers in Special Education, St. Patrick's College, Drumcondra, Dublin 9, 11–14 June.

McDonnell, P. (1994), 'New Perspectives on the History of Modern Sign Languages: Evidence from Irish Sign Language', paper presented at the Second International Conference on Deaf History, Hamburg, 1–4 October.

McDonnell, P. (1995), 'Integration in Education in Ireland: Rhetoric and Reality', paper presented at the European Conference on Educational Research, University of Bath, September 14–17.

McDonnell, P. (1996), *Verb Categories in Irish Sign Language*, unpublished Ph.D. thesis, University of Dublin, Trinity College.

McDonnell, P. (1996*a*), 'Suitable Cases for Treatment: Institutionalising Difference in 19th century Ireland', paper presented at a seminar Culture, Difference and Inclusion, Education Division, University of Sheffield, 16–19 February.

McDonnell, P. (2000), 'Inclusive Education in Ireland', in D. Armstrong, F. Armstrong and L. Barton (eds.), *Inclusive Education: Policy, Contexts and Comparative Perspectives*, London: David Fulton, 12–26.

McDonnell, P. (2000*a*), 'Deep Structures in Deaf Education: Implications for Policy', in L. Leeson (ed.), *Looking Forward: The Deaf Citizen in the 21st Century*, Coleford, Glos.: Forest Books, 100–15.

McDonnell, P. (2003), 'Education Policy', in S. Quin and B. Redmond (eds.), *Disability and Social Policy in Ireland*, Dublin: University College Dublin Press, 28–44.

McDonnell, P. (2003*a*), 'Developments in Special Education in Ireland: Deep Structures and Policy Making', *International Journal of Inclusive Education*, 7(3), 259–69.

McDonnell, P. and Saunders, H. (1993), 'Sit on your Hands: Strategies to Prevent Signing', in R. Fischer and H. Lane (eds.), *Looking Back: A Reader on the History of Deaf Communities and their Sign Languages*, Hamburg: Signum Press, 255–60.

McDowell, R. (1989), 'Administration and the Public Services', in W.E. Vaughan (ed.), *New History of Ireland, Vol. V*, Oxford: Oxford University Press, 538–61.

McDowell, R. (1994), 'Ireland on the Eve of the Famine', in R.D. Edwards and T.D. Williams (eds.), *The Great Irish Famine: Studies in Irish History, 1845–1852*, new edition, Dublin: The Lilliput Press, 3–86.

McGeachie, J. (1999), ' "Normal" Development in an "Abnormal" Place: Sir William Wilde and the Irish School of Medicine', in E. Malcolm and G. Jones (eds.), *Medicine, Disease and the State in Ireland, 1650–1940*, Cork: Cork University Press, 85–101.

McGee, P. (1990), 'Special Education in Ireland', *European Journal of Special Educational Needs*, 3(1), 48–63.

MacKenzie, D. (1981), *Statistics in Britain 1865–1930: The Social Construction of Scientific Knowledge*, Edinburgh: Edinburgh University Press.

McLaren, A. (1990), *Our Own Master Race: Eugenics in Canada, 1885–1945*, Ontario: McClelland and Stewart.

McLellan, D. (1995), *Ideology*, 2nd edition, Buckingham: Open University Press.

McManus, A. (2003), 'Social Security and Disability', in S. Quin and B. Redmond (eds.), *Disability and Social Policy in Ireland*, Dublin: University College Dublin Press, 57–67.

McSweeney, C. (1929), 'The Case against Sterilization of Mental Defectives', *The Catholic Medical Guardian*, 7(3), 92–5.

Malcolm, E. (1991), 'Women and Madness in Ireland 1600–1850', in M. MacCurtain and M. O'Dowd (eds.), *Women in Early Modern Ireland*, Dublin: Wolfhound Press, 318–34.

Malcolm, E. (1999), '"The House of Strident Shadows": The Asylum, the Family and Emigration in Post-Famine Rural Ireland', in E. Malcolm and G. Jones (eds.), *Medicine, Disease and the State in Ireland, 1650–1940*, Cork: Cork University Press, 177–91.

Malcolm, E. and Jones, G. (eds.) (1990), *Medicine, Disease and the State in Ireland, 1650–1940*, Cork: Cork University Press.

Malthus, T. (1803), *An Essay on the Principle of Population*, selected and introduced by D. Winch using the 1803 edition, Cambridge: Cambridge University Press.

Maxwell, C. (1956), *Dublin under the Georges*, 1714–1830, rev. edition, London: Faber.

Mayer, J. (1983), 'Notes towards a Working Definition of Social Control in Historical Analysis', in S. Cohen and A. Scull (eds.), *Social Control and the State*: *Historical and Comparative Essays*, Oxford: Martin Robinson, 17–38.

Meadmore, D. (1993), 'Divide and Rule: A Study of two Dividing Practices in Queensland Schools', in R. Slee (ed.), *Is There a Desk with My Name on It? The Politics of Integration*, London: The Falmer Press, 27–38.

Medoff, M. (1982), *Children of a Lesser God*, new edition, Ambergate, Darbyshire: Amber Lane Press.

Meekosha, H. and Jakubowicz, A. (1996), 'Disability, Participation, Representation and Social Justice', in C. Christensen and F. Rizvi (eds.), *Disability and the Dilemmas of Education and Justice*, Buckingham: Open University Press, 79–95.

Mercer, J. (1974), *Labelling the Mentally Retarded*, Berkeley: University of California Press.

Miller, M. (1996), *Terminating the 'Socially Inadequate': The American Eugenicists and the German Race Hygienists, California to Cold Spring Harbor, Long Island to Germany*, Commack, NY: Malamud-Rose.

Mollat, M. (1986), *The Poor in the Middle Ages*, translated by Arthur Goldhammer, New Haven, Yale University Press.

Moore, J. (2004), 'The Fortunes of Eugenics', in D. Brunton (ed.), *Medicine Transformed: Health, Disease and Society in Europe 1800–1930*,

Manchester: Manchester University Press in association with the Open University, 204–28.

More, T. (2002), *Utopia* (in G. Logan and R. Adams (eds.), Cambridge Texts in the History of Political Thought), rev. edition, Cambridge: Cambridge University Press.

Morris, J. (1991), *Pride against Prejudice*, London: The Women's Press.

Morris, J. (1993), 'Gender and Disability', in J. Swain *et al.* (eds.), *Disabling Barriers – Enabling Environments*, London: Sage, 85–92.

Morris, J. (1993a), *Independent Lives? Community Care and Disabled People*, London: Macmillan.

Morris, J. (1994), 'The Shape of Things to Come: User-Led Social Services', Social Services Policy Forum, Paper No. 3, London: National Institute for Social Work.

Morris, J. (ed.) (1996), *Encounters with Strangers: Feminism and Disability*, London: The Women's Press.

Munck, T. (1990), *Seventeenth Century Europe: States, Conflict and the Social Order in Europe, 1598–1700*, Basingstoke: Macmillan.

Murphy-Lawless, J. (1988), 'The Silencing of Women in Childbirth or Let's Hear it from Bartholomew and the Boys', *Women's Studies International Forum*, 11(4), 293–8.

Murphy-Lawless, J. (1991), 'Images of "Poor" Women in the Writing of Irish Men Midwives', in M. MacCurtain and M. O'Dowd (eds.), *Women in Early Modern Ireland*, Dublin: Wolfhound Press, 291–303.

Murphy-Lawless, J. (1998), *Reading Birth and Death: A History of Obstetric Thinking*, Cork: Cork University Press.

Murray, B. (1998), *An Analysis of the Promotion of Equality of Opportunity for Occupational Integration of People with Disabilities*, unpublished dissertation, Master of Equality Studies, School of Equality and Social Justice, University College Dublin.

National Disability Authority (2002), *Public Attitudes to Disability in the Republic of Ireland*, Dublin: Author.

National Economic and Social Council (1987), *Community Care Services: An Overview*, Dublin: Author.

National Institution for the Education of Deaf and Dumb Children of the Poor in Ireland, Annual Reports 1817–, Dublin: Author.

National Rehabilitation Board (1994), *Equal Status: A Blueprint for Action*, Submission to the Commission on the Status of People with Disabilities, Dublin: Author.

Nesbitt, Dr (1912), 'Report of the Transactions of the Royal Academy of Medicine in Ireland', *Dublin Journal of Medical Science*, vol. 133, April, 293.

Nettleton, S. (1995), *The Sociology of Health and Illness*, Cambridge: Polity Press.

Neufeldt, A. and Albright, A. (1998), *Disability and Self-Directed Employment*, Ontario: Caftus University Publications.

Nicholas, D. (1997), *The Late Medieval City 1300–1500*, London: Longman.

Nicholls, G. (1854), *A History of the English Poor Law*, London: John Murray.

Nicholls, G. (1856), *A History of the Irish Poor Law*, London: John Murray.

Nirje, B. (1969), 'The Normalisation Principle and its Human Management Implications', in R. Kugel and W. Wolfensberger (eds.), *Changing Patterns in Residential Services for the Mentally Retarded*, Washington: President's Committee on Mental Retardation, 227–254.

Nixon, C. (1912), 'Statement of Evidence Given before the Royal Commission on the Care and Control of the Feeble-minded', *Dublin Journal of Medical Science*, vol. 134, 192–215.

Nolan, B. (2003), *On Rights Based Services for People with Disabilities*, Dublin: The Economic and Social Research Institute.

Nolan, M. J. (1912), 'Presidential address given at the Royal Academy of Medicine in Ireland', *Dublin Journal of Medical Science*, vol. 133, March, 170-80.

Norberg, K. (1985), *Rich and Poor in Grenoble, 1600–1814*, Berkeley: University of California Press.

Nussbaum, M. (1995), 'Emotions and Women's Capabilities', in M. Nussbaum and J. Glover (eds.), *Women, Culture and Development*, Oxford: Clarendon Press, 360–95.

Nye, R. (1984), *Crime, Madness and Politics in Modern France: The Medical Concept of National Decline*, Princeton, NJ: Princeton University Press.

O'Brien, E. (1987), *The Charitable Infirmary, Jervis Street, 1718–1987*, Dublin: The Anniversary Press.

O'Brien, G. (1999), 'State Intervention and the Medical Relief of the Irish Poor, 1787– 1850', in E. Malcolm and G. Jones (eds.) (1990), *Medicine, Disease and the State in Ireland, 1650–1940*, Cork: Cork University Press, 195–207.

O'Brien, G. (1999a), 'Protecting the Social Body: Use of the Organism Metaphor in Fighting the "Menace of the Feebleminded"', *Mental Retardation*, 37(3), 188–200.

O'Carroll, J. (1987), 'Contemporary Attitudes towards the Homeless Poor, 1725–1775', in D. Dickson (ed.), *The Gorgeous Mask: Dublin 1700–1850*, Dublin: Trinity History Workshop, 64–85.

O'Carroll-Burke, P. (2000), *Colonial Discipline: The Making of the Irish Convict System*, Dublin: Four Courts Press.

O'Ciosáin, N. (1998), 'Boccoughs and God's Poor: Deserving and Undeserving Poor in Irish Popular Culture', in T. Foley and S. Ryder (eds.), *Ideology and Ireland in the Nineteenth Century*, Dublin: Four Courts Press, 93–9.

O'Connor, J. (1995), *The Workhouses of Ireland*, Dublin: Anvil Books.

O'Connor, S. (1987), *Community Care Services: An Overview, Part II*, Dublin: National Economic and Social Council.

O'Donnell, M.J. (1920), 'Sociology, Health Bill and Eugenics', *The Irish Theological Quarterly*, 15: 139–54.

O'Donovan, O. (1997), 'Contesting Concepts of Care: The Case of the Home Help Service in Ireland', in A. Cleary and M. Treacy (eds.), *The Sociology of Health and Illness in Ireland*, Dublin: University College Dublin Press, 141–155.

O'Gráda, C. (1989), 'Poverty, Population and Agriculture 1801–1845', in W.E. Vaughan (ed.), *New History of Ireland, Vol. V*, Oxford: Oxford University Press, 108–36.

O'Gráda, C. (1995), 'The Rotunda and the People of Dublin, 1745–1995: Glimpses from the Hospital Records', in A. Browne (ed.), *Masters, Midwives and Ladies-in-Waiting: The Rotunda Hospital 1745–1995*, Dublin: A. & A. Farmar, 240–63.

O'Hanlon, C. (1994), 'The Special Education Review Committee: An Outsider's View', in B. Spelman and S. Griffin (eds.), *Special Educational Needs – Issues for the White Paper*, Dublin: Education Department, University College Dublin and The Educational Studies Association of Ireland, 44–67.

Oliver, M. (1989), 'Disability and Dependency: A Creation of Industrial Societies', in L. Barton (ed.), *Disability and Dependency*, London: Falmer Press.

Oliver, M. (1990), *The Politics of Disablement*, London: Macmillan.

Oliver, M. (1992), 'Changing the Social Relations of Research Production?', *Disability and Society*, 7(2), 101–14.

Oliver, M. (1996), *Understanding Disability: From Theory to Practice*, London: Macmillan.

Oliver, M. (1996a), 'A Sociology of Disability or a Disablist Sociology?', in L. Barton (ed.), *Disability and Society: Emerging Issues and Insights*, London: Longman, 18–42.

Oliver, M. (2002), 'Emancipatory Research: A Vehicle for Social Transformation or Policy Development?', in *Using Emancipatory Research Methodologies in Disability Research*, Conference Proceedings, Inaugral NDA Disability Research Conference, Dublin: National Disability Authority, 15–23.

Oliver, M. and Barnes, C. (1998), *Disabled People and Social Policy: From Exclusion to Inclusion*, London: Longman.

O'Neill, P. (1931), 'Casti Connubii', *Irish Ecclesiastical Record*, vol. 37, March, 225–40.

O'Rahilly, A. (1916), 'Race and Super-Race', *The Dublin Review*, 159(318), 125–40.

Orpen, C. (1828), *The Contrast between Atheism, Paganism and Christianity Illustrated, or, The Deaf and Dumb as Heathens Compared with Those Who Have Been Instructed in Language and Revelation and Taught by the Holy Spirit as Christians*, Dublin: Goodwin.

Orpen, C. (1832), *Address to the Public on the State of the Poor*, Dublin: Goodwin and Co.

Orpen, C. (1836), *Anecdotes and Annals of the Deaf and Dumb*, 2nd edition, London: Tims.

O'Shea, E. and Gillespie, P. (2006), 'Health Policy in Ireland', in S. Healy, B. Reynolds and M. Collins (eds.), *Social Policy in Ireland: Principles, Practice and Problems*, rev. edition, Dublin: The Liffey Press, 271–95.

O'Sullivan, E. (1998), 'Juvenile Justice and the Regulation of the Poor "restored to virtue, to society and to God"', in I. Bacik, and M. O'Connell (eds.), *Crime and Poverty in Ireland*, Dublin: Round Hall Sweet and Maxwell, 68–91.

Owen, D. (1999), 'Power, Knowledge and Ethics: Foucault', in S. Glendinning (ed.), *The Edinburgh Encyclopedia of Continental Philosophy*, Edinburgh: Edinburgh University Press, 593–604.

Padden, C. and Humphries, T. (1990), *Deaf in America: Voices from a Culture*, Cambridge, MA: Harvard University Press.

Park, D. and Radford, J. (1998), 'From the Case Files: Reconstructing a History of Involuntary Sterilisation', *Disability and Society*, 13(3), 317–42.

Paterson, K. and Hughes, B. (1999), 'Disability Studies and Phenomenology: The Carnal Politics of Everyday Life', *Disability and Society*, 14(5), 597–610.

Pelling, M. (1997), 'Unofficial and Unorthodox Medicine', in I. Loudon (ed.), *Western Medicine*, Oxford: Oxford University Press, 264–76.

Pelling, M. (1998), *The Common Lot: Sickness, Medical Occupations and the Urban Poor in early Modern England*, Harlow: Addison Wesley Longman.

Persson, B. (1998), 'Who Needs Special Education?', *International Journal of Educational Research*, vol. 29, 107–17.

Peters, S. (1996), 'The Politics of Disability Identity', in L. Barton (ed.), *Disability and Society: Emerging Issues and Insights*, Harlow, Essex: Addison Wesley Longman, 215–34.

Petersen, E. (1997), 'The Wrath of God: Christian IV and Poor Relief in the Wake of Danish Intervention in the Thirty Years' War', in O. Grell and A. Cunningham (eds.), *Health Care and Poor Relief in Protestant Europe 1500–1700*, London: Routledge, 147–66.

Petty, W. (1691), *The Political Anatomy of Ireland*, London [(1970), Shannon, Ireland: Irish University Press].

Phelan, D. (1835), *A Statistical Inquiry into the Present State of the Medical Charities of Ireland*, Dublin: Hodges and Smith.

Philips, D. (1983), '"A Just Measure of Crime, Authority, Hunters and Blue Locusts": The "Revisionist" Social History of Crime and Law in Britain, 1780–1850', in S. Cohen and A. Scull (eds.), *Social Control and the State: Historical and Comparative Essays*, Oxford: Martin Robinson, 50–74.

Phillips, A. (1995), *The Politics of Presence*, Oxford: Clarendon Press.

Phtiaka, H. (1997), *Special Kids for Special Treatment? or How Special Do You Need to be to Find Yourself in a Special School?* London: The Falmer Press.

Pick, D. (1989), *Faces of Degeneration: A European Disorder, c.1848–c.1918*, Cambridge: Cambridge University Press.

Pilgrim, D. and Rogers, A. (1999), *A Sociology of Mental Health and Illness*, 2nd edition, Buckingham: Open University Press.

Pim, J. (1864), 'On the Necessity of a State Provision for the Education of the Deaf and Dumb, the Blind and Imbeciles', *Journal of the Statistical and Social Inquiry Society of Ireland*, 4, 26–41.

Piven, F.F. and Cloward, R.A. (1972), *Regulating the Poor: The Functions of Public Welfare*, London: Tavistock Publications.

Porter, D. (1999), *Health, Civilization and the State: A History of Public Health from Ancient to Modern Times*, London: Routledge.

Porter, D. (1999a), 'Eugenics and the Sterilization Debate in Sweden and Britain before World War II', *Scandanavian Journal of History*, 24, 145–62.

Porter, R. (ed.) (1985), *Patients and Practitioners: Lay Perceptions of Medicine in Pre-Industrial Society*, Cambridge: Cambridge University Press.

Porter, R. (1989), 'The Gift Relation: Philanthropy and Provincial Hospitals in Eighteenth Century England', in L. Granshaw and R. Porter (eds.), *The Hospital in History*, London: Routledge, 149–78.

Porter, R. (1995), 'The Eighteenth Century', in L. Conrad *et al.*, *The Western Medical Tradition: 800BC to AD 1800*, Cambridge: Cambridge University Press, 371–476.

Porter, R. (1995a), *Disease, Medicine and Society in England, 1550–1860*, 2nd edition, Cambridge: Cambridge University Press.

Porter, R. (1997), *The Greatest Benefit to Mankind: A Medical History of Humanity from Antiquity to the Present*, London: HarperCollins.

Porter, R. (2000), *Enlightenment: Britain and the Creation of the Modern World*, London: Allen Lane.

Potts, P. (1983), 'Medicine, Morals and Mental Deficiency', *Oxford Review of Education*, 9(3), 181–96.

Powell, F. (1992), *The Politics of Irish Social Policy 1600–1990*, Lampeter, Dyfed: The Edward Mellon Press.

Preston, M. (1998), 'Discourse and Hegemony: Race and Class in the Language of Charity in Nineteenth Century Dublin', in T. Foley and S. Ryder (eds.), *Ideology and Ireland in the Nineteenth Century*, Dublin: Four Courts Press, 100–12.

Prior, L. (1991), 'Mind, Body and Behaviour: Theorisations of Madness and the Organisation of Therapy', *Sociology*, 25(3), 403–22.

Quin, S. and Redmond, B. (eds.), *Disability and Social Policy in Ireland*, Dublin: University College Dublin Press.

Quinn, G, with Bruce, A. (2003), 'Towards Free and Inclusive Societies for People with Disabilities', in S. Quin and B. Redmond (eds.), *Disability and Social Policy in Ireland*, Dublin: University College Dublin Press, 182–99.

Rabinow, P. (ed.) (1991), *The Foucault Reader*, London: Penguin.

Radford, J. (1991), 'Sterilization versus Segregation: Control of the "Feebleminded", 1900–1938', *Social Science and Medicine*, 33(4), 449–58.

Radford, J. (1994), 'Intellectual Disability and the Heritage of Modernity', in M. Rioux and M. Bach (eds.), *Disability is Not Measles*, Ontario: L'Institut Roeher Institute, 9–27.

Raftery, M. and O' Sullivan, E. (1999), *Suffer the Little Children: The Inside Story of Ireland's Industrial Schools*, Dublin: New Island Books.

Report of the Association for the Suppression of Mendicity in the City of Dublin for the Year 1818 (1819), Dublin: Thom.

Report of the Royal Commission on the Care and Control of the Feeble-minded, HC 1908 (4202) XXXIX.

Reuber, M. (1999), 'Moral Management and the "Unseen Eye": Public Lunatic Asylums in Ireland, 1800–1845', in E. Malcolm and G. Jones (eds.), *Medicine, Disease and the State in Ireland, 1650–1940*, Cork: Cork University Press, 207–233.

Reynolds, J. (1992), *Grangegorman: Psychiatric Care in Dublin Since 1815*, Dublin: Institute of Public Administration.

Rich, N. (1977), *The Age of Nationalism and Reformation 1850–1890*, 2nd edition, New York: W.W. Norton.

Richardson, R. (1987), *Death, Dissection and the Destitute: A Political History of the Human Corpse*, London: Routledge and Kegan Paul.

Riddell, S. (1996), 'Theorising Special Educational Needs in a Changing Political Climate', in L. Barton (ed.), *Disability and Society: Some Emerging Issues*, Harlow, Essex: Addison Wesley Longman, 83–106.

Riis, T. (1997), 'Poor Relief and Health Care Provision in Sixteenth-Century Denmark', in O. Grell, and A. Cunningham (eds.), *Health Care and Poor Relief in Protestant Europe, 1500–1700*, London: Routledge, 129–46.

Risse, G. (1996), 'Perspectives in Hospital History', in N. Finzsch and R. Jütte (eds.), *Institutions of Confinement: Hospitals, Asylums and Prisons in Western Europe and North America, 1500–1950*, Cambridge: Cambridge University Press, 75–96.

Robins, J. (1980), *The Lost Children: A Study of Charity Children in Ireland 1700–1900*, Dublin: Institute of Public Administration.

Robins, J. (1986), *Fools and Mad: History of the Insane in Ireland*, Dublin: Institute of Public Administration.

Robins, J. (1992), *From Rejection to Integration: A Centenary of Service of Daughters of Charity to Persons with a Mental Handicap*, Dublin: Gill and Macmillan.

Robins, J. (1995), *The Miasma: Epidemic and Panic in 19th Century Ireland*, Dublin: Institute of Public Administration.

Robitscher, J. (ed.) (1973), *Eugenic Sterilization*, Springfield, Ill.: Charles C. Thomas.

Roll-Hansen, N. (1996), 'Norwegian Eugenics: Sterilization as Social Reform', in G. Broberg and N. Roll-Hansen (eds.), *Eugenics and the Welfare State: Sterilization Policy in Denmark, Sweden, Norway and Finland*, East Lansing: Michigan State University Press, 151–94.

Roll-Hansen, N. (1996a), 'Conclusion: Scandanavian Eugenics in the International Context', in G. Broberg and N. Roll-Hansen (eds.), *Eugenics and the Welfare State: Sterilization Policy in Denmark, Sweden, Norway and Finland*, East Lansing: Michigan State University Press, 259–72.

Rose, N. (1985), *The Psychological Complex*, London: Macmillan.

Rose, N. (1986), 'Law, Rights and Psychiatry', in P. Miller and N. Rose (eds.), *The Power of Psychiatry*, Cambridge: Polity Press.

Rose, N. (1990), *Governing the Soul: The Shaping of the Private Self*, London: Routledge.

Rose, N. (1996), *Inventing Our Selves: Psychology, Power and Personhood*, Cambridge: Cambridge University Press.

Rosen, G. (1974), *From Medical Police to Social Medicine: Essays on the History of Health Care*, New York: Science History Publications.

Rothman, D. (1983), 'Social Control: The Uses and Abuses of the Concept in the History of Incarceration', in S. Cohen and A. Scull (eds.), *Social Control and the State: Historical and Comparative Essays*, Oxford: Martin Robinson, 106–17.

Royall, M. (1999), *The Petworth House of Correction: A History of the West Sussex Bridewell*, Author.

Russell, C.W. and Prendergast, J.P. (1872), *Calendar of the State Papers Relating to Ireland 1603–1606*, London: Longman and Co. and Trübner and Co.

Ryan, J. and Thomas, F. (1987), *The Politics of Mental Handicap*, Harmondsworth: Penguin Books.

Ryan, M. (2001), 'Divisions of Poverty in Early Modern Dublin', in J. Augusteijn and M. Lyons (eds.), *Irish History: A Research Yearbook*, No. 1, Dublin: Four Courts Press.

Said, E. (1978), *Beginnings: Intention and Method*, Baltimore: John Hopkins University Press.

St. Mary's School for the Deaf (1946), *Good Tidings: Centenary Memorial 1846–1946*, Dublin: St. Mary's School for the Deaf, Cabra.

Samorodov, A. (1996), 'Indicators of Cost-effectiveness of Policy Options for Workers with Disabilities', Labour Market Papers No. 11, Geneva: International Labour Office.

Saunders, H. (1997), *Growing up Deaf in Ireland*, unpublished M.Phil. in Applied Linguistics, Centre for Language and Communication Studies, University of Dublin, Trinity College.

Saxton, M. (1993), 'What's at Stake', *The Disability Rag*, May/June, 4–5.

Sayer, A. (2003), Seminar: Recognition and Redistribution, Equality Studies Centre, University College Dublin, February 3.

Scally, J. (2002), 'A Little Genetic Knowledge is a Dangerous Thing: Eugenics and the Genetic Revolution', *Studies*, 91(361), 15–27.

Scally, R. (1995), *The End of Hidden Ireland*, Oxford: Oxford University Press.

School of Education and Lifelong Learning, University College Dublin (2006–07) Master's Degree in Special Educational Needs, Course Handbook.

Scull, A. (1977), *Decarceration: Community Treatment and the Deviant, A Radical View*, London: Prentice Hall.

Scull, A. (1979), *Museums of Madness: Social Organisation of Insanity in 19th Century England*, London: Allen Lane.

Scull, A. (1983), 'Humanitarianism or Control? Some Observations on the Historiography of Anglo-American Psychiatry', in S. Cohen and A. Scull (eds.), *Social Control and the State: Historical and Comparative Essays*, Oxford: Martin Robinson, 118–40.

Scull, A. (1993), *The Most Solitary of Afflictions: Madness and Society in Britain, 1700–1900*, New Haven, Conn.: Yale University Press.

Searle, G. (1976), *Eugenics and Politics in Britain, 1900–1914*, Leyden: Noordhoff International Publishing.

Shakespeare, T. (1994), 'Cultural Representations of Disabled People: Dustbins for Disavowal', *Disability and Society*, 9(3), 283–301.

Shakespeare, T. (1996), 'Power and Prejudice: Issues of Gender, Sexuality and Disability', in L. Barton (ed.), *Disability and Society: Emerging Issues and Insights*, London: Longman, 191–214.

Shakespeare, T. (ed.) (1998), *The Disability Reader: Social Science Perspectives*, London: Cassell.

Shakespeare, T. (1999), '"Losing the Plot?" Medical and Activist Discourses of Contemporary Genetics and Disability', *Sociology of Health and Illness*, 21(5), 669–88.

Shakespeare, T., Gillespie-Sells, K. and Davies, D. (1996), *The Sexual Politics of Disability*, London: Cassell.

Shakespeare, T. and Watson, N. (1997), 'Defending the Social Model', *Disability and Society*, 12(2): 293–300.

Shapiro, J. (1993), *No Pity: How the Disability Rights Movement is Changing America*, New York: Times Books.

Sharpe, J. (1995), 'Social Strain and Social Dislocation, 1585–1603', in J. Guy (ed.), *The Reign of Elizabeth I: Court and Culture in the Last Decade*, Cambridge: Cambridge University Press.

Shaw, H. (1850), *The Dublin Pictorial Guide and Directory of 1850*, republished 1988, Belfast: Friar's Bush Press.

Sigelman, C., Budd, E., Spanhel, C. and Schoenrock, C. (1981), 'Asking Questions of Retarded Persons: A Comparison of Yes-No and Either-Or Formats', *Applied Research in Mental Retardation*, 2, 347–57.

Skrtic, T. (ed.) (1995), *Disability and Democracy: Reconstructing (Special) Education for Postmodernity*, New York: Teachers College Press.

Slack, P. (1988), *Poverty and Policy in Tudor and Stuart England*, Harlow: Longman.

Slater, T. (1911), 'Eugenics and Moral Theology', *Irish Theological Quarterly*, vol. 6, October, 401–13.

Slee, R. (1995), *Changing Theories and Practices of Discipline*, London: The Falmer Press.

Slee, R. (1996), 'Clauses of Conditionality: the "Reasonable" Accommodation of Language', in L. Barton (ed.), *Disability and Society: Emerging Issues and Insights*, London: Longman, 107–22.

Slee, R. (1997), 'Imported or Important Theory? Sociological Interrogations of Disablement and Special Education', *British Journal of Sociology of Education*, 18(3), 407–19.

Smart, B. (1985), *Michel Foucault*, Chichester: Ellis Horwood.

Soly, H. (1997), 'Continuity and Change: Attitudes towards Poor Relief in Early Modern Antwerp', in O. Grell and A. Cunningham (eds.), *Health Care and Poor Relief in Protestant Europe, 1500–1700*, London: Routledge, 84–101.

Spedding, J., Ellis, R. and Heath, D. (eds.) (1868), *The Works of Francis Bacon*, vol. XI, London: Longmans, Green, Reader and Dyer.

Spender, D. (1980), *Man Made Language*, London: Routledge and Kegan Paul.

Stanley, E.G. (1831), 'Letter to the Duke of Leinster', in A. Hyland and K. Milne, (eds.) (1987), *Irish Educational Documents*, vol. 1, Dublin: Church of Ireland College of Education, 100–1.

Steele, Robert (ed.) (1910), *A Bibliography of Royal Proclamations of the Tudor and Stuart Sovereigns and of Others 1485–1714, Vol. II, Part I: Ireland*, Oxford: Clarendon Press.

Stewart Institution for Idiotic and Imbecile Children (1875), Sixth Annual Report, Dublin: Author.

Stoker, C. (1863), 'On the Necessity of a State Provision for the Education of the Deaf and Dumb of Ireland', *Journal of the Statistical and Social Inquiry Society of Ireland*, 3, 456–60.

Stokoe, W. (1960), *Sign Language Structure: An Outline of the Visual Communication Systems of the American Deaf*, Occasional Papers No. 8, University of Buffalo.

Stone, D. (1985), *The Disabled State*, London: Macmillan.

Stuart, O. (1993), 'Double Oppression: An Appropriate Starting Point', in J. Swain *et al.* (eds.), *Disabling Barriers – Enabling Environments*, London: Sage, 93–100.

Swain, J. and Cameron, C. (1999), 'Unless Otherwise Stated: Discourses in Labelling and Identity in Coming Out', in M. Corker and S. French (eds.), *Disability Discourse*, Buckingham: Open University Press, 68–78.

Swain, J., Finklestein, V., French, S. and Oliver, M. (eds.) (1993), *Disabling Barriers – Enabling Environments*, London: Sage, in association with the Open University.

Symonds, A. (1998), 'Social Construction and the Concept of "Community"', in A. Symonds and A. Kelly (eds.), *The Social Construction of Community Care*, London: Macmillan, 7–17.

Szasz, T. (1971), *The Manufacture of Madness*, London: Routledge and Kegan Paul.

Szivros, S. (1992), 'The Limits to Integration?', in H. Brown and H. Smith (eds.), *Normalisation: A Reader for the Nineties*, London: Routledge, 112–133.

Talbot, J. (1978), *The Death of the Asylum: A Critical Study of State Hospital Management, Services and Care*, New York: Grune and Stratton.

Thomas, C. (1999), *Female Forms: Experiencing and Understanding Disability*, Buckingham: Open University Press.

Thomas, C. (2002), 'Disability Theory: Key Ideas, Issues and Thinkers', in C. Barnes, M. Oliver, and L. Barton (eds.), *Disability Studies Today*, Cambridge: Polity Press, 38–57.

Thomas, C. and Corker, M. (2002), 'A Journey around the Social Model', in M. Corker and T. Shakespeare (eds.), *Disability/Postmodernity: Embodying Disability Theory*, London: Continuum, 18–31.

Thomas, D. (1978), *The Social Psychology of Childhood Disability*, London: Methuen.

Tomlinson, S. (1982), *A Sociology of Special Education*, London: Routledge and Kegan Paul.

Tomlinson, S. (1985), 'The Expansion of Special Education', *Oxford Review of Education*, 11, 157–165.

Tomlinson, S. (1996), 'Conflicts and Dilemmas for Professionals in Special Education', in C. Christensen and F. Rizvi (eds.), *Disability and the Dilemmas of Education and Justice*, Buckingham: Open University Press, 175–86.

Thompson, J. (1990), *Ideology and Modern Culture: Critical Social Theory in the Era of Mass Communication*, Cambridge: Polity Press.

Thompson, S. (2006), *The Political Theory of Recognition: A Critical Introduction*, Cambridge: Polity Press.

Thomson, M. (1998), *The Problem of Mental Deficiency: Eugenics, Democracy and Social Policy in Britain c.1870–1959*, Oxford: Clarendon Press.

Toolin, D. (2003), 'An Emerging Rights Perspective for Disabled People in Ireland: An Activist's View', in S. Quin and B. Redmond (eds.), *Disability and Social Policy in Ireland*, Dublin: University College Dublin Press, 171–81.

Topliss, E. (1979), *Provision for the Disabled*, 2nd edition, Oxford: Blackwell and Martin Robertson.

Tregaskis, C. (2002), 'Social Model Theory: The Story so far ...', *Disability and Society*, 17(4), 457–70.

Trent, J. (1994), *Inventing the Feeble Mind: A History of Mental Retardation in the United States*, Berkeley, CA: University of California Press.

Tröhler, U. and Prüll, C.R. (1997), 'The Rise of the Modern Hospital', in I. Loudon (ed.), *Western Medicine*, Oxford: Oxford University Press, 160–75.

Troyna, B. and Vincent, C. (1996), ' "The Ideology of Expertism": The Framing of Special Education and Racial Equality Policies in the Local State', in C. Christensen and F. Rizvi (eds.), *Disability and the Dilemmas of Education and Justice*, Buckingham: Open University Press, 131–44.

Turner, R. (1961), 'Modes of Social Ascent through Education: Sponsored and Contest Mobility', in A. Halsey, J. Floud and C. Anderson (eds.), *Education, Economy and Society*, Glencoe, Ill.: Free Press, 121–39.

Tussing, D. and Wren, M.A. (2006), *How Ireland Cares: The Case for Health Care Reform*, Dublin: New Island.

Tyne, A. (1992), 'Normalisation: from Theory to Practice', in H. Brown and H. Smith (eds.), *Normalisation: A Reader for the Nineties*, London: Routledge, 33–46.

Tyor, P. and Bell, L. (1984), *Caring for the Retarded in America: A History*, Westport, Conn.: Greenwood Press.

Vail, D. (1966), *Dehumanisation and the Institutional Career*, Springfield, Ill.: Charles C. Thomas.

Valentine, P. (1993), 'Thomas Hopkins Galluadet: Benevolent Paternalism and the Origins of the American Asylum', in J. Van Cleeve (ed.), *Deaf History Unveiled: Interpretations from the New Scholarship*, Washington, DC: Gallaudet University Press, 53–73.

Vlachou, A. (1997), *Struggles for Inclusive Education: An Ethnographic Study*, Buckingham: Open University Press.

Waddington, K. (2000), *Charity and the London Hospitals, 1850–1898*, Woodbridge, Sussex: The Boydell Press.

Walmsley, J. and Johnson, K. (2003), *Inclusive Research with People with Learning Disabilities: Past, Present and Futures*, London: Jessica Kingsley.

Walmsley, S. (1989), 'The Need for Safeguards', in H, Brown and A. Craft (eds.), *Thinking the Unthinkable: Papers on Sexual Abuse and People with Learning Difficulties*, London: FPA, 5–17.

Walsh, O. (1999), 'Lunatic and Criminal Alliances in Nineteenth Century Ireland', in Bartlett, P. and Wright, D. (eds.), *Outside the Walls of the Asylum: The History of Care in the Community 1750–2000*, London: The Athlone Press, 132–52.

Ward, L. (ed.) (2001), *Considered Choices: The New Genetics, Prenatal Testing and People with Learning Disabilities*, Kidderminster: British Institute of Learning Disabilities.

Warnock Report, the (1978), Special Educational Needs, London: HMSO.

Weber, M. (1930), *The Protestant Ethic and the Spirit of Capitalism*, London: Allen and Unwin.

Weindling, P. (1999), 'International Eugenics: Swedish Sterilization in Context', *Scandanavian Journal of History*, 24: 179–97.

Weingart, P. (1999), 'Science and Political Culture: Eugenics in Comparative Perspective', *Scandanavian Journal of History*, 24,163–77.

Weiss, S. (1987), *Race Hygiene and National Efficiency: The Eugenics of Wilhelm Schallmeyer*, Berkeley, CA: University of California Press.

Wendell, S. (1996), *The Rejected Body*, New York: Routledge.

Whitehead, S. (1992), 'The Social Origins of Normalisation', in H. Brown and H. Smith (eds.), *Normalisation: A Reader for the Nineties*, London: Routledge, 47–59.

Whiting, J. (1979), *A House of Correction*, Gloucester: Alan Sutton.

Wilson, A. and Beresford, P. (2002), 'Madness, Distress and Postmodernity: Putting the Record Straight', in M. Corker and T. Shakespeare (eds.), *Disability/Postmodernity: Embodying Disability Research*, London: Continuum, 143–58.

Winzer, M. (1993), *The History of Special Education: From Isolation to Integration*, Washington, DC: Gallaudet University Press.

Wolfensberger, W. (1972), *The Principle of Normalisation in the Human Services*, Ontario: National Institute on Mental Retardation.

Wolfensberger, W. (1989), 'Human Service Policies: the Rhetoric Versus the Reality', in L. Barton (ed.), *Disability and Dependence*, Lewes: Falmer Press, 23–41.

Wolfensberger, W. and Thomas, S. (1987), 'The Principle of Normalization in the Human Services: a Brief Overview', in E. Reinach (ed.), *Normalisation*, Aberdeen: Department of Social Work, University of Aberdeen, 10–22.

Wollstonecraft, M. (1798), 'The Wrongs of Woman: or Maria. A Fragment', in J. Todd and M. Butler (eds.) (1989), *The Works of Mary Wollstonecraft, Vol. 1*, London: Pickering, 74–184.

Woods, A. (1998), *Dublin Outsiders: A History of the Mendicity Institution 1818–1998*, Dublin: A. & A. Farmar.

Woods, M. (1996), 'Researching Disability: An Overview of the Issues', paper prepared for the Commission on the Status of People with Disabilities, Equality Studies Centre, University College Dublin.

Woolf, S. (1986), *The Poor in Western Europe in the Eighteenth and Nineteenth Centuries*, London: Methuen.

Wren, Maev-Ann (2003), 'A Two-Tier System', *The Irish Times*, 2 June.

Wrigley, O. (1996), *The Politics of Deafness*, Washington, DC: Gallaudet University Press.

Young, I. (1990), *Justice and the Politics of Difference*, Princeton, NJ: Princeton University Press.

Zenderland, L. (1998), *Measuring Minds: Henry Herbert Goddard and the Origins of American Intelligence Testing*, Cambridge: Cambridge University Press.

# Index